FDA Acronyms, Abbreviations and Terminology

Human and Veterinary Regulatory Reference

FDA Acronyms, Abbreviations and Terminology

Human and Veterinary Regulatory Reference

FDA Acronyms, Abbreviations and Terminology: Human and Veterinary Regulatory Reference

Copyright © 2009 by PharmaLogika, Inc

PharmaLogika

PharmaLogika, Inc.
PO Box 461
Willow Springs, NC 27592

www.pharmalogika.com

Author / Editor: Mindy J. Allport-Settle

Published by PharmaLogika, Inc.

Printed in the United States of America. First Printing.

ISBN 0-9821476-1-9
ISBN-13 978-0-9821476-1-0

Contents

PART II

Preface

About this Book

The FDA Acronyms and Abbreviations database located on the FDA's website provides a quick reference to acronyms and abbreviations related to Food and Drug Administration (FDA) activities. This book is designed to combine all of those acronyms and abbreviations (with a few not included in the databse) and relevant industry terminology in one location.

The emphasis is on scientific, regulatory, government agency, and computer application terms. The database includes some FDA organizational and program acronyms. For more information about FDA's organization, please see the "FDA Organization" web page.

We have included some terms that are not strictly acronyms because of their relevance to FDA activities. Acronyms for journal titles do not appear in the database.

The FDA Acronyms and Abbreviations database is available for download online at http://www.fda.gov/AboutFDA/FDAAcronymsAbbreviations/default.htm

The included overview of the FDA (*The Food and Drug Administration* section of this chapter) is designed to provide a foundation for understanding the background of the FDA and its regulations.

This book was designed to be used both as a reference for experienced industry representatives and as a training resource for those new to the industry.

Included Documents and Features

FDA Acronyms and Abbreviations

- *Over 3,500 acronyms and abbreviations commonly used by the FDA and industry*

Combined Glossary

- *Over 800 common FDA and industry terms*

Reference Tools

- *FDA and CGMP overview*

About the Reference Tools

FDA and CGMP Overview

This overview (*The Food and Drug Administration* section of this chapter) provides the reader with a brief history of the FDA and explains not only what good manufacturing practices are, but why we have them and how they came to be.

The overview also lists all of the titles within Title 21 of the U.S. Code of Federal Regulations.

Combined Glossary

The Combined Glossary includes terminology from all of the glossaries of each regulation and guidance listed alphabetically rather than by document.

When a word or term appears multiple times in the regulation and guidance documents, the word will appear multiple times in the Combined Glossary when the definitions differ. Each duplicate entry is addressed with the earliest reference to the entry listed first. The source for each entry is bracketed (i.e., [21 CFR § 211]) for ease of reference. While the definitions are similar from one regulatory or guidance document to the next, they are not always identical.

The Food and Drug Administration (FDA)

The United States Food and Drug Administration (FDA) is responsible for protecting and promoting the nation's public health.

The programs for safety regulation vary widely by the type of product, its potential risks, and the regulatory powers granted to the agency. For example, the FDA regulates almost every facet of prescription drugs, including testing, manufacturing, labeling, advertising, marketing, efficacy and safety. FDA regulation of cosmetics, however, is focused primarily on labeling and safety. The FDA regulates most products with a set of published standards enforced by a combination of facility inspections, voluntary company reporting standards, and public and consumer watchdog activity.

The FDA frequently works in conjunction with other Federal agencies including the Department of Agriculture, Drug Enforcement Administration, Customs and Border Protection, and Consumer Product Safety Commission.

Historical Origins of Federal Food and Drug Regulation

Up until, there were few federal laws regulating the contents and sale of domestically produced food and pharmaceuticals before the 20th century (with one exception being the short-lived Vaccine Act of 1813). Some state laws provided varying degrees of protection against unethical sales practices, such as misrepresenting the ingredients of food products or therapeutic substances.

The history of the FDA can be traced to the latter part of the 19th century and the U.S. Department of Agriculture's Division of Chemistry (later Bureau of

Chemistry). Under Harvey Washington Wiley, appointed chief chemist in 1883, the Division began conducting research into the adulteration and misbranding of food and drugs on the American market. Although they had no regulatory powers, the Division published its findings from 1887 to 1902 in a ten-part series entitled Foods and Food Adulterants. Wiley used these findings, and alliances with diverse organizations (such as state regulators, the General Federation of Women's Clubs, and national associations of physicians and pharmacists) to lobby for a new federal law to set uniform standards for food and drugs to enter into interstate commerce.

Wiley's advocacy came at a time when the public had become alert to hazards in the marketplace by journalists and became part of a general trend for increased federal regulation in matters pertinent to public safety during the Progressive Era.[1] The 1902 Biologics Control Act was put in place after diphtheria antitoxin was collected from a horse named Jim who also had tetanus, resulting in several deaths.

The 1906 Food and Drug Act and creation of the FDA

In June 1906, President Theodore Roosevelt signed into law the Food and Drug Act, also known as the "Wiley Act" after its chief advocate.[2] The Act prohibited, under penalty of seizure of goods, the interstate transport of food which had been "adulterated," with that term referring to the addition of fillers of reduced "quality or strength," coloring to conceal "damage or inferiority," formulation with additives "injurious to health," or the use of "filthy, decomposed, or putrid" substances. The act applied similar penalties to the interstate marketing of "adulterated" drugs, in which the "standard of

---

[1] A History of the FDA at www.FDA.gov.
[2] A History of the FDA at www.FDA.gov.

strength, quality, or purity" of the active ingredient was not either stated clearly on the label or listed in the United States Pharmacopoeia or the National Formulary. The act also banned "misbranding" of food and drugs.[3] The responsibility for examining food and drugs for such "adulteration" or "misbranding" was given to Wiley's USDA Bureau of Chemistry.[4] Strength, quality, identity, potency, and purity (SQuIPP) are currently the key product safety standards, with only two measures added since 1906 Act.

Wiley used these new regulatory powers to pursue an aggressive campaign against the manufacturers of foods with chemical additives, but the Chemistry Bureau's authority was soon checked by judicial decisions, as well as by the creation of the Board of Food and Drug Inspection and the Referee Board of Consulting Scientific Experts as separate organizations within the USDA in 1907 and 1908 respectively. A 1911 Supreme Court decision ruled that the 1906 act did not apply to false claims of therapeutic efficacy,[5] in response to which a 1912 amendment added "false and fraudulent" claims of "curative or therapeutic effect" to the Act's definition of "misbranded." However, these powers continued to be narrowly defined by the courts, which set high standards for proof of fraudulent intent.[6] In 1927, the Bureau of Chemistry's regulatory powers were reorganized under a new USDA body, the Food, Drug, and Insecticide organization. This name was shortened to the Food and Drug Administration (FDA) three years later.[7]

---

[3] Text in quotation marks is the original text of the 1906 Food and Drugs Act and Amendments.
[4] A History of the FDA at www.FDA.gov.
[5] United States v. Johnson (31 S. Ct. 627 May 29, 1911, decided).
[6] A History of the FDA at www.FDA.gov.
[7] Milestones in U.S. Food and Drug Law History at www.FDA.gov.

The 1938 Food, Drug, and Cosmetic Act

By the 1930s, muckraking journalists, consumer protection organizations, and federal regulators began mounting a campaign for stronger regulatory authority by publicizing a list of injurious products which had been ruled permissible under the 1906 law, including radioactive beverages, cosmetics which caused blindness, and worthless "cures" for diabetes and tuberculosis. The resulting proposed law was unable to get through the Congress of the United States for five years, but was rapidly enacted into law following the public outcry over the 1937 Elixir Sulfanilamide tragedy, in which over 100 people died after using a drug formulated with a toxic, untested solvent. The only way that the FDA could even seize the product was due to a misbranding problem: an "Elixir" was defined as a medication dissolved in ethanol, not the diethylene glycol used in the Elixir Sulfanilamide.

President Franklin Delano Roosevelt signed the new Food, Drug, and Cosmetic Act (FD&C Act) into law on June 24, 1938. The new law significantly increased federal regulatory authority over drugs by mandating a pre-market review of the safety of all new drugs, as well as banning false therapeutic claims in drug labeling without requiring that the FDA prove fraudulent intent. The law also authorized factory inspections and expanded enforcement powers, set new regulatory standards for foods, and brought cosmetics and therapeutic devices under federal regulatory authority. This law, though extensively amended in subsequent years, remains the central foundation of FDA regulatory authority to the present day.[8]

Early FD&C Act amendments: 1938-1958

Soon after passage of the 1938 Act, the FDA began to designate certain drugs as safe for use only under the

---

[8] A History of the FDA at www.FDA.gov.

supervision of a medical professional, and the category of 'prescription-only' drugs was securely codified into law by the 1951 Durham-Humphrey Amendment.[9] While pre-market testing of drug efficacy was not authorized under the 1938 FD&C Act, subsequent amendments such as the Insulin Amendment and Penicillin Amendment did mandate potency testing for formulations of specific lifesaving pharmaceuticals.[10] The FDA began enforcing its new powers against drug manufacturers who could not substantiate the efficacy claims made for their drugs, and the United States Court of Appeals for the Ninth Circuit ruling in Alberty Food Products Co. v. United States (1950) found that drug manufacturers could not evade the "false therapeutic claims" provision of the 1938 act by simply omitting the intended use of a drug from the drug's label. These developments confirmed extensive powers for the FDA to enforce post-marketing recalls of ineffective drugs.[11] Much of the FDA's regulatory attentions in this era were directed towards abuse of amphetamines and barbiturates, but the agency also reviewed some 13,000 new drug applications between 1938 and 1962. While the science of toxicology was in its infancy at the start of this era, rapid advances in experimental assays for food additive and drug safety testing were made during this period by FDA regulators and others.[12]

Good Manufacturing Practices vs. Current Good Manufacturing Practices

The terms "Good Manufacturing Practices (GMPs)" and "Current Good Manufacturing Practices (CGMPs or

---

[9] A History of the FDA at www.FDA.gov.
[10] Milestones in U.S. Food and Drug Law History at www.FDA.gov
[11] A History of the FDA at www.FDA.gov.
[12] A History of the FDA at www.FDA.gov.

cGMPs[13])" are often used interchangeably both in industry and by FDA inspectors.

"Good Manufacturing Practices" generally refers to the legal mandates detailed in Title 21 of the Code of Federal Regulations (21CFR). "Current Good Manufacturing Practices" refers not only to the legal requirements, but to the guidance provided by the FDA and the standards practiced in industry that are not memorialized as law.

Organizational Structure

The FDA is an agency within the United States Department of Health and Human Services responsible for protecting and promoting the nation's public health. It is organized into the following major subdivisions, each focused on a major area of regulatory responsibility:

- *The Office of the Commissioner (OC)*

- *The Center for Drug Evaluation and Research (CDER)*

- *The Center for Biologics Evaluation and Research (CBER)*

- *The Center for Food Safety and Applied Nutrition (CFSAN)*

- *The Center for Devices and Radiological Health (CDRH)*

- *The Center for Veterinary Medicine (CVM)*

- *The National Center for Toxicological Research (NCTR)*

- *The Office of Regulatory Affairs (ORA)*

---

[13] The lower case "c" was coined in industry to differentiate between the law, emphasized with capital letters, and the current accepted industry practice not mandated by law.

- *The Office of Criminal Investigations (OCI)*

How does the FDA communicate with Industry?

Code of Federal Regulations[14]

The Code of Federal Regulations (CFR) is the codification of the general and permanent rules and regulations (sometimes called administrative law) published in the Federal Register by the executive departments and agencies of the Federal Government of the United States. The CFR is published by the Office of the Federal Register, an agency of the National Archives and Records Administration (NARA).

The CFR is divided into 50 titles that represent broad areas subject to Federal regulation. Title 21 is the portion of the Code of Federal Regulations that governs food and drugs within the United States for the Food and Drug Administration (FDA), the Drug Enforcement Administration (DEA), and the Office of National Drug Control Policy (ONDCP).

It is divided into three chapters:

- *Chapter I — Food and Drug Administration*

- *Chapter II — Drug Enforcement Administration*

- *Chapter III — Office of National Drug Control Policy*

Guidance Documents

Guidance documents represent the Agency's current thinking on a particular subject. They do not create or confer any rights for or on any person and do not operate to bind FDA or the public. An alternative approach may be used if such approach satisfies the

---

[14] Available CFR Titles on GPO Access at
http://www.access.gpo.gov/nara/cfr/cfr-table-search.html#page1

requirements of the applicable statute, regulations, or both. For information on a specific guidance document, please contact the originating office. Another method of obtaining guidance documents is through the Division of Drug Information.

Federal Register

The Federal Register (since March 14, 1936), abbreviated FR, or sometimes Fed. Reg.) is the official journal of the federal government of the United States that contains most routine publications and public notices of government agencies. It is a daily (except holidays) publication.

The Federal Register is compiled by the Office of the Federal Register (within the National Archives and Records Administration) and is printed by the Government Printing Office.

There are no copyright restrictions on the Federal Register as it is a work of the U.S. government. It is in the public domain.[15]

Citations from the Federal Register are [volume] FR [page number] ([date]), e.g., 65 FR 741 (2000-10-01).

Direct Communication and Letters

The FDA interacts with consumers, health professionals, and industry representatives through letters, meetings (requested by either the FDA or the industry representatives), and telephone calls.

While not all questions can be answered over the phone, the FDA prefers telephone interactions over physical meetings (when a teleconference can reasonably replace a face-to-face meeting).

---

[15] The Federal Register at the GPO, online in both text and PDF, from 1994 on.

www.FDA.gov

The FDA maintains a website at www.fda.gov that is focused on three key audiences:

- *consumers*

- *health professionals*

- *industry representatives*

Through collaboration with users in testing site-wide designs, FDA.gov provides online access to its guidance documents, communication with industry, consumers, and health professionals. Information is categorized by topic, with related subjects consolidated in sections on the site.

Additionally, FDA.gov provides a search engine for Title 21 of the CFR that makes finding keyword references throughout the title more accessible.

Conferences

The FDA routinely sends speakers to industry conferences where they are available to answer questions on their particular area of expertise.

False Statement to a Federal Agency

The U.S. Code of Federal Regulations (CFR) makes it a federal crime for anyone willfully and knowingly to make a false or fraudulent statement to a department or agency of the United States. The false statement must be related to a material matter, and the defendant must have acted willfully and with knowledge of the falsity. It is not necessary to show that the government agency was in fact deceived or misled. The issue of materiality is one of law for the courts. The maximum penalty is five years' imprisonment and a $10,000 fine.

A person may be guilty of a violation without proof that he or she had knowledge that the matter was within the jurisdiction of a federal agency. A businessperson may violate this law by making a false statement to another firm or person with knowledge that the information will be submitted to a government agency. Businesses must take care to avoid exaggerations in the context of any matter that may come within the jurisdiction of a federal agency.

CFR Title 21 - Food and Drugs: Parts 1 to 1499[16]

General

(1) General enforcement regulations

(2) General administrative rulings and decisions

(3) Product jurisdiction

(5) Organization

(7) Enforcement policy

(10) Administrative practices and procedures

(11) Electronic records; electronic signatures

(12) Formal evidentiary public hearing

(13) Public hearing before a public board of inquiry

(14) Public hearing before a public advisory committee

(15) Public hearing before the commissioner

(16) Regulatory hearing before the food and drug administration

(17) Civil money penalties hearings

---

[16] All of the 21CFR regulations can be searched online for no charge at http://www.accessdata.fda.gov/scripts/cdrh/cfdocs/cfcfr/cfrsearch.cfm

(19) Standards of conduct and conflicts of interest

(20) Public information

(21) Protection of privacy

(25) Environmental impact considerations

(26) Mutual recognition of pharmaceutical good manufacturing practice

(50) Protection of human subjects

(54) Financial disclosure by clinical investigators

(56) Institutional review boards

(58) Good laboratory practice for nonclinical laboratory studies

(60) Patent term restoration

(70) Color additives

(71) Color additive petitions

(73) Listing of color additives exempt from certification

(74) Listing of color additives subject to certification

(80) Color additive certification

(81) General specifications and general restrictions for provisional color additives for use in foods, drugs, and cosmetics

(82) Listing of certified provisionally listed colors and specifications

(83-98) [reserved]

(99) Dissemination of information on unapproved/new uses for marketed drugs, biologics, and devices

Foods

(100) General

(101) Food labeling

Foods

(102) Common or usual name for nonstandardized foods

(104) Nutritional quality guidelines for foods

(105) Foods for special dietary use

(106) Infant formula quality control procedures

(107) Infant formula

(108) Emergency permit control

(109) Unavoidable contaminants in food for human consumption and food-packaging material

(110) Current good manufacturing practice in manufacturing, packing, or holding human food

(111) Current good manufacturing practice in manufacturing, packaging, labeling, or holding operations for dietary supplements

(113) Thermally processed low-acid foods packaged in hermetically sealed containers

(114) Acidified foods

(115) Shell eggs

(119) Dietary supplements that present a significant or unreasonable risk

(120) Hazard analysis and critical control point (HACCP) systems

(123) Fish and fishery products

(129) Processing and bottling of bottled drinking water

(130) Food standards: general

(131) Milk and cream

(133) Cheeses and related cheese products

(135) Frozen desserts

(136) Bakery products

(137) Cereal flours and related products

(139) Macaroni and noodle products

(145) Canned fruits

(146) Canned fruit juices

(150) Fruit butters, jellies, preserves, and related products

(152) Fruit pies

(155) Canned vegetables

(156) Vegetable juices

(158) Frozen vegetables

(160) Eggs and egg products

(161) Fish and shellfish

(163) Cacao products

(164) Tree nut and peanut products

(165) Beverages

(166) Margarine

(168) Sweeteners and table syrups

(169) Food dressings and flavorings

(170) Food additives

(171) Food additive petitions

(172) Food additives permitted for direct addition to food for human consumption

(173) Secondary direct food additives permitted in food for human consumption

(174) Indirect food additives: general

(175) Indirect food additives: adhesives and components of coatings

(176) Indirect food additives: paper and paperboard components

(177) Indirect food additives: polymers

(178) Indirect food additives: adjuvants, production aids, and sanitizers

(179) Irradiation in the production, processing and handling of food

(180) Food additives permitted in food or in contact with food on an interim basis pending additional study

(181) Prior-sanctioned food ingredients

(182) Substances generally recognized as safe

(184) Direct food substances affirmed as generally recognized as safe

(186) Indirect food substances affirmed as generally recognized as safe

(189) Substances prohibited from use in human food

(190) Dietary supplements

(191-199) [reserved]

Drugs

(200) General

(201) Labeling

(202) Prescription drug advertising

(203) Prescription drug marketing

(205) Guidelines for state licensing of wholesale prescription drug distributors

(206) Imprinting of solid oral dosage form drug products for human use

(207) Registration of producers of drugs and listing of drugs in commercial distribution

(208) Medication guides for prescription drug products

(209) Requirement for authorized dispensers and pharmacies to distribute a side effects statement

(210) Current good manufacturing practice in manufacturing, processing, packing, or holding of drugs; general

(211) Current good manufacturing practice for finished pharmaceuticals

(216) Pharmacy compounding

(225) Current good manufacturing practice for medicated feeds

(226) Current good manufacturing practice for type A medicated articles

(250) Special requirements for specific human drugs

(290) Controlled drugs

(299) Drugs; official names and established names

New Drugs and Over-the-Counter Drug Products

(300) General

(310) New drugs

(312) Investigational new drug application

(314) Applications for FDA approval to market a new drug

(315) Diagnostic radiopharmaceuticals

(316) Orphan drugs

(320) Bioavailability and bioequivalence requirements

(328) Over-the-counter drug products intended for oral ingestion that contain alcohol

---

(330) Over-the-counter (OTC) human drugs which are generally recognized as safe and effective and not misbranded

(331) Antacid products for over-the-counter (OTC) human use

(332) Antiflatulent products for over-the-counter human use

(333) Topical antimicrobial drug products for over-the-counter recognized as safe and effective and not misbranded

(335) Antidiarrheal drug products for over-the-counter human use

(336) Antiemetic drug products for over-the-counter human use

(338) Nighttime sleep-aid drug products for over-the-counter human use

(340) Stimulant drug products for over-the-counter human use

(341) Cold, cough, allergy, bronchodilator, and antiasthmatic drug products for over-the-counter human use

(343) Internal analgesic, antipyretic, and antirheumatic drug products for over-the-counter human use

(344) Topical OTIC drug products for over-the-counter human use

(346) Anorectal drug products for over-the-counter human use

(347) Skin protectant drug products for over-the-counter human use

(348) External analgesic drug products for over-the-counter human use

(349) Ophthalmic drug products for over-the-counter human use

(350) Antiperspirant drug products for over-the-counter human use

(352) Sunscreen drug products for over-the-counter human use [stayed indefinitely]

(355) Anticaries drug products for over-the-counter human use

(357) Miscellaneous internal drug products for over-the-counter human use

(358) Miscellaneous external drug products for over-the-counter human use

(361) Prescription drugs for human use generally recognized as safe and effective and not misbranded: drugs used in research

(369) Interpretative statements re warnings on drugs and devices for over-the-counter sale

(370-499) [reserved]

Veterinary Products

(500) General

(501) Animal food labeling

(502) Common or usual names for nonstandardized animal foods

(509) Unavoidable contaminants in animal food and food-packaging material

(510) New animal drugs

(511) New animal drugs for investigational use

(514) New animal drug applications

(515) Medicated feed mill license

(516) New animal drugs for minor use and minor species

(520) Oral dosage form new animal drugs

(522) Implantation or injectable dosage form new animal drugs

(524) Ophthalmic and topical dosage form new animal drugs

(526) Intramammary dosage forms

(529) Certain other dosage form new animal drugs

(530) Extralabel drug use in animals

(556) Tolerances for residues of new animal drugs in food

(558) New animal drugs for use in animal feeds

(564) [reserved]

(570) Food additives

(571) Food additive petitions

(573) Food additives permitted in feed and drinking water of animals

(579) Irradiation in the production, processing, and handling of animal feed and pet food

(582) Substances generally recognized as safe

(584) Food substances affirmed as generally recognized as safe in feed and drinking water of animals

(589) Substances prohibited from use in animal food or feed

(590-599) [reserved]

Biologics

(600) Biological products: general

(601) Licensing

(606) Current good manufacturing practice for blood and blood components

(607) Establishment registration and product listing for manufacturers of human blood and blood products

(610) General biological products standards

(630) General requirements for blood, blood components, and blood components, and blood derivatives

(640) Additional standards for human blood and blood products

(660) Additional standards for diagnostic substances for laboratory tests

(680) Additional standards for miscellaneous products

Cosmetics

(700) General

(701) Cosmetic labeling

(710) Voluntary registration of cosmetic product establishments

(720) Voluntary filing of cosmetic product ingredient composition statements

(740) Cosmetic product warning statements

(741-799) [reserved]

Medical Devices

(800) General

(801) Labeling

(803) Medical device reporting

(806) Medical devices; reports of corrections and removals

(807) Establishment registration and device listing for manufacturers and initial importers of devices

(808) Exemptions from federal preemption of state and local medical device requirements

(809) In vitro diagnostic products for human use

(810) Medical device recall authority

(812) Investigational device exemptions

(813) [reserved]

(814) Premarket approval of medical devices

(820) Quality system regulation

(821) Medical device tracking requirements

(822) Postmarket surveillance

(860) Medical device classification procedures

(861) Procedures for performance standards development

(862) Clinical chemistry and clinical toxicology devices

(864) Hematology and pathology devices

(866) Immunology and microbiology devices

(868) Anesthesiology devices

(870) Cardiovascular devices

(872) Dental devices

(874) Ear, nose, and throat devices

(876) Gastroenterology-urology devices

(878) General and plastic surgery devices

(880) General hospital and personal use devices

(882) Neurological devices

(884) Obstetrical and gynecological devices

(886) Ophthalmic devices

(888) Orthopedic devices

(890) Physical medicine devices

(892) Radiology devices

(895) Banned devices

(898) Performance standard for electrode lead wires and patient cables

Mammography

(900) Mammography

Radiological Health

(1000) General

(1002) Records and reports

(1003) Notification of defects or failure to comply

(1004) Repurchase, repairs, or replacement of electronic products

(1005) Importation of electronic products

(1010) Performance standards for electronic products: general

(1020) Performance standards for ionizing radiation emitting products

(1030) Performance standards for microwave and radio frequency emitting products

(1040) Performance standards for light-emitting products

(1050) Performance standards for sonic, infrasonic, and ultrasonic radiation-emitting products

Regulations under Certain Other Acts

(1210) Regulations under the federal import milk act

(1230) Regulations under the federal caustic poison act

(1240) Control of communicable diseases

(1250) Interstate conveyance sanitation

(1251-1269) [reserved]

(1270) Human tissue intended for transplantation

(1271) Human cells, tissues, and cellular and tissue-based products

(1272-1299) [reserved]

Controlled Substances

(1300) Definitions

(1301) Registration of manufacturers, distributors, and dispensers of controlled substances

(1302) Labeling and packaging requirements for controlled substances

(1303) Quotas

(1304) Records and reports of registrants

(1305) Orders for schedule I and II controlled substances

(1306) Prescriptions

(1307) Miscellaneous

(1308) Schedules of controlled substances

(1309) Registration of manufacturers, distributors, importers and exporters of List I chemicals

(1310) Records and reports of listed chemicals and certain machines

(1311) Digital certificates

(1312) Importation and exportation of controlled substances

(1313) Importation and exportation of list I and list II chemicals

(1314) Retail sale of scheduled listed chemical products

(1315) Importation and production quotas for ephedrine, pseudoephedrine, and phenylpropanolamine

(1316) Administrative functions, practices, and procedures

Office of National Drug Control Policy

(1400) [reserved]

(1401) Public availability of information

(1402) Mandatory declassification review

(1403) Uniform administrative requirements for grants and cooperative agreements to state and local governments

(1404) Governmentwide debarment and suspension (nonprocurement)

(1405) Governmentwide requirements for drug-free workplace (financial assistance)

(1406-1499) [reserved]

Part I
Acronyms &
Abbreviations

FDA Acronyms & Abbreviations

1932	FDA form for veterinary adverse drug reaction, lack of effectiveness, product defect report--mandatory
348	FDA form for sponsored travel
482	FDA form for notice of inspection
483	FDA form used as a written notice of deficiencies found in inspections
2301	FDA form for transmittal of periodic reports and promotional material for new animal drugs
3500	FDA form for voluntary reporting of adverse events
WPADP	ISBT Working Party on Automation and Data Processing
[NA]TAG	[North American] Technical Advisory Group
§	Section – shorthand symbol used to designate a section in a legal document; as in §201(m) of the FD&C Act.
§§	Sections – shorthand symbol used to designate sections in a legal document; as in §§201(m), 301(k) of the FD&C Act.
1932a	FDA form for veterinary adverse drug reaction, lack of effectiveness, product defect report--voluntary
3500A	FDA form for mandatory reporting of adverse events
356V	FDA form for new animal drug appication

3Rs	Recruitment and Relocation bonuses and Retention allowances
406B	Section of the FDA Modernization Act dealing with getting feedback from our stakeholders
505(b)(2)	A new drug application that contains full reports of investigations of safety and effectiveness but where at least some of the information required for approval comes from studies not conducted by or for the applicant and for which the applicant has not obtained a right of reference.
510(k)	Section of the Food, Drug, and Cosmetic Act that deals with premarket notification

A

A/L	Annual Leave
A2LA	American Association for Laboratory Accreditation
AAA	Abdominal Aortic Aneurysm
AAALAC	Association for Assessment and Accreditation of Laboratory Animal Care international
AAAP	American Association of Avian Pathologists
AAAS	American Association for the Advancement of Science
AABB	American Association of Blood Banks
AABP	American Association of Bovine Practitioners
AACR	American Association for Cancer Research
AADA	Abbreviated Antibiotic Drug Application
AAEP	American Association of Equine Practitioners

AAFCO	Association of American Feed Control officials
AAFP	American Academy of Family Physicians
AAHA	American Animal Hospital Association
AAI	American Association of Immunologists
AALAS	American Association for Laboratory Animal Science
AAMI	American Association for Medical instrumentation
AANN	American Association of Neurosciences Nurses
AANS	American Association of Neurological Surgeons
AAO	American Academy of Ophthalmology
AAP	American Academy of Pediatrics
AAP	American Academy of Peridontology
AAPHP	American Association of Public Health Physicians
AAPM	American Association of Physicists in Medicine
AAPS	American Association of Pharmaceutical Scientists
AAR	After Action Review
AARP	American Association of Retired Persons
AAS	Acute Abdominal Series
AASP	American Association of Swine Practitioners
AASRP	American Association of Small Ruminant Practitioners
AATB	American Association of Tissue Banks
AAVLD	American Association of Veterinary Laboratory Diagnosticians
AAVMC	Association of American Veterinary Medical Colleges
AB (CDRH)	Analysis Branch (CDRH)
ABC	American Blood Commission
ABC	America's Blood Centers
ABE	Adverse Biologic Experience

ABG	Arterial Blood Gas
ABI	Automated Broker interface (U.S. Customs)
Abifarma	Brazilian Association of the Pharmaceutical industry
ABM	Application Briefing Meeting
ABPI	Association of the British Pharmaceutical industry
ABRA	American Blood Resource Association
AC	Advisory Committee
ACB (CDRH)	Accreditation and Certification Branch (CDRH)
ACBSA	Advisory Committee on Blood Safety and Availability (HHS)
ACC	RCHSA (Radiation Control for Health and Safety Act) Accession Number (ORA AofC Code)
ACCME	Accreditation Council for Continuing Medical Education
ACCP	American College of Clinical Pharmacology
ACE	Adverse Clinical Event
ACE	Association of Clinical Embryologists
ACE	Automated Commercial Environment (Customs and Border Protection)
ACEP	American College of Emergency Physicians
ACF	Administration for Children and Families (DHHS)
ACG	American College of Gastroenterology
ACGME	Accreditation Council for Graduate Medical Education
ACIL	American Council of independent Laboratories
ACIP	Advisory Committee on Immunization Practices (CDC)
ACLA	American Clinical Laboratory Association

ACLAD	American Committee on Laboratory Animal Diseases
ACLAM	American College of Laboratory Animal Medicine
ACMP	American College of Medical Physics
ACOL	Acceptable Carry-Over Limit
ACP	American College of Physicians
ACPE	Accreditation Council for Pharmacy Education
ACPM	American College of Preventive Medicine
ACR	American College of Radiology
ACRA (ORA)	Associate Commissioner for Regulatory Affairs (ORA)
ACRPI	Association of Clinical Research for the Pharmaceutical industry
ACS	Automated Commercial System (U.S. Customs)
ACS	American Chemical Society
ACS (CBER)	Analytical Chemistry Staff (CBER)
ACS (CDER)	Advisors and Consultants Staff (CDER)
ACSM	American College of Sports Medicine
ACT	Applied Clinical Trials
ACT	AIDS Clinical Trials
ACTB (NCTR)	Analytical Chemical Techniques Branch (NCTR)
ACTH	Adrenocorticotropic Hormone
ACTIS	Aids Clinical Trials information Service
ACUS	Administrative Conference of the United States
ACWA	Administrative Careers With America (OPM)
AD	Action Due
ad lib	As Much As Needed
ADA	Americans With Disabilities Act of 1990
ADA	American Dental Association
ADAA	Animal Drug Availability Act of 1996
ADaM	Analysis Dataset Model (CDISC)

ADAMHA	Alcohol, Drug Abuse and Mental Health Administration (Now SAMHSA)
ADCOM	Advisory Committee
ADE	Adverse Drug Event
ADE	Adverse Drug Experience
ADE/ADER	Adverse Drug Experience/Adverse Drug Experience Report
ADEC	Australian Drug Evaluation Committee
AdEERS	Adverse Event Expedited Reporting System (NCI)
ADH	Antidiuretic Hormone
ADI	Acceptable Daily intake
ADME	Absorption, Distribution, Metabolism, and Excretion
ADMIA (CBER)	Associate Director for Medical and international Affairs (CBER)
ADP	Automated Data Processing
ADP (CBER)	Associate Director for Policy (CBER)
ADR	Adverse Drug Report
ADR	Adverse Drug Reaction
ADR (CBER)	Associate Director for Research (CBER)
ADRAC	Adverse Drug Reactions Advisory Committee (TGA)
ADRM (CBER)	Associate Director for Review Management (CBER)
ADRP	Association of Donor Recruitment Professionals
ADRS	Adverse Drug Reporting System
ADSA	American Dairy Science Association
ADUFA	Animal Drug User Fee Act of 2003
AdvaMed	Advanced Medical Technology Association
AE	Approvable
AE	Adverse Event
AEA	Actual Expense Allowance
AER	Adverse Event Report
AERS	Adverse Event Reporting System

AF	Atrial Fibrillation
AF	Administrative File
AFAB	Absorbable Fibrin Adhesive Bandage
AFDO	Association of Food and Drug officials
AFGE	American Federation of Government Employees
AFIA	American Feed industry Association
AFIP	Armed forces institute of Pathology (DoD)
AFP	Alpha-Fetoprotein
AGRICOLA	Agricultural online Access (USDA)
AHA	American Hospital Association
AHCPR	Agency for Health Care Policy and Research (Now AHRQ)
AHF	Antihemophilic Factor
AHFS	American Hospital formulary Service
AHI	Animal Health institute
AHIC	American Health information Community
AHRQ	Agency for Healthcare Quality and Research (formerly AHCPR) (DHHS)
AHU	Air Handling Unit
AICRC	Association of independent Clinical Research Contractors (UK)
AID	Agency for international Development
AIDS	Acquired Immune Deficiency Syndrome
AIM	Active ingredient Manufacturer
AIM	Association for Automatic Identification and Mobility
AIMBE	American institute for Medical and Biological Engineering
AIMDD	Active Implantable Medical Device Directive
AIMS	Agency information Management System
AIN	Food Additive Identification Number (ORA AofC Code)
AIP	Abbreviated inspection System
AIP	Application integrity Policy

A

AIRIO	Agency intramural Research integrity Officer (NIH)
AIS	Automated information System
aka	Also Known As
AL	Annual Leave
ALARA	As Low As Reasonably Achievable
ALFB (CBER)	Acess Litigation and FOI Branch (CBER)
ALJ	Administrative Law Judge
ALJ (OC)	Office of the Administrative Law Judge (OC)
ALL	Acute Lymphocytic Leukemia
alt	Alanine Aminotransferase
AMA	American Medical Association
AMA	Agricultural Marketing Act of 1946 (USDA)
AMA-DE	American Medical Association's Drug Evaluations
AMB (CDRH)	Adminstrative Management Branch (CDRH)
AMDUCA	Animal Medicinal Drug Use Clarification Act
AME	Absorption, Metabolism, Excretion
AMF	Administrative Management of Files
AmFAR	American Foundation for AIDS Research
AMG	Arzeneimittelgesetz (West Germany Drug Law)
AMHPS	Association of Minority Health Professionals Schools
AMI	American Meat institute
AML	Acute Myelogenous Leukemia
AMP	Average Manufacturer Price
AMPI	Associated Milk Producers, inc.
AMS	Agricultural Marketing Service (USDA)
AMS	Aseptic Meningitis Syndrome
AMT (OC)	Asset Management Team (OC)
ANA	Antinuclear Antibody

ANA	Abbreviated New Animal Drug Number (ORA AofC Code)
ANADA	Abbreviated New Animal Drug Application
ANCOVA	Analysis of Covariance
AND	Abbreviated New Drug Application Number (ORA AofC Code)
ANDA	Abbreviated New Drug Application
ANOVA	Analysis of VAriance
ANPR	Advance Notice of Proposed Rulemaking
ANPRM	Advanced Notice of Proposed Rule Making
ANRC	American National Red Cross
ANSI	American National Standards institute
ANZFA	Australia New Zealand Food Authority
AO	Administrative Officer
AoA	Administration on Aging (DHHS)
AOAC	Association of official Analytical Chemists
AOB (OC)	Accounting Operations Branch (OC)
AODM	Adult onset Diabetes Mellitus
AofC	Affirmation of Compliance [Codes] (ORA)
AOPC	Agency/organization Program Coordinator
APA	Administrative Procedures Act
APAC	Allergenic Products Advisory Committee (CBER)
apap	N-Acetyl-Para-Amino-Phenol
APBI	Association of the British Pharmaceutical industry
APEC	Asia-Pacific Economic Cooperation Council
APhA	American Pharmaceutical Association
APHA	American Public Health Association
APHIS	Animal and Plant Health inspection Service (USDA)
APHL	Association of Public Health Laboratories
API	Active Pharmaceutical ingredient

APIC	Active Pharmaceutical ingredients Committee of CEFIC (European Chemical industry Council)
APIFARMA	Association of the Portuguese Pharmaceutical industries
APLB (CBER)	Advertising and Promotional Labeling Branch (CBER)
APR	Annual Product Review
APSB (OC)	Accounting Policy and Systems Branch (OC)
APTF	Application Policy Task force
APUA	Alliance for Prudent Use of Antibiotics
AQL	Acceptable Quality Level
AR	Approvable Letter
ARAB (OC)	Accounting Reports and Analysis Branch (OC)
ARC	American Red Cross
ARCH	Administrative Resources Core Hub (CFSAN)
ARCRT	American Registry of Clinical Radiography Technologists
ARDB (CDRH)	Anesthesiology and Respiratory Devices Branch (CDRH)
ARDS	Acute Respiratory Distress Syndrome
ARENA	Applied Research Ethics National Association
ARF	Acute Renal Failure
ARIES	Administrative Resources information Exchange System
ARL (ORA)	Arkansas Regional Laboratory (ORA)
ARNet	Acquisition Reform Network
ARPA	Advanced Research Projects Agency (DoD)
ARRT	American Registry of Radiologic Technologists
ARS	Agricultural Research Service (USDA)
ART	Assisted Reproductive therapy
ART	Assisted Reproductive Technology

ARTCA	Antimicrobial Regulations Technical Correction Act of 1998
AS	Aortic Stenosis
AS (CVM)	Administrative Staff (CVM)
ASA	American Society of Anesthesiologists
ASA	American Statistical Association
ASA	Americans for Safe Access
ASA	Aminosalicylic Acid
ASAP	As Soon As Possible
ASAP	Administrative Systems Automation Project
ASAS	American Society of Animal Science
ASB (OC)	Accounting Services Branch (OC)
ASB (OC)	Administrative Services Branch (OC)
ASBPO	Armed Services Blood Program Office
ASC	Advertising Standards Council (Canada)
ASCII	American Standard Code for information interchange (Computer Files)
ASCO	American Society for Clinical oncology
ASCP	American Society for Clinical Pathology
ASCPT	American Society for Clinical Pharmacology and therapeutics
ASCVD	Atherosclerotic Cardiovascular Disease
ASD	Atrial Septal Defect
ASD (HD)	Assistant Secretary of Defense for Homeland Defense
ASGE	American Society for Gastrointestinal Endoscopy
ASHD	Atherosclerotic Heart Disease
ASHRAE	American Society of Heating, Refrigeration & Air Conditioning Engineers
ASIA	American Sheep industry Association
ASICS	Application Specific integrated Circuit(S)
ASLAP	American Society of Laboratory Animal Practitioners
ASM	American Society for Microbiology

A

ASR	Analyte Specific Reagent
ASRM	American Society for Reproductive Medicine
ASTHO	Association of State and Territorial Health officials
ASTM	American Society for Testing and Materials
AT (OC)	Acquisitions Team (OC)
ATC	Anatomical therapeutic Chemical (Drug Classification System) (Who)
ATF	Bureau of Alcohol, tobacco and Firearms (U.S. Department of Justice)
ATM	Automatic Teller Machine
ATPA	American Technology Pre-Eminence Act of 1991
ATPM	Association of Teachers and Preventive Medicine
ATS (CDER)	Applied Technologies Staff (CDER)
ATSDR	Agency for toxic Substances and Disease Registry (CDC)
AUC	Area Under the Curve
AUSA	Assistant United States Attorney
AV	Atrioventricular
A-V	Arteriovenous
AVA	American Veal Association
AVDA	American Veterinary Distributors Association
AVEG	Aids Vaccine Evaluation Group
AVMA	American Veterinary Medical Association
A-VO2	Arteriovenous Oxygen
AWOL	Absent Without official Leave
AWP	Average Wholesale Price
AWS	Alternate Work Schedule

B

B&F (CVM)	Budget and Finance Team (CVM)
BA/BE	Bioavailability/Bioequivalence
BAC	Billing Agency Code
BaCON	Bacterial Contamination Study
BACPAC	Bulk Activities Postapproval Changes
BAER	Brief Adverse Event Report Review (CDRH)
BAH	Booz-Allen & Hamilton
BAM	Bacteriological Analytical Manual
BARC	Beltsville Area Agricultural Research Service (USDA)
BARDA	Biomedical Advanced Research and Development Authority
BARQA	British Association of Research Quality Assurance
BARS (CDER)	Business Analysis and Reporting Staff (CDER)
BASIS	Blood Availability and Safety inventory System (HHS)
BATF	Bureau of Alcohol, tobacco and Firearms (U.S. Department of Justice)
BB IND	Biological investigational New Drug
BBB	Bundle Branch Block
BBR	Bureau of Biologics and Radiopharmaceuticals (Canada)
BBS	Bulletin Board System
BC/BS	Blue Cross and Blue Shield Association Health insurance
BCA	Blood Center of America
BCAA	Branched-Chain Amino Acids
BCB (CFSAN)	Bioanalytical Chemistry Branch (CFSAN)
BCE	Beneficial Clinical Event
BCP	Bureau of Consumer Protection (FTC)
BCPT	Breast Cancer Prevention Trial

B

BDB	Biologic Devices Branch (CBER)
BDB (CDRH)	Bacteriology Devices Branch (CDRH)
BDLS	Blood Donor Locator Service
BDPA	Bureau of Drug Policy and Administration (China)
BDR	Budget Data Request
BDS	Bureau of Drug Surveillance (Canada)
BDSS	Biologics Decision Support System
BEA	Bureau of Economic Analysis (U.S. Department of Commerce)
BECON	Bioengineering Consortium (NIH)
BECS	Blood Establishment Computer Software
BENS	Business Executives for National Security
BEq	Bioequivalence
BER	Blood Establishment Registration and Product Listing (CBER)
BEST	Biomonitoring of Environmental Status and Trends Program (U.S. Geological Survey)
BFAC	Biologics Field Advisory Committee (CBER)
BFAD	Bureau of Food & Drug Administration (Philippines)
BfArM	Bundesinstitut Fur Arzneimittel Und Medizinprodukte (German Ministry of Health)
BFL	Biologic Establishment License Number (ORA AofC Code)
BGA	Bundesgesundheitsamt (German Federal Health Office)
BGH	Bovine Growth Hormone
BGMA	British Generic Manufacturer's Association
BHPr	Bureau of Health Professions (HRSA)
BIA	Bureau of indian Affairs (U.S. Department of the interior)
BID	Two Times Per Day

BIG	Blacks in Government
BIMO	Bioresearch Monitoring
BIMS	Biologic ind Management System
BIND	Biological investigational New Drug
BIO	Biotechnology industry Association
BIOB (CFSAN)	Biostatistics Branch (CFSAN)
BIRA	the British institute of Regulatory Affairs
BIRAMS	Biologics investigational and Related Applications Management System
BISTI	Biomedical information Science and Technology initiative (NIH)
BISTIC	Biomedical information Science and Technology initiative Consortium (NIH)
BIVAS	Body Image Visual Analog Scale
BLA	Biologics License Application (CBER)
BLM	Bureau of Land Management (U.S. Department of the interior)
BLS	Biologics License Supplement
BLST (CFSAN)	Building and Laboratory Services Team (CFSAN)
BLT	Blood Logging and Tracking System (CBER)
BMB (CFSAN)	Bioanalytical Methods Branch (CFSAN)
BMBL	Biosafety in Microbiological and Biomedical Laboratories (CDC)
BMI	Body Mass index
BMIS	Bioresearch Monitoring information System (CDER)
BMR	Basal Metabolic Rate
BMS (OC)	Broadcast Media Staff (OC)
BNA	Bureau of National Affairs
BNF	Biotechnology Notification File
BOCB (CFSAN)	Biological and organic Chemistry Branch (CFSAN)
BOP	Boards of Pharmacy
BOS (CBER)	Building Operations Staff (CBER)

B

BOS-DO (ORA)	Boston (Massachusetts) District Office (ORA)
BP	Blood Pressure
BP	British Pharmacopoeia
BPA	Bureau of Pharmaceutical Assessment (Canada)
BPA	Blanket Purchase Agreement
BPAC	Blood Products Advisory Committee (CBER)
BPB (CBER)	Blood and Plasma Branch (CBER)
BPC	Bulk Pharmaceutical Chemical
BPC	Bureau of Policy and Coordination (Canada)
BPCA	Best Pharmaceuticals for Children Act
BPD	Biological Product Deviation
BPD	Broncho-Pulmonary Dysplasia
BPE	Bulk Pharmaceutical Excipient
BPH	Benign Prostatic Hyperplasia
BPHC	Bureau of Primary Health Care (HRSA)
BPL	Biologic Product License Number (ORA AofC Code)
BPM	Beats Per Minute
BPR	Business Process Re-Engineering
BPSRG	Biomedical and Pharmaceutical Sciences Research Group (UK)
BrAPP	British Association of Pharmaceutical Physicians
BRCC	Biologics Research Coordinating Committee (CBER)
BRFSS	Benavioral Risk Factor Surveillance System (CDC)
BRMAC	Biological Response Modifiers Advisory Committee (CBER)
BRMD	Bureau of Radiation and Medical Devices (Canada)
BRMS	Biologics Regulatory Management System
BSA	Body Surface Area

BSB (CFSAN)	Biotechnology Studies Branch (Chicago, Illinois) (CFSAN)
BSC	Business Service Centers
BSC	Biological Safety Cabinet
BSC	Blood Safety Committee
BSD	Blood Service Directive
BSE	Bovine Spongiform Encephalopathy (Mad Cow Disease)
BSL	Biosafety Level
BST	Bovine Somatotropin
BT	Bioterrorism
Bt	Bacillus Thuringiensis
BT Act	Bioterrorism Act (Public Health Security and Bioterrorism Preparedness and Response Act of 2002)
BTA	the Bioterroism Act of 2002
BTCB (CBER)	Blood and Tissue Compliance Branch (CBER)
BTR	Blood and Tissue Registration System
BUF-DO (ORA)	Buffalo (New York) District Office (ORA)
BUN	Blood Urea Nitrogen
BUS	Bims User Support Group
BVB (CBER)	Bacterial Vaccine and Allergenic Products Branch (CBER)
BVC	British Veterinary Codex
BW	Body Weight
BWM	Biologics Workload Management
BWM	Basic Workload Measurement
BX	Biopsy

B

C

c	With
C & R	Corrections and Removals
C & S	Culture and Sensitivity
C of A	Certificate of Analysis
C/CC	Career or Career Conditional
C3I	Communications, Command, Control, and intelligence
CA	Chemical Abstracts
CA	Committee Assignment
CA	Competent Authority (U.K.)
CAAT	Center for Alternatives to Animal Testing (Johns Hopkins)
CAB	Conformity Assessment Body
CAB (OC)	Computer Applications Branch (OC)
CABE	Corrective Action(S) Being Effected
CABG	Coronary Artery Bypass Graft
caBIG	Cancer Biomedical informatics Grid (NIH)
CABs	Conformity Assessment Bodies
CAC	Carcinogenicity Assessment Committee (CDER)
CACBERS	Committee for the Advancement of CBER Science
CACTIS	Center ADP/TC Computer Tracking and inventory System (CFSAN)
CAD	Control of Automated Processes
CAD	Coronary Artery Disease
caDSR	Cancer Data Standards Repository (NCI)
CAERS	CFSAN Adverse Event Reporting System
CAERST (CFSAN)	CFSAN Adverse Event Reporting System Team
CAFDAS	Committee for the Advancement of FDA Science
CALA	Computer-Assisted License Application
CAN	Common Accounting Number

CANDA	Computer Assisted New Drug Application
CAO	Change of Appointing Office
CAP	Color Additive Petition
CAP	Corrective Action Plan
CAP	College of American Pathologists
CAPA	Corrective and Preventive Action
CAPD	Continuous Ambulatory Peritoneal Dialysis
CAPLA	Computer Assisted Product License Application
CAPLAR	Computer-Assisted Product License Application Review
CAPRA	Canadian Association of Professional Regulatory Affairs
CARS	Compliance Achievement Reporting System
CARTS	CFSAN Automated Research Tracking System
CAS	Chemical Abstracts Service
CAs	Competent Authorities
CASE	Computer Aided Software Engineering
CASPER	Center Automated System Process Exchange and Reporting (CFSAN)
CAST	Calf Antibiotic and Sulfonamide Test
CAST	Council for Agricultural Science
CAT	Computerized Axial tomography
CATCH	Child and Adolescent Trial for Cardiovascular Health (NIH)
CBC	Complete Blood Count
CBCTN	Community-Based Clinical Trials Network (Amfar)
CBE	Changes Being Effected
CBER	Center for Biologics Evaluation and Research (FDA)
CBG	Capillary Blood Gas
CBIAC	Chemical and Biological Defense information Analysis Center (DoD)

C

CBO	Congressional Budget Office (U.S.)
CBP	Customs and Border Protection (U.S. Department of Homeland Security)
CBRA	California Biomedical Research Association
CBRG	Cancer Biomarkers Research Group (NCI)
CBSC	Cord Blood Stem Cells
CBT	Computer-Based Training
CC	Clinical Center (NIH)
CC	Chief Complaint
CC	Coordinating Committee
CC	Conference Call
CC	Commissioned Corps
CC/RVDF	Codex Committee on Residues of Veterinary Drugs in Foods
CCA	Clinger-Cohen Act (formerly the information Technology Management Reform Act)
CCB (CFSAN)	Color Certification Branch (CFSAN)
CCBC	Council of Community Blood Centers
CCC	Compliance Coordinating Committee (CDER)
CCC	Commodity Credit Corporation (FSA)
CCC	Chinese Ceramicware Factory Code (ORA AofC Code)
CCEHRP	Committee to Coordinate Environmental Health and Related Programs (PHS)
CCFAC	Codex Committee on Food Additives and Contaminants
CCFICS	Codex Committee on Food Import and Export Certification and inspection Systems
CCFL	Codex Committee on Food Labeling
CCHIT	Certification Commission for Healthcare information Technology
CCI	Corrected Count increment

CCOHTA	Canadian Coordinating Office for Health Technology Assessment
CCOP	Community Clinical oncology Program (NCI)
CCP	Critical Control Point
CCPR	Codex Committee on Pesticide Residues
CCR	Center for Cancer Research (NCI)
CCR	CDER Request for Collaborative Review
CCRA	Clinical Contract Research Association (UK)
CCRC	Certified Clinical Research Coordinator
CCST (CFSAN)	Clinical Chemistry Support Team (CFSAN)
CCU	Clean Catch Urine
CCU	Cardiac Care Unit
CCVDF	Codex Committee on Veterinary Drugs in Foods
CDA	Clinical Document Architecture
CDASH	Clinical Data Acquisition Standards Harmonization
CDC	Centers for Disease Control and Prevention (DHHS)
CDDI	Collaboration for Drug Development Improvement
CDDTB (CBER)	Career Development and Directed Training Branch (CBER)
CDER	Center for Drug Evaluation and Research (FDA)
CDIS	Component Distribution information System
CDISC	Clinical Data interchange Standards Consortium
CDM	Clinical Data Management
CDP	Candidate Development Program (SES)
CDP	Career Development Plan
CDR	Central Document Room
CDR	Clinical Drug Request

C

C

CDRH	Center for Devices and Radiological Health (FDA)
CD-ROM	Compact Disc Read-only Memory
CDRS (CFSAN)	Case Development and Recall Staff (CFSAN)
CDSA	Controlled Drugs and Substances Act (Canada)
CDUS	Clinical Data Update System (NCI)
CE	Continuing Education
CE Mark	CE (Conformite Europeene or European Conformity) Marking
CEA	Council of Economic Advisers
CEARS	CBER Error and Accident Reporting System
CEB (CDER)	Clinical Evaluation Branch (CBER)
CEB (CFSAN)	Compliance and Enforcement Branch (CFSAN)
CEDR	Comprehensive Epidemiologic Data Resource (U.S. Department of Energy)
CEF	Chick Embryo Fibroblast
CEFIC	European Chemical industry Council
CEMB (CDRH)	Cardiac Electrophysiology and Monitoring Devices Branch (CDRH)
CEN	Comite Europeen De Normalisation (European Committee for Standardization)
CENELEC	Comite Europeen De Normalisation Electrotechnique (European Committee for Electrotechnical Standardization)
CEO	Chief Executive Officer
CEPPO	Chemical Emergency Preparedness and Prevention Office (EPA)
CEQ	Council on Environmental Quality
CERCLIS	Comprehensive Environmental Response, Compensation and Liability information System (EPA)
CERG	CBER Emergency Relocation Group
CERT	Community Emergency Response Team

CERTS	Centers for Education and Research on therapeutics (DHHS)
CES (CFSAN)	Consumer Education Staff (CFSAN)
CET (CFSAN)	Clinical Evaluation Team (CFSAN)
CEU	Continuing Education Units
CF	Cystic Fibrosis
CFA	Catfish Farmers of America
CFC	Combined Federal Campaign
CFC	Chlorofluorohydrocarbons
CFDA	Catalog of Federal Domestic Assistance
CFG	Certificate for foreign Government
CFG	Center for Functional Genomics (NCTR)
CFIA	Canadian Food inspection Agency
CFN	Central File Number (ORA)
CFO	Chief Financial Officer
CFO (OC)	Chief Financial Officer (OC)
CFOC	Chief Financial Officers Council
CFR	Code of Federal Regulations
CFR	Code of Federal Regulations Section (ORA AofC Code)
CFSAN	Center for Food Safety and Applied Nutrition (FDA)
CFU	Colony forming Unit
CGCS	Computer-Generated Cover Sheet
CGI	Common Gateway interface
CGL	Chronic Granulocytic Leukemia
cGMP	Current Good Manufacturing Practice
CGMPR	Current Good Manufacturing Practices Regulations
CGS (ORA)	Contract and Grants Staff (ORA)
CGTP	Current Good Tissue Practice
CH	Clinical Hold
CHAMPVA	Civilian Health and Medical Program of the Department of Veterans Affairs
CHAT (CFSAN)	Chemical Hazards Assessment Team (CFSAN)

C

CHCB (CFSAN)	Chemical Contaminants Branch (CFSAN)
CHF	Congestive Heart Failure
CHI	Consolidated Health informatics initiative
CHID	Combined Health information Database (NIH)
CHISSA	Center for High integrity Software System Assurance
ChLIA	Chemi-Luminescent Immunoassay
CHO	Carbohydrate
CHPA	Consumer Healthcare Products Association
CHSB (CFSAN)	Chemical Hazards Science Branch (CFSAN)
CI	Criminal investigator
CI	Confidential informant
CI	Clinical investigator
CI/KR	Critical infrastructure and Key Resources
CIA	Corporate integrity Agreement
CIA	Central intelligence Agency (U.S.)
CIAC	Computer incident Advisory Capability (U.S. Department of Energy)
CIAO	Critical infrastructure Assurance Office
CIB	Clinical investigator's Brochure
CIB (CFSAN)	Compliance information Branch (CFSAN)
CIN	Color index Number (ORA AofC Code)
CINAHL	Cumulative index to Nursing and Allied Health Literature
CIO	Chief information Officer
CIOMS	Council for international organizations of Medical Sciences (WHO)
CIP	Clean in Place
CIP	Critical infrastructure Protection
CIPP	Critical infrastructure Protection Program
CIR	Cosmetic ingredient Review
CIRMS	Council on Ionizing Radiation Measurements and Standards

CIRS	Center information Retrieval System (CDRH)
CIS	Cancer information Service (NCI)
CIS	Catastrophic incident Supplement (FEMA)
CISET	Committee on international Science, Engineering and Technology
CIT	Center for information Technology (NIH)
CITES	Convention on international Trade in Endangered Species of Wild Fauna and Flora
CJD	Creutzfeldt Jakob Disease
CLA	Conference Lodging Allowance
CLIA	Clinical Laboratory Improvement Amendments of 1988
CLSI	Clinical and Laboratory Standards institute
CM	Committee Meeting
CM	Configuration Management
CM	Case Management
CM	Chemistry and Manufacturing (Canada)
CMA	Chemical Manufacturers Association
CMC	Chemistry, Manufacturing, and Control
CMCCC	Chemistry and Manufacturing Controls Coordinating Committee (CDER)
CME	Continuing Medical Education
CMGB (CDER)	Cae Management and Guidance Branch (CDER)
CMHS	Center for Mental Health Services (SAMHSA)
CMO	Contract Management organization
CMP	Civil Money Penalty
CMP/ HMO	Comprehensive Medical Plan/Health Maintenance organization
CMS	Centers for Medicare and Medicaid Services (DHHS) (formerly HCFA)
CMV	Cytomegalovirus
CN	Cranial Nerves

C

C

CND (CDRH)	Cardiovascular/Neurological Devices Branch (CDRH)
CNPP	Center for Nutrition Policy and Promotion (USDA)
CNS	Central Nervous System
CNS	Congress of Neurological Surgeons
CO	Commissioned Officer
CO	Contract Officer
CO	Compliance Officer
COA	Commissioned Officers Association (PHS)
COA	Certificate of Analysis
COB	Close of Business
COB (OC)	Contract Operations Branch (OC)
COBRA	Consolidated Omnibus Budget Reconciliation Act
COBTA	Council on Biologics and therapeutic Agents (of AVMA)
COCB (CFSAN)	Communication and Coordination Branch (CFSAN)
CODB (CDRH)	Cardiovascular and Ophthalmic Devices Branch (CDRH)
CODEX	Codex Alimentarius
COE	Certificate of Exportability
CoE	Center of Excellence
COFEPRIS	Comisión Federal Para La Protección Contra Riesgos Sanitarios (Federal Commission for the Protection Against Sanitary Risks) (Mexico)
COI	Conflict of interest
COLA	Cost of Living Allowance
COLD	Chronic Obstructive Lung Disease
COMAH	Control of Major Accident Hazards Regulations 1999
COMIS	Center-Wide ORAcle Management information System
COMSTAT	Compliance Status information System
CONOPS	Concept of Operations

CONSER	Cooperative online Serials
CONUS	Continental United States
COOL	Country-of-origin Labeling
COOP	Continuity of Operations Plan
COP	Clean Out of Place
COP	Continuation of Pay
COP	Coastal Ocean Program (NOAA)
COPD	Chronic Obstructive Pulmonary Disease
COPR	Council of Public Representatives (NIH OD)
COPTRG	Community oncology and Prevention Trials Research Group (NCI)
CORE	EASE Central Repository Module
CoS	Certificate of Suitability
COS	Cosmetic Registration Number (ORA AofC Code)
COS (CFSAN)	Cosmetics Staff (CFSAN)
COSTART	Coding Symbols for thesaurus of Adverse Reaction Terms
COTA	Career Opportunities Training Agreement (HHS)
COTB (CBER)	Communication Technology Branch (CBER)
COTS	Commercial off-the-Shelf Software
COTT	Committee of Ten Thousand
CP	Cerebral Palsy
CP	Chest Pain
CP	Compliance Program
CP	Citizen Petition
CPAC	Central Pharmaceutical Affairs Council (Japan)
CPAP	Continuous Positive Airway Pressure
CPB (CFSAN)	Compliance Programs Branch (CFSAN)
CPC	Compliance Policy Council
CPCSEA	Committee for the Purpose of Control and Supervision on Experiments on Animals (india)

C

CPDF	Central Personnel Data File (OPM)
CPE	Continuing Professional Education
CPFP	Cancer Prevention Fellowship Program (NCI)
CPG	Compliance Policy Guide
CPGM	Compliance Program Guidance Manual
CPI	Consumer Price index
CPID	Certified Product information Document (Canada)
CPK	Creatinine Phosphokinase
CPMP	Committee for Proprietary Medicinal Products (EMEA)
CPP	Critical Process Parameter
CPP	Certificate of Pharmaceutical Product
CPR	Cardiopulmonary Resuscitation
CPS	Compendium of Pharmaceuticals and Specialties (Canada)
CPSA	Consumer Product Safety Act
CPSC	Consumer Product Safety Commission
CPT	Current Procedural Terminology (Ama)
CR	Collection Report
CRA	Clinical Research Associate
CRADA	Cooperative Research and Development Agreement
CRB (CBER)	Clinical Review Branch (CBER)
CRC	Clinical Research Coordinator
CRC	Civil Rights Center (U.S. Department of Labor)
CRCL	Creatinine Clearance
CRCPD	Conference of Radiation Control Program Directors
CRF	Case Report form
CRF	Chronic Renal Failure
CRIS	Clinical Research information System (NIH)
CRISP	Computer Retrieval of information on Scientific Projects (Database) (NIH)

CRIX	Clinical Research information Exchange (FDA and NCI)
CRM	Corporate Records Management
CRMT (OC)	Cosmetics toxicology Branch (CFSAN)
CRMTS	CBER Regulatory Meetings Management Tracking System
CRO	Contract Research organization
CRO	Clinical Research organization
CRP	C-Reactive Protein
CRR	Consult Review Request
CRS	Contamination Response System
CRS	Congressional Research Service
CRT	Case Report Tabulations
CRTP	Clinical Research Training Program
CRU	Center Recall Unit
CRWG	Hurricane Katrina Comprehensive Review Working Group
CS	Civil Service
CS	Clinically Significant
CS (CVM)	Communications Staff (CVM)
CS (OC)	Communications Staff (OC)
CSA	Controlled Substances Act
CSA	Clinical Study Agreement
CSAP	Center for Substance Abuse Prevention (SAMHSA)
CSAT	Center for Substance Abuse Treatment (SAMHSA)
CSB	Chemical Safety and Hazard investigation Board
CSB (OC)	Customer Support Branch (OC)
CSB (ORA)	Customer Support Branch (ORA)
CSDD	Center for the Study of Drug Development (Tufts University)
CSF	Cerebrospinal Fluid
CSG	Counterterrorism Security Group
CSI	Consumer Safety inspector
CSM	Committee on Safety of Medicines (UK)

C

CSO	Consumer Safety Officer
CSPDB (CDRH)	Circulatory Support and Prosthetic Devices Branch (CDRH)
CSPI	Center for Science in the Public interest
CSR	Center for Scientific Review (NIH)
CSR	Customer Service Records
CSR	Customer Service Representative (EASE)
CSR	Clinical Study Report
CSREES	Cooperative State Research, Education and Extension Services (USDA)
CSS (CDER)	Controlled Substance Staff (CDER)
CST	Consumer Safety Technician
CST (CFSAN)	Consumer Studies Team (CFSAN)
CSTE	Council of State and Territorial Epidemiologists
CSV	Comma Separated VAlue (File format)
CSV	Computer System Validation
CT	Computed tomography
CT	Clinical Trial
CTA	Clinical Trial Application
CTA	Clinical Trial Agreement
CTAP	Career Transition Assistance Plan
CTB (CBER)	Cell therapies Branch (CBER)
CTC	Clinical Trial Certificate
CTC	Common toxicity Criteria
CTC	Chlortetracycline
CTD	Common Technical Document
CTDB 1 (CDRH)	Chemistry and toxicology Devices Branch 1 (CDRH)
CTDB 2 (CDRH)	Chemistry and toxicology Devices Branch 2 (CDRH)
CTEB (CFSAN)	Cosmetics Technology Branch (CFSAN)
CTEP	Cancer therapy Evaluation Program
CTFA	Cosmetic, toiletry and Fragrance Association

CTIA	Cellular Telecommunications and internet Association
CTM	Clinical Trials Materials
CTO	Clinical Trial Outline
CTOB (CFSAN)	Cosmetics toxicology Branch (CFSAN)
C-TPAT	Customs-Trade Partnership against Terrorism
CTS	Correspondence Tracking System
CTS	Counseling and Testing Site
CTTB (CBER)	Cellular and Tissue therapy Branch (CBER)
CTX	Clinical Trials Exemption (UK)
CU	Consumers Union
CUE	Confidential Unit Exclusion
CUF	Commissione Unica Del Farmaco (Italy)
CUVP	Committee for Veterinary Medicinal Products (EMEA)
CV	Curriculum Vitae
CV	Cardiovascular
CVA	Costovertebral Angle
CVA	Cerebrovascular Accident
CVM	Center for Veterinary Medicine (FDA)
CVMP	Committee on Veterinary Medical Products (EMEA)
CVP	Central Venous Pressure
CXR	Chest X-Ray
CY	Calendar Year

C

D

D & C	Dilation and Curettage
D0AF (CDRH)	Division of Planning, Analysis and Finance (CDRH)
DA (OC)	Division of Accounting (OC)
DAA	Designated Approving Authority
DAARP (CDER)	Division of Anesthesia, Analgesia, and Rheumatology Products (CDER)
DAC (CFSAN)	Division of of Analytical Chemistry (CFSAN)
DADS	Developers and Distributors System
DADS (CDER)	Division of Applications Development and Services (CDER)
DAE (OC)	Division of Applied Engineering (OC)
DAEA II	Division of Adverse Event Analysis 2 (CDER)
DAF (CVM)	Division of Animal Feeds (CVM)
DAFM (CVM)	Division of Animal and Food Microbiology (CVM)
DAGID (CDRH)	Division of Anesthesiology, General Hospital, infection Control, and Dental Devices (CDRH)
DAIDS	Division of AIDS (NIAID)
DailyMed	NLM-Based Database of information on Marketed Drugs including FDA-Approved Labels.
DAIOP (CDER)	Division of Anti-infective and Ophthalmology Products (CDER)
DAL	Defect Action Level
DAPR (CDER)	Division of Applied Pharmacology Research (CDER)
DAR (CVM)	Division of Animal Research (CVM)
DARPA	Defense Advanced Research Projects Agency (DoD)
DARRTS	Document Archiving, Reporting and Regulatory Tracking System

DART	Developmental and Reproductive toxicology
DAS (CFSAN)	Division of Administrative Services Management (CFSAN)
DAS (NCTR)	Division of Administrative Services (NCTR)
DAT	Diet As tolerated
DATS	Document Accountability and Tracking System (CBER)
DAVP (CDER)	Division of Anti-Viral Products (CDER)
DAWN	Drug Abuse Warning Network
DB	Double-Blind
DB (CBER)	Division of Biostatistics (CBER)
DB (CDRH)	Division of Biology (CDRH)
DB I (CDER)	Division of Biometrics I (CDER)
DB II (CDER)	Division of Biometrics II (CDER)
DB III (CDER)	Division of Biometrics III (CDER)
DB IV (CDER)	Division of Biometrics IV (CDER)
DB V (CDER)	Division of Biometrics V (CDER)
DB VI (CDER)	Division of Biometrics VI (CDER)
dba	Doing Business As
DBA (CBER)	Division of Blood Applications (CBER)
DBC (CFSAN)	Division of Bioanalytical Chemistry (CFSAN)
DBCP (CBER)	Division of Blood Collection and Processing (CBER)
DBE (CDER)	Division of Bioequivalence (CDER)
DBEC (OC)	Division of Budget Execution and Control (OC)
DBEPA (CBER)	Division of Blood Establishment and Product Applications (CBER)
DBGNR (CFSAN)	Division of Biotechnology and GRAS Notice Review (CFSAN)
DBGNR (CFSAN)	Division of Biotechnology and GRAS Notice Review (CFSAN)
DBM (CDRH)	Division of Bioresearch Monitoring (CDRH)

D

D

DBMS	Database Management System
DBOP (CDER)	Division of Biologic oncology Products (CDER)
DBPAP (CBER)	Division of Bacterial, Parasitic and Allergenic Products (CBER)
DBRA (NCTR)	Division of Biometry and Risk Assessment (NCTR)
DBS (CDRH)	Division of Biostatistics (CDRH)
DBT (NCTR)	Division of Biochemical toxicology (NCTR)
DC	Discontinue
DC	Discharge
DC (CVM)	Division of Compliance (CVM)
DC (NCTR)	Division of Chemistry (NCTR)
DC I (CDER)	Division of Chemistry I (CDER)
DC II (CDER)	Division of Chemistry II (CDER)
DC III (CDER)	Division of Chemistry III (CDER)
DCB (CFSAN)	Domestic Compliance Branch (CFSAN)
DCC	Document Control Center
DCC (CBER)	Document Control Center (CBER)
DCC (CFSAN)	Division of Cosmetics and Compliance (CFSAN)
DCC (OC)	Division of Customer Care (OC)
DCCA (CBER)	Division of Communication and Consumer Affairs (CBER)
DCCT (CFSAN)	Division of Color Certification and Technology (CFSAN)
DCD (CDRH)	Division of Cardiovascular Devices (CDRH)
DCEPT (CBER)	Division of Clinical Evaluation and Pharmacology/toxicology (CBER)
DCF	Data Clarification Request form
DCGM (OC)	Division of Contracts and Grants Management (OC)
DCGT (CBER)	Division of Cell and Gene therapies (CBER)
DCIA	Debt Collection Act of 1996

DCIQA (ORA)	Division of Compliance information and Quality Assurance (ORA)
DCIS	Design Control inspection Strategy
DCLD (CDRH)	Division of Clinical Laboratory Devices (CDRH)
DCM (CBER)	Division of Case Management (CBER)
DCM (CDRH)	Division of Communications Media (CDRH)
DCMO (ORA)	Division of Compliance Management and Operations (ORA)
DCMS (CDRH)	Division of Chemistry and Material Science (CDRH)
DCP (CFSAN)	Division of Cooperative Programs (CFSAN)
DCP (NCTR)	Division of Contracts and Procurement (NCTR)
DCP (ORA)	Division of Compliance Policy (ORA)
DCP 1 (CDER)	Division of Clinical Pharmacology 1 (CDER)
DCP 2 (CDER)	Division of Clinical Pharmacology 2 (CDER)
DCP 3 (CDER)	Division of Clinical Pharmacology 3 (CDER)
DCP 4 (CDER)	Division of Clinical Pharmacology 4 (CDER)
DCP 5 (CDER)	Division of Clinical Pharmacology 5 (CDER)
DCPA (CBER)	Division of Congressional and Public Affairs (CBER)
DCPS	Defense Civilian Pay System
DCRER (CFSAN)	Division of Chemistry Research and Environmental Review (CFSAN)
DCRMS (CDER)	Division of Compliance Risk Management and Surveillance (CDER)
DCRP (CDER)	Division of Cardiovascular and Renal Products (CDER)
DCSC (OC)	Division of Construction and Service Contracts (OC)

D

D

DCT (CDER)	Division of Counter-Terrorism (CDER)
DCTD (CDRH)	Division of Chemistry and toxicology Devices (CDRH)
DCU	Document Control Unit
DD	Division Director
DD	Department of Drugs (Swedish Regulatory Agency)
DD (CVM)	District Director
DDA	Division of Drug Analysis (CDER)
DDB (CDRH)	Dental Devices Branch (CDRH)
DDB (CDRH)	Diagnostic Devices Branch (CDRH)
DDDP (CDER)	Division of Dermatology and Dental Products (CDER)
DDE	Dynamic Data Exchange
DDES (CFSAN)	Division of Dairy and Egg Safety (CFSAN)
DDI (CDER)	Division of Drug information (CDER)
DDM (NCTR)	Deputy Director for Management (NCTR)
DDM (OC)	Division of Dockets Management (OC)
DDMAC (CDER)	Division of Drug Marketing, Advertising and Communication (CDER)
DDMS (CDER)	Division of Database Management and Services (CDER)
DDOM (CBER)	Division of Disclosure and Oversight Management (CBER)
DDOP (CDER)	Division of Drug oncology Products (CDER)
DDR	Donor Deferral Registry
DDRE (CDER)	Division of Drug Risk Evaluation (CDER)
DDSPC (CFSAN)	Division of Dietary Supplement Programs and Compliance (CFSAN)
DE (CBER)	Division of Epidemiology (CBER)
DE (CFSAN)	Division of Enforcement (CFSAN)
DEA	Drug Enforcement Administration (U.S. Department of Justice)
DEB (CFAN)	Dairy and Egg Branch (CFSAN)

DEC (CFSAN)	Division of Education and Communication (CFSAN)
DEEM	Dietary Exposure Evaluation Model
DEHP	Di(2-Ethylhexyl)Phthalate
DEIO (ORA)	Division of Emergency and investigational Operations (ORA)
DEMO (CDRH)	Division of Ethics and Management Operations (CDRH)
DEN	Drug Experience Network
DEOD (CDRH)	Dental, Ear, Nose, Throat and Ophthalmic Devices Branch (CDRH)
DEP	Data Evaluation Project
DEPI (CBER)	Division of Ethics and Program integrity (CBER)
DEPI (CDER)	Division of Epidemiology (CDER)
DER	Drug Experience Report
DES	Diethylstilbestrol
DES	Drug Eluting Stent
DES (CVM)	Division of Epidemiology and Surveillance (CVM)
DES (OC)	Division of Engineering Services (OC)
DESE (CDRH)	Division of Electrical and Software Engineering (CDRH)
DESI	Drug Efficacy Study Implementation
DETTD (CBER)	Division of Emerging and Transfusion Transmitted Diseases (CBER)
DEV	Device Registration Number (ORA AofC Code)
DFCN (CFSAN)	Division of Food Contact Notifications (CFSAN)
DFEM (NCTR)	Division of Facilities Engineering and Maintenance (NCTR)
DFLSC (CFSAN)	Division of Food Labeling, Standards, and Compliance (CFSAN)
DFM (NCTR)	Division of Financial Management (NCTR)
DFO	Designated Federal official
DFO (OC)	Division of Field Operations (OC)

D

D

DFOI (OC)	Division of Freedom of information (OC)
DFPG (CFSAN)	Division of Field Programs and Guidance (CFSAN)
DFPP (CFSAN)	Division of Food Processing and Packaging (Chicago, Illinois) (CFSAN)
DFPST (CFSAN)	Division of Food Processing Science and Technology (CFSAN)
DFRM	Drug Facility Registration Module (Furls)
DFS	Division File System
DFS (ORA)	Division of Field Science (ORA)
DGFPS	Direccion General De Farmacia Y Productos Sanitarios (Directorate General of Pharmacy and Sanitary Products) (Spain)
DGP (CDER)	Division of Gastroenterology Products (CDER)
DGRND (CDRH)	Division of General, Restorative and Neurological Devices (CDRH)
DGRT (NCTR)	Division of Genetic and Reproductive toxicology (NCTR)
DGSS (CFSAN)	Division of General Scientific Support (CFSAN)
DH (CBER)	Division of Hematology (CBER)
DHC	Dioxin Health Certificate (ORA AofC Code)
DHCP	Dear Healthcare Professional (Type of Letter)
DHCP	Dynamic Host Configuration Protocol
DHF	Design History File
DHFS (CVM)	Division of Human Food Safety (CVM)
DHHS	Department of Health and Human Services (U.S.)
DHR	Device History Record
DHRD (ORA)	Division of Human Resources Development (ORA)
DHS	Department of Homeland Security (U.S.)
DHSS	Department of Health and Social Security (U.K.)

DHT (CBER)	Division of Human Tissues (CBER)
DI	Diabetes insipidus
DI	Deionized Water
DIA	Drug information Association
DIA	Defense intelligence Agency (U.S.)
DIAM (CDRH)	Division of Imaging and Applied Mathematics (CDRH)
DIB	Directory, investigations Branch
DIC	Disseminated intravascular Coagulation
DICOM	Digital Imaging and Communications in Medicine
DID (CBER)	Division of information Development (CBER)
DIDP (CBER)	Division of information Disclosure Policy (CDER)
DIHD (CDRH)	Division of Immunology and Hematology Devices (CDRH)
DIMS (CFSAN)	Data information Management Staff (CFSAN)
DIMS (OC)	Division of infrastructure Management and Services (OC)
DIN	Drug Identification Number (Canada)
DIO (CBER)	Division of information Operations (CBER)
DIO (OC)	Division of infrastructure Operations (OC)
DIOP (ORA)	Division of Import Operations and Policy (ORA)
DIRM (CFSAN)	Division of information Resources Management (CFSAN)
DIS (CBER)	Division of inspections and Surveillance (CBER)
DIS (CDER)	Division of information Services (CDER)
DIT (CDRH)	Division of information Technology (CDER)
DIT (NCTR)	Division of information Technology (NCTR)
DIVBT (CFSAN)	Division of in Vitro and Biochemical toxicology (CFSAN)

D

DJD	Degenerative Joint Disease
DKA	Diabetic Ketoacidosis
dL	Deciliter
DLI	Donor Lymphocyte infusion
DLPS (CDER)	Division of Labeling and Program Support (CDER)
DLR	Drug Listing Rule
DLS	Document Logging System (CBER)
DLS	Drug Listing Number (ORA AofC Code)
DM	Diabetes Mellitus
DM (CFSAN)	Division of Mathematics (CFSAN)
DM (CFSAN)	Division of Microbiology (CFSAN)
DM (NCTR)	Division of Microbiology (NCTR)
DMA	Danish Medicines Agency
DMA (CDER)	Division of Monoclonal Antibodies (CDER)
DMARDS	Disease-Modifying Antirheumatic Drug
DMAT	Disaster Medical Assistance Team
DMAT (CBER)	Division of Manufacturers Assistance and Training (CBER)
DMB	Dockets Management Branch
DMB (CDER)	Division of Management and Budget (CDER)
DMB (CFSAN)	Division of Molecular Biology (CFSAN)
DMC	Data Monitoring Committee
DMD (CDRH)	Division of Microbiology Devices (CDRH)
DME	Durable Medical Equipment
DME (NCTR)	Division of Molecular Epidemiology (NCTR)
DMEP (CDER)	Division of Metabolism and Endocrinology Products (CDER)
DMETS (CDER)	Division of Medical Errors and Technical Support (CDER)
DMF	Drug Master File
DMIHP (CDER)	Division of Medical Imaging and Hematology Products (CDER)

DMIRDP (CDER)	Division of Medical Imaging and Radiopharmaceutical Drug Products (CDER)
DMO (CFSAN)	Division of Management Operations (CFSAN)
DMO (ORA)	Division of Management Operations (ORA)
DMORT	Disaster Mortuary Operational Response Team
DMPQ (CBER)	Division of Manufacturing and Product Quality (CBER)
DMPQ (CDER)	Division of Manufacturing and Product Quality (CDER)
DMQRP (CDRH)	Division of Mammography Quality and Radiation Programs (CDRH)
DMR	Device Master Record
DMS (CDER)	Division of Management Services (CDER)
DMS (CFSAN)	Division of Microbiological Studies (CFSAN)
DMS (OC)	Division of Management Systems (OC)
DMSO	Dimethylsulfoxide
DMST (CFSAN)	Division of Market Studies (CFSAN)
DMT (CVM)	Division of Manufacturing Technologies (CVM)
DNA	Deoxyribonucleic Acid
DNCE (CDER)	Division of Nonprescripton Clinical Evaluation (CDER)
DNDLC (CDER)	Division of New Drugs and Labeling Compliance (CDER)
DNP (CDER)	Division of Neurology Products (CDER)
DNP (CFSAN)	Division of Natural Products (CFSAN)
DNPL (CFSAN)	Division of Nutrition Programs and Labeling (CFSAN)
DNR	Do Not Resuscitate
DNRD (CDER)	Division of Nonprescription Regulation Development (CDER)
DNS	Domain Name Server

D

DNT (NCTR)	Division of Neurotoxicology (NCTR)
DO	District Office (FDA)
DO	Disbursing Officer
DOA	Drugs of Abuse
DOA	Dead on Arrival
DOC	Department of Commerce (U.S.)
DOC	Documentary Sample
DoD	Department of Defense (U.S.)
DODP (CDER)	Division of oncologic Drug Products (CDER)
DOE	Department of Energy (U.S.)
DOE	Design of Experiment
DOE	Dyspnea on Exertion
DOE A (CDRH)	Division of Enforcement A (CDRH)
DOE B (CDRH)	Division of Enforcement B (CDRH)
DOEd	Department of Education (U.S.)
DOED (CDRH)	Division of Ophthalmic, Ear, Nose and Throat Devices (CDRH)
DOI	Department of the interior (U.S.)
DOJ	Department of Justice (U.S.)
DOL	Department of Labor (U.S.)
DOS	Department of State (U.S.)
DOT	Department of Transportation (U.S.)
DOT (CFSAN)	Division of toxicology (CFSAN)
DP	Drug Product
DP (CDRH)	Division of Physics (CDRH)
DP (NCTR)	Division of Planning (NCTR)
DPA (CDER)	Division of Pharmaceutical Analysis (CDER)
DPA (CDER)	Division of Public Affairs (CDER)
DPA I (CDER)	Division of Pre-Marketing Assessment I (CDER)
DPA II (CDER)	Division of Pre-Marketing Assessment II (CDER)
DPAMS (CDER)	Division of Pre-Marketing Assessment III and Manufacturing Science (CDER)

DPAP (CDER)	Division of Pulmonary and Allergy Products (CDER)
DPC-PTR Act	Drug Price Competition and Patent Trade Restoration Act of 1984
DPD (CVM)	Division of Production Drugs (CVM)
DPD (OC)	Division of Portfolio Development (OC)
DPDD (CDER)	Division of Pediatric Drug Development (CDER)
DPDFS (CFSAN)	Division of Plant and Dairy Food Safety (CFSAN)
DPE (CDER)	Division of Post-Marketing Development (CDER)
DPEB (CBER)	Division of Planning, Evaluation and Budget (CBER)
DPEM (ORA)	Division of Planning, Evaluation and Management (ORA)
DPEPOPD (CFSAN)	Division of Programs and Enforcement Policy (OPDFB) (CFSAN)
DPEPOS (CFSAN)	Division of Programs and Enforcement Policy (OS) (CFSAN)
DPFRM (CFSAN)	Division of Planning and Financial Resources Management (CFSAN)
DPHB (CFSAN)	Division of Public Health and Biostatistics (CFSAN)
DPI	Dry Powder inhaler
DPIC (CFSAN)	Division of Pesticides and industrial Chemicals (CFSAN)
DPL	Drug Product Licensing (Canada)
DPMU	Disaster Portable Morgue Unit (PHS)
DPP (CDER)	Division of Psychiatry Products (CDER)
DPPS (CFSAN)	Division of Plant Product Safety (CFSAN)
DPQ (CBER)	Division of Product Quality (CBER)
DPQR (CDER)	Division of Product Quality Research (CDER)
DPR (CFSAN)	Division of Petition Review (CFSAN)
DPRF	Drug Product Reference File
DPS (CBER)	Division of Program Services (CBER)

D

DPS (CDRH)	Division of Post-Marketing Surveillance (CDRH)
DPS (CFSAN)	Division of Program Services (CFSAN)
DPT	Diphtheria, Pertussis, and Tetanus
DQ	Design Quality
DQRS	Drug Quality Reporting System (CDER)
DR	Discipline Review [Letter]
DR	Delayed Release [Medication]
DRA (CFSAN)	Division of Risk Assessment (CFSAN)
DRARD (CDRH)	Division of Reproductive, Abdominal and Radiological Devices (CDRH)
DRAT (CFSAN)	Division of Research and Applied Technology (CFSAN)
DRB (CBER)	Devices Review Branch (CBER)
DRC	Disaster Recovery Center
DRC (CVM)	Division of Residue Chemistry (CVM)
DRF	Dose Range Findings (Study)
DRFDD (ORA)	Deputy Regional Food and Drug Director (ORA)
DRG	Diagnosis Related Group
DRG	Disaster Response Group
DRI	Daily Reference intake
DRLM	Device Registration and Listing Module (FURLS)
DRLS	Drug Registration and Listing System
DRM (CDER)	Division of Records Management (CDER)
DRM (OC)	Division of Resource Management (OC)
DRMO (CDRH)	Division of Risk Management Operations (CDRH)
DRMP (CDER)	Division of Review Management and Policy (CDER)
DRP (CBER)	Division of Regulations and Policy (CBER)
DRP I (CDER)	Division of Regulatory Policy I (CDER)
DRP II (CDER)	Division of Regulatory Policy II (CDER)
DRPM	Dispute Resolution Project Manager

DRR (NCTR)	Deputy Director for Research (NCTR)
DRUP (CDER)	Division of Reproductive and Urologic Products (CDER)
DRV	Daily Reference VAlue
DS	Drug Substance
DS (CVM)	Division of Surveillance (CVM)
DSAC (CBER)	Division of Scientific Advisors and Consultants (CBER)
DSATOS (CFSAN)	Division of Science and Applied Technology (OS) (CFSAN)
DSCI (OC)	Division of Systems, Compliance and IMPAC (OC)
DSDB (CDRH)	Diagnostic and Surgical Devices Branch (CDRH)
DSFM (CDRH)	Division of Solid and Fluid Mechanics (CDRH)
DSHEA	Dietary Supplement and Health Education Act of 1994
DSI (CDER)	Division of Scientific investigation (CDER)
DSM	Data Standards Manual (CDER)
DSMB	Data Safety Monitoring Board
DSMICA (CDRH)	Division of Small Manufacturers, international and Consumer Assistance (CDRH)
DSORD	Division of Surgical, orthopedic, and Restorative Devices (CDRH)
DSP	Desktop Standardization Project
DSP (OC)	Division of Strategic Projects (OC)
DSPTP (CDER)	Division of Special Pathogen and Transplant Products (CDER)
DSRCS (CDER)	Division of Surveillance, Research and Communication Support (CDER)
DSRIT (CFSAN)	Dietary Supplement Regulations Implementation Team (CFSAN)
DSS	Decision Support System
DSS (CDRH)	Division of Surveillance Systems (CDRH)
DSS (CFSAN)	Division of Seafood Safety (CFSAN)

D

D

DSS (CFSAN)	Division of Social Sciences (CFSAN)
DSST (CFSAN)	Division of Seafood Science and Technology (CFSAN)
DTaP	Diphtheria, Tetanus, and Pertussis [Vaccine]
DTBIMP (CDER)	Division of therapeutic Biological internal Medicine Products (CDER)
DTBOP (CDER)	Division of therapeutic Biological oncology Products (CDER)
DTC	Direct-to-Consumer
DTD	Document Type Definition (for Electronic interchange)
DTD	Device Tracking Database
DTD (CDER)	Division of Training and Development (CDER)
DTDFA (CVM)	Division of therapeutic Drugs for Food Animals (CVM)
DTDNFA (CVM)	Division of therapeutic Drugs for Non-Food Animals (CVM)
DTNPS (CFSAN)	Division of toxicology and Nutrition Product Studies (CFSAN)
DTP	Direct-to-Patient
DTP (CDER)	Division of therapeutic Proteins (CDER)
DTR	Deep Tendon Reflexes
DTR	Detention Request
DTS	Distribution Tracking System (CBER)
DUPSA (CDRH)	Division of Device User Programs and System Analysis (CDRH)
DUR	Drug Utilization Review
DUSM	Deputy United States Marshal (U.S. Department of Justice)
DV	Daily VAlue
DVA (CFSAN)	Division of Virulence Assessment (CFSAN)
DVD	Digital Video Disc
DVM	Doctor of Veterinary Medicine
DVP (CBER)	Division of Viral Products (CBER)

DVRPA (CBER)	Division of Vaccines and Related Product Applications (CBER)
DVS (CBER)	Division of Veterinary Services (CBER)
DVS (NCTR)	Division of Veterinary Services (NCTR)
DVT	Deep Venous Thrombosis
DWPE	Detention Without Physical Examination
DX	Diagnosis
DXA	Dual-Energy X-Ray Absorptiometry Test

D

E

E2B	Efficacy topics' Data Elements for Transmission of Adverse Drug Reactions Reports (ICH)
EA	Environmental Assistance
EAA	Essential Amino Acids
EAB	Ethics Advisory Board
EAB (CFSAN)	Exposure Assessment Branch (CFSAN)
EAC	Expert Advisory Committee (Canada)
EAR	Export Administration Regulations (U.S. Department of Commerce)
EAS	Emergency Alert System
EAS (CDER)	Enterprise Architecture Staff (CDER)
EASE	Enterprise Administrative Support Environment
EB (CDRH)	Epidemiology Branch (CDRH)
EB (NCTR)	Engineering Branch (NCTR)
EBAA	Eye Bank Association of America
eBPDR	Electronic Biological Product Deviation Reporting
EBS	Emergency Broadcast System
EC	European Community
ECBS	Expert Committee on Biological Standardization (WHO)
eCDT	Electronic Common Technical Document (ICH M2 [Multi-Disciplinary Group 2] EWG [Expert Working Group])
ECE	Economic Commission for Europe
ECG	Electrocardiogram
ECL	Electrochemiluminescence
ECMO	Extra-Corporeal Membrane Oxygenation
e-CRF	Electronic Case Report form
ECRI	Emergency Care Research institute (No Longer Uses Name initials only)

ECRS (CFSAN)	Emergency Coordination and Response Staff (CFSAN)
ECS (OC)	Economics Staff (OC)
ECT	Electroconvulsive therapy
ECT (CFSAN)	Economics Team (CFSAN)
eCTD	Electronic Common Technical Document
ECU	European Currency Unit
ED	Effective Dose
EDI	Electronic Data Exchange
EDIFACT	Electronic Data interchange for Administration, Commerce, and Transportation
EDIPI	Electronic Data interchange Personal Identifier
EDKB	Endocrine Disrupter Knowledge Base
EDMF	European Drug Master File
EDMS	Electronic Document Management System
EDQM	European Directorate for the Quality of Medicines
EDR	Electronic Document Room
EDR	Enhanced Design Review
EDRG	Early Detection Research Group
eDRLS	Electronic Drug Registration and Listing Systems
EEA	European Economic Area
EEC	European Economic Community
EEG	Electroencephalogram
EEO	Equal Employment Opportunity
EEO (CFSAN)	Equal Employment Opportunity Office (CFSAN)
EEO (NCTR)	Equal Employment Opportunity Staff (NCTR)
EEOC	Equal Employment Opportunity Commission
EEPS	Electronic Entry Processing System
EER	Establishment Evaluation Request

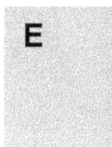

E

E

EES	Establishment Evaluation System
EFD	Engineering Flow Diagram
EFGCP	European forum on Good Clinical Practice
EFOIA	Electronic Freedom of information Act
EFPIA	European Federation of Pharmaceutical industries and Associations
EFT	Electronic Funds Transfer
EFTA	European Free Trade Association
EGA	European Generics Medicines Association
EH & S	Environmental Health and Safety
EHPAS (NCTR)	Environmental Health and Program Assurance Staff (NCTR)
EHPC	Environmental Health Policy Committee (formerly CCEHRP) (Currently inactive)
EHR	Electronic Health Record
EHRP	Enterprise Human Resources and Payroll System
EI	Establishent inspection
EI	Establishment inventory (ORA)
EIA	Environmental Impact Assessment
EIA	Enzyme Immunoassay
EID	Electronic Identification Device
EIF	Expected investment Fund
eIND	Electronic investigational New Drug Application
EINECS	European inventory of Existing Commercial Chemical Substances
EIP	Emerging infections Program (CDC)
EIR	Establishment inspection Report
EIS	Epidemic intelligence Service
EIS	Environmental Impact Statement
EIS (OC)	Ethics and integrity Staff (OC)
EKG	Electrocardiogram
ELA	Establishment License Application
ELDU	Extra-Label Drug Use

---

eLEXNET	Electronic Laboratory Exchange Network
ELINS	European List of Notified Chemical Substances
ELIPS	Electronic Labeling information Processing System (FDA)
ELISA	Enzyme-Linked Immunosorbent Assay
eLIST	Electronic Listing System
ELPS	Establishment Licensing and Product Surveillance
ELS	Establishment License Supplement
EMAC	Emergency Management Assistance Compact
EMBS	Engineering in Medicine and Biology Society (IEEE)
EMC	Electromagnetic Compatibility
EMEA	European Medicines Agency (formerly European Medicines Evaluation Agency)
EMI	Electromagnetic interference
EML	Environmental Measurement Laboratory
EMOPS (OC)	Office of Emergency Operations (OC)
EMS	Emergency Medical Services
EMV	Eye-Motor-Verbal (Glasgow Coma Scale)
ENG (OC)	Engineering Team (OC)
ENL	Erythema Nodosum Leprosum
ENT	Ear, Nose and Throat
ENTB (CDRH)	Ear, Nose, and Throat Devices Branch (CDRH)
EO	Executive order
EOC	Emergency Operations Center (FDA)
EOD	Enter on Duty
eOFP	Electronic official Personnel File
EOM	Extraocular Muscles
EOP1	End-of-Phase 1
EOP2	End-of-Phase 2
EORTC	European organisation for Research and Treatment of Cancer
EOS	End of Study

E

EOS (CDER)	Executive Operations Staff (CDER)
EOS (ORA)	Executive Operations Staff (ORA)
EP	European Pharmacopoeia
EPA	Environmental Protection Agency (U.S.)
EPAR	European Public Assessment Reports (EMEA)
EPC	Evidence-Based Practice Center
EPD (CDRH)	Electronic Product Devices Branch (CDRH)
EPFA	European Plasma Fractionation Association
EPI	Essential Prescribing information
EPIA	Egg Products inspection Act
EPIA	Egg Products inspection Act
EPL	Effective Patent Life
EPMS	Employee Performance Management System
EPO	European Patent Office
EPRG	European Pharmacovigilance Research Group
EPRS	Establishment Product Registration System
EPT (CFSAN)	Epidemiology Team (CFSAN)
ER	Extended Release [Medication]
ER/ES	Electronic Records/Electronic Signatures
ERB	Ethics Review Board
ERB (CFSAN)	Elemental Research Branch (CFSAN)
ERC	Engineering Research Center (NSF)
ERCP	Endoscopic Retrograde Cholangio-Pancreatography
EREA	Export Reform and Enhancement Act of 1996
ERIC	Employee Resource information Center
ERISA	Employee Retirement income Security Act of 1974
ERP	Enterprise Resource Planning

ERR	Entry Review Recommended (ORA AofC Code)
ERS	Electronic Regulatory Submission
ERS	Economic Research Service (USDA)
ERS	Emergency Relocation Site
ERSB (CFSAN)	Emergency Response and Surveillance Branch (CFSAN)
ERSR	Electronic Regulatory Submissions and Review
ERT	Emergency Response Team
ES	Effect Size
ESB (ORA)	Enterprise Systems Branch (ORA)
ESC	Electronic Submission Coodinator
ESD	Electrostatic Discharge
ESF	Emergency Support Function
ESIG	Electronic Signature
ESR	Erythrocyte Sedimentation Rate
ESRA	European Society of Regulatory Affairs
ESS (CBER)	Executive Secretariat Team (CBER)
ESS (NCTR)	Executive Secretariat Staff (NCTR)
ESTRI	Electronic Standards for the Transfer of Regulatory information
ET	Endotracheal
ET	Excepted Trust
ET (CFSAN)	Education Team (CFSAN)
ETA	EASE Time and Attendance Module
ETASU	Elements to Assure Safe Use
EtoH	Ethanol
ETS	Environmental tobacco Smoke
eTS	Etravel Services Vendors
ETT	Exercise tolerance Test
ETT	Endotracheal Tube
EU	European Union
EU	Endotoxin Unit
EUA	Examination Under Anesthesia
EUA	Emergency Use Authorization

E

E

EUCOMED	European Confederation of Medical Devices Associations
EUP	Experimental Use Permit
EVA	Entry Validation Application
EVS (OC)	Evaluation Staff (OC)
EWG	Expert Working Group

F

FA	Filing Action
FAA	Federal Aviation Administration (U.S. Department of Transportation)
FAAN	Food Allergy and Anaphylaxis Network
FACA	Federal Advisory Committee Act 1972
FACS (CFSAN)	Food Advisory Committee Staff (CFSAN)
FACT	Food Animal Concerns Trust
FACT	Functional Assessment of Cancer therapy
FACTS	Field Accomplishments and Compliance Tracking System
FACTS	Frequency of Agents Communicable By Transfusion Study
FACTS@FDA	System for Electronically Communicating Approved Drug Labeling and for Disseminating Prescribing information
FAEMS	Foods Adverse Event Monitoring System
FAHCT	Foundation for Accreditation of Hematopoietic Cell therapy
FAI	Further Action indicated
FAIR	Federal Activities inventory Reform Act of 1998
FALCPA	Food Allergen Labeling and Consumer Protection Act
FAM	Foreign Affairs Manual
FAME	Formula for Achieving Managerial Excellence
FAN	Food Allergy Network
FAO	Food and Agriculture organization of the United Nations
FAP	Food Additive Petition
FAP	Food Additive Petition Approval Number (ORA AofC Code)
FAPMC	Food Animal Production Medicine Consortium

F

FAQ	Frequently Asked Questions
FAR	Federal Acquisition Regulations
FARAD	Food Animal Residue Avoidance Databank
FARM	Food Additives Regulatory Management System (CFSAN)
Farmindustria	Association of Italian Pharmaceutical Manufacturers
FASA	Federal Acquisition Streamlining Act of 1994
FASAB	Federal Accounting Standards Advisory Board
FASEB	Federation of American Societies for Experimental Biology
FASS	Federation of Animal Science Societies
FAT	Factory Acceptance Test
FATA	Federal Agency Travel Administrator
FATA	Federal Anti-Tampering Act
FAX	Facsimile
FBI	Federal Bureau of investigation (U.S. Department of Justice)
FBS	Fasting Blood Sugar
FCC	Federal Communications Commission (U.S.)
FCC	French Cheese Facility Certification Number (ORA AofC Code)
FCC	Forensic Chemistry Center
FCCSET	Federal Coordinating Council for Science, Engineering and Technology
FCE	Food Canning Establishment Number (ORA AofC Code)
FCIC	Federal Consumer information Center
FCN	Food Contact Substance Notification
FCO	Federal Coordinating Officer
FCRDC	Frederick Cancer Research and Development Center
FD&C ACT	Federal Food, Drug, and Cosmetic Act of 1938

FD-1932	FDA form for Veterinary Adverse Drug Reaction, Lack of Effectiveness, Product Defect Report--Mandatory
FD-1932a	FDA form for Veterinary Adverse Drug Reaction, Lack of Effectiveness, Product Defect Report--Voluntary
FD-2301	FDA form for Transmittal of Periodic Reports and Promotional Material for New Animal Drugs
FD-356V	FDA form for New Animal Drug Appication
FD-483	FDA form Used As A Written Notice of Deficiencies Found in inspections
FDA	Food and Drug Administration
FDAAA	Food and Drug Administration Amendments Act
FDAGLOBE	Gay, Lesbian, Bisexual, Transgender Employees of the Federal Government within FDA
FDAMA	Food and Drug Administration Modernization Act of 1997
FDARA	FDA Revitalization Act
FDAS	Defense Finance and Accounting Services
FDA-SRS	Spontaneous Reporting System of the Food and Drug Administration
FDASS (OC)	FDA Safety Staff (OC)
FDC	Food, Drug, & Cosmetic
FDCA	Federal Food, Drug, and Cosmetic Act of 1938
FDERA	Food and Drug Export Reform and Enhancement Act of 1996
FDLI	Food and Drug Law institute
FDOT (CFSAN)	Food Defense Oversight Team (CFSAN)
FEB	Federal Executive Board
FECA	Federal Employees' Compensation Act
FedGLOBE	Gay, Lesbian, Bisexual, Transgender Employees of the Federal Government

F

F

FEDRIP	Federal Research in Progress Database
FedRooms	Federal Premier Lodging Program
FEEA	Federal Employee Assistance and Education Fund
FEGLI	Federal Employees Group Life insurance
FEHB	Federal Employees Health Benefits [Program]
FEHBP	Federal Employees Health Benefits Program
FEI	FDA Establishment Identifier (ORA)
FEMA	Federal Emergency Management Agency
FERC	Federal Energy Regulatory Commission
FERN	Food Emergency Response Network
FERS	Federal Employees Retirement System
FES (OC)	Financial Enterprise Solutions (OC)
FF	Fogarty Fellow
FFD & C	Federal Food, Drug and Cosmetic Act of 1938
FFDCA	Federal Food, Drug, and Cosmetic Act of 1938
FFLA	Family Friendly Leave Act
FFP	Fresh Frozen Plasma
FFRM	Food Facility Registration Module (Furls)
FFS	Fee for Service
FGIS	Comisión Federal Para La Protección Contra Riesgos Sanitarios (Federal Commission for the Protection Against Sanitary Risks) (Mexico)
FHA	Federal Health Architecture
FHSA	Federal Hazardous Substances Act (Consumer Product Safety Commission)
FIC	John E. Fogarty international Center (NIH)
FICA	Federal insurance Contributions Act
FIFO	First in First Out
FIFR	First-in-First Reviewed

FIFRA	Federal insecticide, Fungicide, and Rodenticide Act
FIH	First-in-Human [Clinical Trials]
FIREBIRD	Federal investigator Registry for Bioinformatics Research Data
FIRSt	FDA information Retrieval System
FIS	Field information System
FISMA	Federal information Security Management Act
FIT	FDA internet Improvement Team
FLC	Federal Laboratory Consortium
FLETC	Federal Law Enforcement Training Center
FLQ	Fluoroquinolone
FLSA	Fair Labor Standards Act
FLSS (CFSAN)	Food Labeling and Standards Staff (CFSAN)
FLTCIP	Federal Long Term Care insurance Program
FM	Filing Meeting
FM	Final Monograph
FMB (CDRH)	Financial Management Branch (CDRH)
FMCS	Federal Mediation and Conciliation Service
FMD	Field Management Directives
FMD	Foot and Mouth Disease
FMEA	Failure Modes and Effect Analysis
FMECA	Failure Modes Effects and Criticality Analysis
FMFIA	Federal Management Financial integrity Act of 1982
FMI	Food Marketing institute
FMIA	Federal Meat inspection Act
FML	Firms Master List (ORA)
FMLA	Family Medical Leave Act of 1993
FMRI	Functional Magnetic Resonance Imaging

F

F

FMS	Financial Management Service (U.S. Department of the Treasury)
FNCS	Food, Nutrition, and Consumer Services
FNH	Febrile Non-Hemolytic Reaction
FNS	Food and Nutrition Service
FOB	Federal Office Building
FOI	Freedom of information
FOIA	Freedom of information Act
FOIB (CDRH)	Freedom of information Branch (CDRH)
FONSI	Finding of No Significant Impact
FOP	Financial Operating Plan
FORCG	Foodborne Outbreak Response Coordinating Group
FOUO	for official Use only
FPA	Food Products Association
FPB (CDRH)	Field Programs Branch (CDRH)
FPB (CFSAN)	Field Programs Branch (CFSAN)
FPB (CFSAN)	Food Processing Branch (Chicago, Illinois) (CFSAN)
FPBR (CFSAN)	Food Packaging Branch (Chicago, Illinois) (CFSAN)
FPET (CFSAN)	Food Processing Evaluation Team (CFSAN)
FPIF	Finnish Pharmaceutical industry Association
FPL	Final Printed Label
FPLA	Fair Packaging and Labeling Act (1967)
FPLP	Federal Premier Lodging Program
FPS	Federal Protective Service (Department of Homeland Security)
FPVST (OC)	Facilities Planning and Voice Services Team (OC)
FQ	Fluoroquinolone
FQPA	Food Quality Protection Act of 1996
FR	Federal Register
Fr.P.	Pharmacopee Francaise (French Pharmacopoeia)

FRAC	FDA Research Animal Council
FRC	Federal Records Center (Suitland)
FRC	Functional Residual Capacity
FRDTS	Federal Register Document Tracking System
FRP	Federal Response Plan (FEMA)
FS	Federal Standard (U.S.)
FS	Feasibility Study
FSA	Farm Service Agency (USDA)
FSANZ	Food Standards Australia New Zealand
FSH	Follicle-Stimulating Hormone
FSI	Food Safety initiative (CFSAN)
FSIS	Food Safety and inspection Service (USDA)
FSPS (ORA)	Federal-State Program Staff (ORA)
FSTA	Federal Supervisory Travel Approver
FT (OC)	Financial Team (OC)
FTA	Fault Tree Analysis
FTB (CFSAN)	Food Technology Branch (CFSAN)
FTC	Federal Trade Commission (U.S.)
FTCA	Federal Trade Commission Act
FTE	Full-Time Equivalent
FTIM	First Time in Man
FTP	File Transfer Protocol
FTR	Federal Travel Regulations
FTS	Federal Telecommunications System
FTT	Failure to Thrive
FU	Farmacopea Ufficiale (Italian Pharmacopoeia)
FUO	Fever of Unknown origin
FURLS	FDA Uniform Registration & Listing System
FVC	forced Vital Capacity
FWP	Federal Women's Program
Fx	Fracture
FY	Fiscal Year

F

F

FYI   For Your information

G

GAAP	Greater Access to Affordable Pharmaceuticals Act of 2003
GADPTRA	Generic Animal Drug and Patent Term Restoration Act
GAMP	Good Automated Manufacturing Practice
GAO	Government Accountability Office (U.S.)
GAO	General Accounting Office
GAPS	Good Agricultural Practices
GARR	Grants Application Review Request
GAT	Genome Amplification Testing
GATT	General Agreement of Tariffs and Trade
GBL	Government Bill of Lading
GC	Gonorrhea
GC	General Counsel (FDA)
GC	Gas Chromatography
GCBS	Global Collaboration for Blood Safety (WHO)
GCC	Government Coordinating Council [of the Food and Agriculture Sector]
GCLP	Good Clinical Laboratory Practice
GCP	Good Clinical Practice
GCPB I (CDER)	Good Clinical Practice Branch I (CDER)
GCPB II (CDER)	Good Clinical Practice Branch Ii (CDER)
GCPP (OC)	Good Clinical Practice Program (OC)
GCRC	General Clinical Research Centers
GCSL (CFSAN)	Gulf Coast Seafood Laboratory (Dauphin Island, Alabama) (CFSAN)
GDEA	Generic Drug Enforcement Act of 1992
GDS	Global Distribution System
GEBAT	Government Excess Baggage Authorization Ticket
GeMCRIS	Genetic Modification Clinical Research information System (NIH)
GEO	Genetically Engineered organism

G

GEP	Good Engineering Practice
GG	Goal Group
GGP	Good Guidance Practice
GHC	Group Health Cooperative
GHDB (CDRH)	General Hospital Devices Branch (CDRH)
GHS	Globally Harmonised System of Classification and Labelling of Chemicals (UN)
GHTF	Global Harmonization Task force
GI	Gastrointestinal
GIF	Graphics interchange format
GILS	Government information Locator Service
GIPSA	Grain inspection, Packers & Stockyards Administration (USDA)
GIS	Geographical information System
GLP	Good Laboratory Practice
GLPBB (CDER)	Good Laboratory Practices and Bioequivalence investigations Branch (CDER)
GM	Genetically Modified
GMA	Grocery Manufacturers Association
GMDN	Global Medical Device Nomenclature
GME	Graduate Medical Education
G-MED (LNE)	Medical Device Assessment Group (Laboratoire National De Metrologie Et d'Essias)
GMID	Global Market information Database
GMO	Grants Management Officer
GMO	Genetically Modified organism
GMP	Good Manufacturing Practice
GOCO	Government-Owned Contractor-Operated
GOCRG	Gastrointestinal and Other Cancer Research Group
GOTS	Government off-the-Shelf
GOVCC	Government Travel Charge Card

GOVTRIP	Government Travel Website Operated By Northrop Grumman
GPEA	Government Paperwork Elimination Act
GPhA	Generic Pharmaceutical Association
GPO	Government Printing Office (U.S.)
GPO	Group Purchasing organization
GPP	Good Programming Practices
GPRA	Government Performance Results Act of 1993
GPRD	General Practice Research Database
GRAS	Generally Recognized As Safe
GRAS/E	Generally Recognized As Safe and Effective
GRC	Gerontology Research Center
GRDB (CDRH)	Gastroenterology and Renal Devices Branch (CDRH)
GRNs	Generally Recognized As Safe Notifications
GRP	Good Review Practice
GRS	General Records Schedule
GS	General Schedule
GSA	General Services Administration (U.S.)
GSDB (CDRH)	General Surgery Devices Branch (CDRH)
GSFA	General Standard for Food Additives
GSP	Good Statistics Practice
gt	Drops
GTB (CBER)	Gene therapies Branch (CBER)
GTIB (CBER)	Gene Transfer and Immunogenicity Branch (CBER)
GTIS	Gene therapy information System
GTL (NCTR)	Genetic toxicology Laboratory (NCTR)
GTT	Glucose tolerance Test
gtt	Drops
GU	Genitourinary
GUI	Graphical User interface

G

G

GWQAP	Government Wide Quality Assurance Program
GxP	Good "X" Practices
GXT	Graded Exercise tolerance (Stress Test)

H

H/H	Henderson-Hasselbach Equation
H/H	Hemoglobin/Hematocrit
HA	Headache
HAA	Hepatitis-Associated Antigen
HAART	Highly Active Antiretroviral therapy – the Name Commonly Given to Combinations of Anti-HIV Drugs
HAB (CFSAN)	Hazard Assessment Branch (CFSAN)
HAC	Health Administration Center (VA)
HACCP	Hazard Analysis Critical Control Point
HAD	Hospital Anxiety and Depression [Scale]
HAI	Health Action international
HAM/TSP	HTLV-I-Associated Myelopathy / Tropical Spastic Paraparesis
HARTS	Hoechst Adverse Reaction Terminology System
HAV	Hepatitis A Virus
HAZMAT	Hazardous Material
HAZOP	Hazard and Operability
HBOC	Hemoblogin-Based Oxygen Carrier
HBP	High Blood Pressure
HBV	Hepatitis B Virus
HCDB (CDRH)	Hematology and Cytology Devices Branch (CDRH)
HCFA	Health Care Financing Administration (Now CMS)
HCG	Human Chorionic Gonadotropin
HCI	Human-Computer interaction
HCO	Health Care organization
HCP	Healthcare Provider
HCT	Hematocrit
HCT/P	Human Cellular and Tissue-Based Products

H

HCTERS	Human Cell and Tissue Establishment Registration System
HCTRS	Human Cell and Tissue Establishment Registration System
HCTZ	Hydrochlorothiazide
HCV	Hepatitis C Virus
HDC	High Dose Chemotherapy
HDE	Humanitarian Use Exemptions (CDRH)
HDL	High Density Lipoprotein
HDMA	Healthcare Distribution Management Association
HDP	Hydroxymethylene Diphosphonate
HDPE	High Density Polyethylene
HEENT	Head, Eyes, Ears, Nose, Throat
HEO	Hispanic Employee organization
HEPA	High Efficiency Particulate Air (Filter)
hERG	Human Ether-A-Go-Go Gene
HF	Mail Code for FDA Office of the Commissioner
HF	High Frequency
HFA	Hemophilia Federation of America
HFA	Hydrofluoroalkane
HFD	Mail Code for CDER
HFEB (CDRH)	Human Factors Engineering Branch (CDRH)
HFES	Human Factors and Ergonomics Society
HFM	Mail Code for CBER
HFS	Mail Code for CFSAN
HFT	Mail Code for NCTR
HFV	Mail Code for CVM
HFZ	Mail Code for CDRH
Hgb	Hemoglobin
HGH	Human Growth Hormone
HHE	Health Hazard Evaluation
HHI	Herth Hope index
HHMI	Howard Hughes Medical institute

HHS	Health and Human Services (U.S. Department of)
HHS SERT	Health and Human Services Secretary's Emergency Response Team
HIBCC	Health industry Business Communication Council
HIMA	Health industry Manufacturers Association
HIMSS	Healthcare information Management Systems Society
HIPAA	Health insurance Portability and Accountability Act of 1996
HIRS	Health information Resources Service
HISB	Health informatics Standards Board
HISPC	Health information Security and Privacy Collaboration
HITSP	Health information Technology Standards Panel
HIV	Human Immunodeficiency Virus
HL7	Health Level 7
HLBT	Heat Labile Bacterial toxins
HLGT	High Level Group Term
HLT	High Level Term
HLT	Hurricane Liaison Team (FEMA)
HMO	Health Maintenance organization
HNK cells	Human Neonatal Kidney Cells
HPB	Health Protection Board (Canada)
HPB	Hematological Products Branch (CBER) (Defunct)
HPC	Hematopoietic Progenitor Cells
HPC	Human Progenitor Cells
HPFB	Health Products and Food Branch (Canada's FDA)
HPK	Human Pharmacokinetic
HPLC	High Performance Liquid Chromatography
HPO	High Performance organization

H

HPUS	Homeopathic Pharmacopeia of the United States
HPV	Human Papillomavirus
HR	Heart Rate
HR	Human Resources
HRG	Health Research Group
HRRC	Human Research Review Committee
HRSA	Health Resources and Services Administration (DHHS)
HS	At Bedtime
HS	Handling Statement
HS	High Structure
HSA	Health Services Administration
HSBT	Heat Stable Bacterial toxins
HSC	Homeland Security Council
HSIN	Homeland Security information Network
HSOC	Homeland Security Operations Center
HSPD	Homeland Security Presidential Directive
HSS	Hemophilia Surveillance System (CDC)
HSUS	Humane Society of the United States
HSV	Herpes Simplex Virus
HTLV	Human T-Lymphotropic Virus
HTLV-III	Human Lymphotropic Virus, Type III (AIDS Agent, HIV)
HTM	Health Technical Memorandum
HTML	Hypertext Markup Language
HTN	Hypertension
HTRB (CBER)	Human Tissue and Reproduction Branch (CBER)
HTTP	Hypertext Transfer Protocol
HUD	Humanitarian Use Device (CDER)
HUD	Department of Housing and Urban Development (U.S.)
HVAC	Heating, Ventilating, and Air Conditioning
Hx	History

I

I & D	Incision and Drainage
I & O	Intake and Output
IA	Import Administration (U.S. Department of Commerce)
IAB (CDRH)	Information and Analysis Branch (CDRH)
IAB (ORA)	Infrastructure Applications Branch (ORA)
IACUC	Institutional Animal Care and Use Committee
IAG	Interagency Agreement
IAL	Informal Action Levels
IAMFES	International Association of Milk, Food and Environmental Sanitarians
IARC	International Agency for Research on Cancer (WHO)
IAS (CFSAN)	Industry Activities Staff (CFSAN)
IAS (CFSAN)	International Affairs Staff (CFSAN)
IAS (OC)	International Agreements Staff (OC)
IAST (CFSAN)	International Activities Staff (CFSAN)
IATA	International Air Transport Association
IAVG	Interagency Vaccine Group
IAW	In Accordance With
IB	Investigator's Brochure
IB (CFSAN)	Immunobiology Branch (CFSAN)
IB (ORA)	International Branch (ORA)
IBB (CFSAN)	Instrumentation and Biophysics Branch (CFSAN)
IBE	Individual Bioequivalence
IBP	Indian Black Pepper Certificate (ORA AofC Code)
IBR (CFSAN)	Import Branch (CFSAN)
IC	Informed Consent
ICA	Intelligent Console Architecture
ICA	Inter-Center Agreement

I

ICAM	International Cooperative Agreements Manual
ICAO	International Civil Aviation organization
ICB (CDRH)	Inspection and Compliance Branch (CDRH)
ICB (CFSAN)	Implementation and Compliance Branch (CFSAN)
ICCBBA	International Council for Commonality in Blood Banking Automation, inc.
ICCVAM	Interagency Coordinating Committee on Validation of Alternative Methods
ICD	Informed Consent Document
ICD-9-CM	International Classification of Diseases, Ninth Revision, Clinical Modification
ICDB (CDRH)	Infection Control Devices Branch (CDRH)
ICDB (CDRH)	Interventional Cardiology Devices Branch (CDRH)
ICDRA	International Conference of Drug Regulatory Authorities
ICE	Immigration and Customs Enforcement (Department of Homeland Security)
ICH	International Conference on Harmonisation (of Technical Requirements for Registration of Pharmaceuticals for Human Use)
ICIB (CDRH)	Intraocular and Corneal Implants Branch (CDRH)
ICL	Idiopathic CD4+ T-Lymphocytopenia
ICLAS	International Council for Laboratory Animal Science
ICMJE	International Committee of Medical Journal Editors
ICPEMC	International Commission for Protection Against Environmental Mutagens and Carcinogens
ICRP	International Commission on Radiological Protection
ICRU	International Commission on Radiation Units and Measurements

ICS	Incident Command System
ICSR	Individual Case Safety Reports
ICTAP	Interagency Career Transition Assistance Plan
ICU	Intensive Care Unit
ID	Identification
IDC	Information and Data Committee
IDDM	Insulin Dependent Diabetes Mellitus
IDE	Investigational Device Exemption (CDRH)
IDE	Investigational Device Exemption Number (ORA AofC Code)
IDE (CDRH)	Investigational Device Exemptions Sections (CDRH)
IDF	International Dairy Federation
IDF	Immune Deficiency Foundation
IDIQ	Indefinite-Delivery, indefinite-Quantity [Contracts]
IDL	International Date Line
IDM	Informational Disclosure Manual
IDP	Individual Development Plan
IDR	Idiosyncratic Drug Reaction
IEC	Independent Ethics Committee (DHHS)
IEE	Intervention Effect Estimate
IEEE	Institute of Electrical and Electronics Engineers
IFA	Investigational Food Additive (File)
IFA	Indirect Fluorescent Antibody
IFAD	International Food Additives Database (CFSAN)
IFE	Import for Export (ORA AofC Code)
IFIC	International Food information Council
IFIP	International Federation for information Processing
IFMFS (CFSAN)	Infant formula and Medical Foods Staff (CFSAN)

I

IFPMA	International Federation of Pharmaceutical Manufacturers Associations
IFT	Institute of Food Technologists
IFU	Instructions for Use
IFWG	Interagency Food Working Group
IG	Immunoglobulin
IG	inspector General
IgA	Immunoglobin A
IgD	Immunoglobin D
IgE	Immunoglobin E
IGF	Insulin-Like Growth Factor
IgG	Immunoglobin G
IGIV	Immune Globulin intravenous
IgM	Immunoglobin M
IHS	Indian Health Service (DHHS)
IIC	Inspector-in-Charge
iiFAR	Incurably Ill for Animal Research
IIG	Inactive ingredient Guide
IIMB (CDRH)	It infrastructure Management Branch (CDRH)
IIMG	Interagency incident Management Group
IIS	Internet information Officer
ILAR	Institute for Laboratory Animal Research
IM	Intramuscular
IMB	Irish Medicines Board
IMB (CDER)	Interface Management Branch (CDER)
IMB (CDRH)	Information Management Branch (CDRH)
IMC	Information Management Consultants, inc.
IMCC	Information Management Coordinating Committee (CBER)
IMDA	Irish Medical Device Association
IMDB (CDRH)	Immunology and Molecular Diagnostics Devices Branch (CDRH)
IMDG	International Maritime Dangerous Goods Code

IMLS	Institute of Museum and Library Services
IMO	International Maritime organisation
IMP	Investigational Medicinal Product
IMPAC	International Merchant Purchase Authorization Card
IMPAC	Information for Management, Planning, Analysis and Coordination
IMPD	Investigational Medicinal Product Dossier (EU)
IMS	Information Management System
IMS	Interstate Milk Shippers
IMS (CDRH)	Issues Management Staff (CDRH)
IMT	International Medical Terminology
IMT	Incident Management Team
IMTS	Industry Meeting Tracking System
INA	Investigational New Animal Drug Number (ORA AofC Code)
INAD	Investigational New Animal Drug
INADA	Investigational New Animal Drug Application
IND	Investigational New Drug
IND	Investigational New Drug Number (ORA AofC Code)
IND	Investigational New Drug Application
INDA	Investigational New Drug Application
INDC	Investigational New Drug Committee
INFARME D	Instituto Nacional Da Farmaciae E Do Medicamento (Portugal)
INN	International Nonproprietary Name
INN	International Approved Names for Pharmacopoeial Substances
INNS	International Neural Network Society
INS	Incident of National Significance
INV sample	Investigational Sample
IO	Immediate Office
IOM	Institute of Medicine of the National Academies

IOM	Investigation Operations Manual
IOTF	Interagency oncology Task force (FDA and NCI)
IP	Internet Protocol
IP	Information Panel
IPC	In Process Control
IPC	Incidental Patient Contact
IPCB (CDER)	Investigations and Preapproval Compliance Branch (CDER)
IPCS	International Programme on Chemical Safety (WHO)
IPEC	International Pharmaceutical Excipients Council
IPO	Initial Public offering
IPOAB (CDRH)	Information Processing and Office Automation Branch (CDRH)
IPPIA	International Plasma Products industry Association
IPRMS (OC)	International Planning and Resource Management Staff (OC)
IPRO	Independent Pharmaceutical Research organization
IPS (OC)	Impac Program Staff (OC)
IPS (OC)	International Policy Staff (OC)
IPU	Irish Pharmaceutical Union
IPV	Inactivated Poliovirus Vaccine
IQ	Installation Qualification
IQA	Institute of Quality Assurance (UK)
IR	Immediate Release
IR	Information Request
IRA	Immediate Response Authority
IRB	Institutional Review Board
IRB	Investigational Review Board
IRC	internet Relay Chat
IRC	Impact Resistance Lens Certification (ORA AofC Code)
IRDM	Insulin Resistant Diabetes Mellitus

IREAS (CDRH)	International Relations and External Affairs Staff (CDRH)
IRIS	International Regulatory Issues Staff (ORA)
IRM	Information Resources Management
IRMC	Information Resources Management College
IRS	Identical, Related, or Similar
IRS	Incident Reporting System
IRS	Internal Revenue Service (U.S. Department of the Treasury)
IRS (OC)	International Relations Staff (OC)
IRTA	Intramural Research Training Award (NIH)
IS	Interstate Commerce
IS	Ingredients Statement
ISA	Information Systems Architecture
ISAC	Information Sharing and Analysis Center
ISASS (OC)	International Scientific Activities and Standards Staff (OC)
ISB (CDRH)	Inspection Support Branch (CDRH)
ISBT	International Society of Blood Transfusion
ISBT 128	international Society of Blood Transfusion Standard for Blood, Tissue, and organ Identification
ISDN	Integrated Services Digital Network
ISE	integrated Summary of Efficiency
ISIS	Import Support and information System
ISMP	Institute for Safe Medication Practices
ISO	International organization for Standardization
ISP	Internet Service Provider
ISPE	International Society for Pharmacoepidemiology
ISPE	International Society for Pharmaceutical Engineering
ISR	Individual Safety Report

I

I

ISS	Integrated Summary of Safety
ISS/ISE	Integrated Summary of Safety and Effectiveness
ISSO	Information Systems Security Officer
IT	Information Technology
ITA	International Trade Administration
ITATMT (OC)	IT Asset Tracking and Management Team (OC)
ITB (CFSAN)	Immunotoxicology Branch (CFSAN)
ITC	International Trade Commission (U.S.)
ITCB (OC)	Information Technology Contracts Branch (OC)
ITCC	Information Technology Coordinating Committee (CDER)
ITDS	International Trade Data System
ITF	Inspection Task force (CBER)
ITGS (OC)	It Governance Staff (OC)
ITIC	Information Technology Implementation Committee (CBER)
ITIPS	Information Technology investment Portfolio System
ITMRA	Information Technology Management Reform Act (Now the Clinger-Cohen Act)
ITS (CBER)	Information Technology Staff (CBER)
ITT	Intent to Treat
ITTT (OC)	Information Technology (IT) Training Team (OC)
IUO	Investigation Use only
IUPAC	International Union of Pure and Applied Chemistry
IV	Intravenous
IV & V	Independent Verification and Validation
IVC	Intravenous Cholangiogram
IVC	Inferior Vena Cava
IVD	In Vitro Diagnostics
IVF	In Vitro Fertilization
IVIG	Intravenous Immunoglobulin

IVMD	In Vitro Medical Device
IVP	Intravenous Pyelogram
IVTB (CFSAN)	In Vitro toxicology Branch (CFSAN)

I

J, K

J/D	Judgment for the Defendant
JAD	Joint Application Development
JAN	Japanese Adopted Names
J-ART	Japanese Adverse Reaction Terminology
JBIG	Joint Bi-Level Image Experts Group
JCAHO	Joint Commission on Accreditation of Health Care organizations
JECFA	Joint (FAO/WHO) Expert Committee on Food Additives
JFHQ	Joint force Headquarters
JFO	Joint Field Office
JFTR	Joint Federal Travel Regulations
JIC	Joint information Center
JIFSAN	Joint institute for Food Safety and Applied Nutrition
JIFSAN (CFSAN)	JIFSAN Liaison Staff (CFSAN)
JINAD	Generic investigational New Animal Drug File
JLCS (OC)	Jefferson Laboratory Complex Staff (OC)
JMO	Japanese Maintenance organization
JMPR	Joint FAO/WHO Meeting of Pesticide Residues
JP	Japanese Pharmacopoeia
JPEG	Joint Photographic Experts Group
JPMA	Japan Pharmaceutical Manufacturers Association
JRIES	Joint Regional information Exchange System
JTF	Joint Task force
JTR	Joint Travel Regulations
kcal	Kilocalories
Kg	Kilogram
KMT (OC)	Knowledge Management Staff (OC)
KOS	Knowledge organization System

KPS	Karnofsky Performance Status Scale
KS	Kaposi's Sarcoma

L

L & D	Labor and Delivery	
LACF	Low-Acid Canned Foods	
LAF	Laminar Air Flow	
LAN	Local Area Network	
LanguaL	Langua Alimentaria (Language of Foods)	
LAR	Licensing Action Recommendation	
LARD	Licensing Action Recommendation Document	
LASA	Linear Analog Self-Assessment Measure	
LASER	Light Amplification By Stimulated Emission of Radiation	
LASIK	Laser Assisted in Situ Keratomileusis	
LATS	License Application Tracking System	
LBL	Ernest orlando Lawrence Berkeley National Laboratory	
LBP (CBER)	Laboratory of Bacterial Polysaccharides (CBER)	
LBPUA (CBER)	Laboratory of Bacterial, Parasitic and Unconventional Agents (CBER)	
LBVB (CBER)	Laboratory of Biochemistry and Vascular Biology (CBER)	
LCDC	Laboratory Centre for Disease Control (Canada)	
LCH (CBER)	Laboratory of Cellular Hematology (CBER)	
LCI	Livestock Conservation institute	
LCP (CDER)	Laboratory of Clinical Pharmacology (CDER)	
LCT (CFSAN)	Labeling Compliance Team (CFSAN)	
LD	Lethal Dose	
LD50	Lethal Dose Where 50% of the Animal Population Die	

LDPE	Low-Density Polyethylene
LDV (CBER)	Laboratory of DNA Viruses (CBER)
LEAA	Law Enforcement Alliance of America
LECC	Law Enforcement Coordination Committee
LERN	Library Electronic Reference Network
LES	Leave and Earnings Statement
LESTD (CBER)	Laboratory of Enteric and Sexually Transmitted Diseases (CBER)
LF	Low Frequency
LF1	Low-VAlue Food/Food-Related Products Less Than or Equal to $200 (ORA AofC Code)
LF2	Low-VAlue Food/Food-Related Products Greater Than $200 and Less Than or Equal to $500 (ORA AofC Codes)
LF3	Low-VAlue Food/Food-Related Products Greater Than $500 and Less Than or Equal to $1000 (ORA AofC Code)
LH (CBER)	Laboratory of Hemostasis (CBER)
LHREA (CBER)	Laboratory of Hepatitis and Related Emerging Agents (CBER)
LHV (CBER)	Laboratory of Hepatitis Viruses (CBER)
LI	Learned intermediary
LIB (CBER)	Laboratory of Immunobiochemistry (CBER)
LIMS	Laboratory information Management System
LIR (CBER)	Laboratory of Immunoregulation (CBER)
Lm	Listeria Monocytogenes
LMD (CBER)	Laboratory of Method Development (CBER)
LMDCI (CBER)	Laboratory of Mycobacterial Diseases and Cellular Immunology (CBER)
LMDQC (CBER)	Laboratory of Methods Development and Quality Control (CBER)
LMO	Living Modified organism
LMS	Laboratory Management System

LMV (CBER)	Laboratory of Molecular Virology (CBER)
LNC	Labeling and Nomenclature Committee (CDER)
LNE	Laboratoire National De Metrologie Et d'Essias (National Laboratory of Metrology and Essays)
LOA	Letter of Agreement
LOAEL	Lowest Observed Adverse Effect Level
LOB (ORA)	Laboratory Operations Branch (ORA)
LOC	Level of Concern
LOCF	Last Observation Carried forward
LOD	Limit of Detection
LOINC	Logical Observation Identifier Name Codes (Regenstrief institute)
LOQ	Limit of Quantification
LOV	List of VAlues (EASE)
LPB (OC)	Leasing and Policy Branch (OC)
LPD (CBER)	Laboratory of Plasma Derivatives (CBER)
LPET (CFSAN)	Laboratory Proficiency and Evaluation Team (CFSAN)
LPRVD (CBER)	Laboratory of Pediatric and Respiratory Viral Diseases (CBER)
LPT (CFSAN)	Liaison and Policy Team (CFSAN)
LR (CBER)	Laboratory of Retroviruses (CBER)
LR1	Low-VAlue Non-Rx Radiation-Emitting Products Less Than or Equal to $200 (ORA AofC Code)
LR2	Low-VAlue Non-Rx Radiation-Emitting Products Greater Than $200 and Less Than or Equal to $1000 (ORA AofC Code)
LRA	Local Registration Authority
LRB (CDER)	Labeling Review Branch (CDER)
LRC	Lipid Research Clinic
LRI	Lower Respiratory infection
LRIS	Lot Release Imaging System

J
K
L

L

LRIT (CFSAN)	Labeling Regulations Implementation Team (CFSAN)
LRN	Laboratory Response Network (CDC)
LRP	Low Regulatory Priority
LRPDB (CDRH)	Labeling Research and Policy Development Branch (CDRH)
LRS	Lot Release System
LRSP (CBER)	Laboratory of Respiratory and Special Pathogens (CBER)
LS	Labelling Standard (Canada)
LS (CDRH)	Library Staff (CDRH)
LS/LS	Life Supporting/Life Sustaining
LSHLC	Lipid Soluble Heat Labile Chemicals
LSHSC	Lipid Soluable Heat Stable Chemical
LST	Device Listing Number (ORA AofC Code)
LTE	Less Than Effective
LUACRG	Lung and Upper Aerodigestive Cancer Research Group
LVBD (CBER)	Laboratory of Vector-Borne Diseases (CBER)
LVCH	Local Voucher
LVP	Large-Volume Parenteral – An injection Product Having A Solution Volume Which Exceeds 100 Ml
LWC	Electrode Lead Wire or Patient Cable (ORA AofC Code)
LWOP	Leave without Pay

M

M&IE	Miscellaneous and incidental Expenses
M2	ICH M2 Expert Working Group (EWG) [Electronic Standards for Transmission of Regulatory information]
M204	Model 204 Database Management System (Computer Corporation of America)
M4	ICH M4 Expert Working Group (EWG) [Focusing on Common Technical Documents for Sections of the NDA]
MA	Marketing Authorisation
MAA	Marketing Authorisation Application
mAb	Monoclonal Antibody
MAB (CDER)	Management Analysis Branch (CDER)
MAB (CFSAN)	Methods Application Branch (CFSAN)
MAC	Mental Adjustment to Cancer Scale
MACS (CBER)	Manufacturers Assistance and Communications Staff (CBER)
MAD	Multiple Ascending Dose
MAH	Marketing Authorisation Holder (EC)
MAPP	Manual of Policy and Procedures
MARCS	Mission Accomplishment and Regulatory Compliance Services System (ORA)
MARS	Mobile Automated Regulatory Services (ORA)
MAS cell	Manipulated Autologous Structural Cell
MAT	Modular Antigen Transporter
MATS	Management Assignment Tracking System
MATTB (CBER)	Manufacturers Assistance and Technical Training Branch (CBER)
MAUDE	Manufacturer and User Facility Device Experience Database (CDRH)
MAV	Maximum Allowable VAriation

MB (CFSAN)	Microanalytical Evaluations Branch (CFSAN)
MBC	Minimum Bactericidal Concentration
MCA	Medicines Control Agency (Part of MHRA)
mCAFT	Modified Canadian Aerobic Fitness Test
MCO	Managed Care organization
MDA	Medical Devices Agency (UK)
MDA	Medical Device Amendments of 1976
MDB	Medical Devices Bureau (Canada)
MDB (CFSAN)	Methods Development Branch (CFSAN)
MDD	Maximum Daily Dose
MDD	Medical Devices Directives (EU)
MDDRP	Medical Device Dispute Resolution Panel
MDI	Metered Dose inhaler
MDII	Medical Device innovation initiative
MDL	Model Number (ORA AofC Code)
MDMA	Medical Device Manufacturers Association
MDP	Medical Devices Program (Canada)
MDR	Medical Device Reporting
MDUFA	Medical Device User Fee Amendments of 2007
MDUFMA	Medical Device User Fee and Modernization Act of 2002
MDUFSA	Medical Device User Fee Stabilization Act of 2005
MDV	Medical Device Vigilance
MedDRA	Medical Dictionary for Regulatory Activities
MEDEC	Medical Devices Canada
MEDLARS	Medical Literature Analysis and Retrieval System (NLM)
MedPAC	Medicare Payment Advisory Commission
MEDSA	the Medicine Equity and Drug Safety Act of 2000
MedSuN	Medical Product Safety Network (CDRH)

MEDWATCH	FDA Safety information and Adverse Event Reporting Program
MEFA	Association of the Danish Pharmaceutical industry
MEG	Magnetoencephalography
MEMO	Medicines Evaluation and Monitoring organization
MEO	Most Efficient organization
MERCOSUR	Southern Common Market (South America)
MERP	Medication Error Reporting and Prevention
MERS-TM	Medical Event Reporting System - Transfusion Medicine
MeSH	Medical Subject Headings
MF	Master File
MFA	Medicated Feed Application Number (ORA AofC Code)
MFC	Model Food Code
mfr	Manufacturer
MGB (CFSAN)	Molecular Genetics Branch (CFSAN)
MGSS	Multi-Generation Support System
MHPF	Minority Health Professionals Foundation
MHRA	Medicines and Healthcare Products Regulatory Agency (UK)
MHSB (CFSAN)	Microbial Hazards Science Branch (CFSAN)
MHW	Ministry of Health and Welfare (Japan's Equivalent to the FDA)
MI	Myocardial infarction
MIC	Minimum inhibitory Concentration
MID	Manufacturer Identifier (CBP)
MIP	Management Improvement Plan
MIRA	Medicare innovation Responsiveness Act of 2003
MIS	Management information System
MIS (OC)	Management initiatives Staff (OC)

M

M

MIWG	Mentoring Implementation Working Group
MJ	Major Amendment
ML	Manufacturer's License (UK Pharmaceuticals)
MLD	Minimum Lethal Dose
MMA	Medicare Prescription Drug, Improvement and Modernization Act of 2003
MMAB (CFSAN)	Microbiological Methods Application Branch (CFSAN)
MMDB (CFSAN)	Microbial Methods Development Branch (CFSAN)
MMR	Measles, Mumps and Rubella
MMRB (CFSAN)	Microbiological Methods Research Branch (CFSAN)
MMSB (CFSAN)	Molecular Methods and Subtyping Branch (CFSAN)
MMWR	Morbidity and Mortality Weekly Report - Published By the CDC.
MNVP	Medically Necessary Veterinary Product
MOA	Memorandum of Agreement
MOA	Mode of Action
MOC	Management and Operations Council (FDA)
MOD	Miscellaneous Obligation Document
MOD 1	Module one (Laboratory Facility - CFSAN)
MOD 2	Module Two (Laboratory Facility - CVM)
MON	Memorandum of Need
MOU	Memorandum of Understanding
MPA	Medical Products Agency (Sweden)
MPA	Multiple Projects (Human Subjects) Assurance
MPAB (OC)	Management Programs and Analysis Branch (OC)
MPCC	Medical Policy Coordinating Committee
MPEG	Moving Pictures Experts Group

MPN	Metro Park North
MPQA	Medical Products Quality Assurance
MPR	Moisture Protein Ratio
MPRIS	Mammography Program Reporting and information Systems
MQC	Mammography Quality Control
MQSA	Mammography Quality Standards Act of 1992
MRA	Magnetic Resonance Angiography
MRA	Medical Research Associate
MRA	Mutual Recognition Agreement
MRB	Material Review Board (American National Red Cross)
MRB (CFSAN)	Methods Research Branch (CFSAN)
MRC	Managed Review Committee
MRC	Medical Reserve Corps (U.S. Public Health Service)
MRD	Multiple Rising Dose
MRE	Meal, Ready-to-Eat
MRFG	Mutual Recognition Facilitating Group
MRI	Magnetic Resonance Imaging
MRL	Maximum Residue Limit
MRP	Manufacturing Resource Planning
MRRA (CFSAN)	Microbial Research and Risk Assessment Staff (CFSAN)
MRS	Magnetic Resonance Spectroscopy
MS	Mass Spectroscopy
MS	Milestone
MSAB (CFSAN)	Manufacturing and Storage Adulteration Branch (CFSAN)
MSB (NCTR)	Mass Spectrometry Branch (NCTR)
MSDS	Material Safety Data Sheets
MSI	Magnetic Source Imaging
MSQA	Mammography Quality Standards Act of 1992
MSS (CVM)	Management Support Staff (CDRH)

M

M

MSSO	Maintenance and Support Services organization
MT (CFSAN)	Medical Team (CFSAN)
MTA	Mail Transport Agent
MTA	Material Transfer Agreement
MTBF	Mean Time Between Failures
MTD	Maximum tolerated Dose
MTOS (CFSAN)	Muirkirk Technical Operations Staff (CFSAN)
MUMS	Minor Use Minor Species
MUMS (CVM)	Office of Minor Use and Minor Species (CVM)
MUMS Act	Minor Use and Minor Species Animal Health Act of 2004
MVB (CFSAN)	Molecular Virology Branch (CFSAN)
MVT (CFSAN)	Molecular Virology Team (CFSAN)
MWG	Milk Working Group

N

n.b.	Nota Bene (Note Well)
N/A	Not Applicable
NA	Not Approvable
NAA	National Aquaculture Association
NABR	National Association for Biomedical Research
NACCHO	National Association of County and City Health officials
NACDS	National Association of Chain Drug Stores
NACHO	National Association of County Health officials
NACMCF	National Advisory Committee on Microbiological Criteria for Foods
NAD	Ned Animal Drug Number (ORA AofC Code)
NADA	New Animal Drug Application
NADE	New Animal Drug Evaluation
NAET (CFSAN)	Nutrition Assessment and Evaluation Team (CFSAN)
NAF	Notice of Adverse Findings
NAFTA	North American Free Trade Agreement
NAGC	National Association of Government Communicators
NAHC	National Advisory Health Council
NAI	No Action indicated
NAION	Non-Arteritic Anterior Ischemic Optic Neuropathy
NAL	National Agricultural Library
NALBOH	National Association of Local Boards of Health
NAM	National Agency for Medicines (Finland)
NARA	National Archives and Records Administration (U.S.)

NARB	National Advertising Review Board (Ftc)
NARMS	National Antimicrobial Resistance Monitoring System (CDC)
NAS	National Academy of Sciences (U.S.)
NAS	New Active Substance
NASA	National Aeronautics and Space Administration (U.S.)
NASAR	National Association of Search and Rescue
NASDA	National Association of State Departments of Agriculture
NASS	National Agricultural Statistics Survey
NAT	Nucleic Acid-Based Tests
NBAC	National Bioethics Advisory Commission
NBCS	National Biomedical Computer System (American National Red Cross)
NBDRC	National Blood Data Resource Center
NBII	National Biological information infrastructure
NBS	National Bureau of Standards (Now NIST)
NC	Non-Clinical (Phase, Studies)
NCAB	National Cancer Advisory Board
NCBA	National Cattlemen's Beef Association
NCBDDD	National Center on Birth Defects and Developmental Disabilities (CDC)
NCBI	National Center for Biotechnology information (NCI)
NCC	National Coordinating Committee
NCC	National Chicken Council
NCC MERP	National Coordinating Council for Medication Error Reporting and Prevention
NCCAM	National Center for Complementary and Alternative Medicine (NIH)
NCCDPHP	National Center for Chronic Disease Prevention and Health Promotion (CDC)

NCCLS	National Committee for Clinical Laboratory Standards (Now CLIS)
NCDCP	National Council on Prescription Drug Programs
NCE	New Chemical Entity
NCEH	National Center for Environmental Health (CDC)
NCFST	National Center for Food Safety and Technology
NCHGR	National Center for Human Genome Research (NIH)
NCHM	National Center for Health Marketing (CDC)
NCHS	National Center for Health Statistics (CDC)
NCHSTP	National Center for HIV, STD, and TB Prevention (CDC)
NCI	National Cancer institute (NIH)
NCID	National Center for infectious Diseases (CDC)
NCIE	Notice of Claimed investigational Exemption (CVM)
NCIE	National Center for Import and Export (USDA)
NCIMS	National Conference on interstate Milk Shipments
NCIPC	National Center for injury Prevention and Control (CDC)
NCL	National Consumers League
NCMHD	National Center on Minority Health and Health Disparities (NIH)
NCNR	National Center for Nursing Research (NIH)
NCP	Nonconforming Product
NCPDP	National Council for Prescription Drug Programs
NCPHI	National Center for Public Health informatics (CDC)

N

NCPIE	National Council on Patient information and Education
NCRP	National Council on Radiation Protection and Measurements
NCRR	National Center for Research Resources (NIH)
NCS	Not Clinically Significant
NCS	National Communications System
NCTR	National Center for toxicological Research (FDA)
NCVHS	National Committee on Vital and Health Statistics (DHHS)
NCVIA	National Childhood Vaccine injury Act of 1986
NCWM	National Conference on Weights and Measures
NDA	New Drug Application
NDA	New Drug Application Number (ORA AofC Code)
NDAB	National Drugs Advisory Board (Ireland)
NDAC	Nonprescription Drug Advisory Committee
NDC	National Drug Code (FDA)
NDE	New Drug Evaluation
NDE/MIS	New Drug Evaluation Management information System
NDF-RT	National Drug File Reference Terminology (VA)
NDIRS (CFSAN)	New Dietary ingredients Review Staff (CFSAN)
NDMA	Nonprescription Drug Manufacturers Association (Now CHPA)
NDMS	National Disaster Medical System
NDMS (CDER)	New Drug Microbiology Staff (CDER)
NDRMMP	National Drug Residue Milk Monitoring Program
NDS	New Drug Submission (Canada)
NDS	New Drug Study

NDTI	National Disease and therapeutic index
NEC	Not Elsewhere Classified
NEDSS	National Electronic Disease Surveillance System (CDC)
NEEP	National Exercise and Evaluation Program
NEFARMA	Dutch Association of the innovative Pharmaceutical industry
NEFLE	National Exchange for Food Labeling Education
NEHA	National Environmental Health Association
NEI	National Eye institute (NIH)
NEMA	National Electrical Manufacturers Association
NEMA	National Emergency Management Association
NEP	National Exercise Program (Department of Homeland Security)
NEPA	National Environmental Policy Act
NetBEUI	Netbios Extended User interface
NEXT	Nationwide Evaluation of X-Ray Trends (CDRH)
NF	National formulary
NFPA	National Food Processor Association
NFSS	National Food Safety System
NFT	Notification of foreign Travel
NGA	National Geospatial-intelligence Agency
NGB	National Guard Bureal
NGFA	National Grain and Feed Association
NGO	Non-Governmental organization
NHANES	National Health and Nutrition Examination Survey (NCHS)
NHC	National Hurricane Center
NHF	National Hemophilia Foundation
NHGRI	National Human Genome Research institute (NIH)

N

NHIC	National Health information Center (DHHS)
NHIN	Nationwide Health information Network
NHIS	National institute of Hygienic Sciences (Japan)
NHLBI	National Heart, Lung, and Blood institute (NIH)
NHRIC	National Health Related Items Code (CDRH)
NHW	National Health and Welfare Department (Canada's Equivalent of DHHS)
NIA	National institute on Aging (NIH)
NIAAA	National institute on Alcohol Abuse and Alcoholism (NIH)
NIAID	National institute of Allergy and infectious Disease (NIH)
NIAMS	National institute of Arthritis and Musculoskeletal and Skin Diseases (NIH)
NIBIB	National institute of Biomedical Imaging and Bioengineering (NIH)
NICCL	National incident Communications Conference Line
NICHD	National institute of Child Health and Human Development (NIH)
NIDA	National institute on Drug Abuse (NIH)
NIDCD	National institute on Deafness and Other Communication Disorders (NIH)
NIDCR	National institute of Dental and Craniofacial Research (NIH)
NIDDK	National institute of Diabetes and Digestive and Kidney Diseases (NIH)
NIDPOE	Notice of initiation of Disqualification Proceeding and Opportunity to Explain
NIDR	National institute of Dental Research (See NIDCR)
NIDRR	National institute on Disability and Rehabilitation Research (U.S. Department of Education)

NIEHS	National institute of Environmental Health Sciences (NIH)
NIFC	National interagency Fire Center
NIGMS	National institute of General Medical Sciences (NIH)
NIH	National institutes of Health (DHHS)
NIM	No inspection Made
NIMH	National institute of Mental Health (NIH)
NIMS	National incident Management System (FEMA)
NINDS	National institute of Neurological Disorders and Stroke (NIH)
NINR	National institute of Nursing Research (NIH)
NIOSH	National institute for OCcupational Safety and Health (CDC)
NIP	National Immunization Program (CDC)
NIPP	National infrastructure Protection Plan
NIS	National inpatient Sample
NISAC	National infrastructure Simulation and Analysis Center (Department of Homeland Security)
NIST	National institute of Standards and Technology (U.S. Department of Commerce)
NKCA	Natural Killer Cell Cytotoxic Activity
NLEA	Nutrition Labeling and Education Act of 1990
NLM	National Library of Medicine (NIH)
NLN	Nordic Council on Medicines
NLRC	Nicholson Lane Research Center
NLT	Not Less Than
NMA	National Medical Association
NMDP	National Marrow Donor Program
NME	New Molecular Entity
NMFS	National Marine Fisheries Service
NMI	Non-Medicinal ingredient

N

NMPF	National Milk Producers Federation
NMQAAC	National Mammography Quality Assurance Advisory Committee
NMR	Nuclear Magnetic Resonance Spectroscopy
NMT	Not More Than
NNC	National Notification Center
NNMC	National Naval Medical Center
NOA	Notice of Availability
NOAA	National OCeanographic and Atmospheric Administration (U.S.)
NOAEL	No Observable Adverse Effect Level
NOC	Notice of Compliance (Canada)
NOC	National Operations Center
NOD	Notice of Deficiency (Canada)
NOEL	No Observed Effect Level
NOH	Notice of Hearing
NOMI	Federation of Norwegian Pharmaceutical Manufacturers
NON	Notice of Non-Compliance (Canada)
NONS	Notification of New Substance Regulations 193 (EC)
NOOH	Notice offering An Opportunity for A Hearing
NOP	National organic Program
NOS	Network Operating System
NOSB	National organic Standards Board
NOV	Notice of Violation Letter
NPA	National Prescription Audit
NPA	National Pharmaceutical Association (UK)
NPCC	National Poison Control Center
NPCC	National Pork Producers Council
NPCR	National Program of Cancer Registries
NPG	National Preparedness Goal
NPI	National Provided Identifier (CMS)
NPR	National Performance Review

NPRM	Notice of Proposed Rulemaking
NPS	National Park Service (Department of the interior)
NPS	National Pharmaceutical Stockpile(CDC)
NPS (CFSAN)	Nutrition Programs Staff (CFSAN)
NPSB (CFSAN)	Nutritional Product Studies Branch (CFSAN)
NR	Response to Not Approvable Letter
NR	Non-Compliance Record
NRB	Noninstitutional Review Board
NRC	National Research Council
NRC	Nuclear Regulatory Commission (U.S.)
NRCC	National Response Coordination Center
NREVSS	National Respiratory and Enteric Virus Surveillance System
NRP	National Response Plan (Department of Homeland Security)
NRP-CIS	National Response Plan Catastrophic incident Supplement
NRSP	National Research Support Project
NRTE	Not Ready-to-Eat
NS	Not Significant
NS/EP	National Security and Emergency Preparedness
NSA	National Security Agency (U.S.)
NSAID	Nonsteroidal Anti-inflammatory Drug
NSAPB	National Surgical Adjuvant Breast and Bowel Project
NSAPE	North American Society for Pacing and Electrophysiology
NSC	National Security Council
NSE	Not Substantially Equivalent
NSF	National Science Foundation (U.S.)
NSIP	National Seafood inspection Program
NSN	National Stock Number
NSR	Nonsignificant Risk
NSRT (CFSAN)	Nutrition Science Review Team (CFSAN)

N

NSV-DO (ORA)	Nashville (Tennessee) District Office (ORA)
NSWL	Naval Surface Weapons Laboratory (Now FDA White Oak Campus)
NTA	Notice to Applicants (EC)
NTB (CFSAN)	Neurotoxicology Branch (CFSAN)
NTEU	National Treasury Employees Union
NTF	National Turkey Federation
NTI	Narrow therapeutic index
NTIA	National Telecommunications and information Administration (U.S.)
NTIS	National Technical information Service
NTL	National Testing Laboratory (American National Red Cross)
NTP	National toxicology Program (U.S.)
NUCC	National Uniform Claim Committee (AMA and HCFA)
NVC	National Vaccine Commission
nvCJD	New Variant Creutzfeldt-Jakob Disease
NVICP	National Vaccine injury Compensation Program
NVLAP	National Voluntary Laboratory Accreditation Program (Nist)
NVOAD	National Volunteer organizations Active in Disaster
NVP	National Vaccine Program
NVPO	National Vaccine Program Office (DHHS)
NVSS	National Vital Statistics System
NVTB (CFSAN)	Neurotoxicological and in Vitro toxicology Branch (CFSAN)
NWK-DO (ORA)	Newark District Office (ORA)
NWR	NOAA Weather Radio
NWS	National Weather Service

O

OA	Osteoarthritis
OAGS (OC)	Officeof Acquisitions and Grants Services (OC)
OAI	official Action indicated
OAP (CDER)	Office of Antimicrobial Products (CDER)
OARSA (CFSAN)	Office of Applied Research and Safety Assessment (CFSAN)
OASDI	Old Age, Survivors, and Disability insurance
OASH	Office of the Assistant Secretary for Health (DHHS)
OASIS	Operational and Administrative System for Import Support (CFSAN)
OB (CDER)	Office of Biostatistics (CDER)
OBA	Office of Biotechnology Activities (NIH)
OBE	online Booking Engine
OBE (CBER)	Office of Biostatistics and Epidemiology (CBER)
OBES (OC)	Office of Business Enterprise Solutions (OC)
OBFP (OC)	Office of Budget formulation and Presentation (OC)
OB-GYN	Obstetrics-Gynecology
OBP (CDER)	Office of Biotechnology Products (CDER)
OBPS (CDER)	Office of Business Process Support (CDER)
OBRR (CBER)	Office of Blood Research and Review (CBER)
OC	Office of Compliance
OC	Immediate Office of the Commissioner (OC)
OC	Office of the Commissioner (FDA)
OC (CDER)	Office of Compliance (CDER)
OC (CDRH)	Office of Compliance (CDRH)

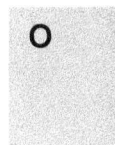

O

O

OC (CFSAN)	Office of Compliance (CFSAN)
OCAC (CFSAN)	Office of Cosmetics and Colors (CFSAN)
OCBQ (CBER)	Office of Compliance and Biologics Quality (CBER)
OCC	Object Class Code
OCC (OC)	Office of the Chief Counsel (OC)
OCD (CDRH)	Office of the Center Director (CDRH)
OCD (CFSAN)	Office of the Center Director (CFSAN)
OCD (CVM)	Office of the Center Director (CVM)
OCER (CDRH)	Office of Communication, Education and Radiological Programs (CDRH)
OCI (ORA)	Office of Criminal investigations (ORA)
OCIO (OC)	Office of the Chief information Officer (OC)
OCM (OC)	Office of Crisis Management (OC)
OCO (CFSAN)	Office of Constituent Operations (CFSAN)
OCP (CDER)	Office of Clinical Pharmacology (CDER)
OCP (OC)	Office of Combination Products (OC)
OCR	Office for Civil Rights (DHHS)
OCTEC (CDER)	Office of Counter-Terrorism and Emergency Coordination (CDER)
OCTGT (CBER)	Office of Cellular, Tissue and Gene therapies (CBER)
OCTMA (CBER)	Office of Communication, Training and Manufacturers Assistance (CBER)
OD	Office of the Director
OD (CBER)	Office of the Director (CBER)
OD (CDER)	Office of the Center Director (CDER)
OD (NCTR)	Office of the Director (NCTR)
ODA	Orphan Drug Act of 1983
ODAC	Oncologic Drugs Advisory Committee
ODE	Office of Drug Evaluation (CDER)
ODE (CDRH)	Office of Device Evaluation (CDRH)
ODE I	Office of Drug Evaluation I (CDER)
ODE II	Office of Drug Evaluation II (CDER)
ODE III	Office of Drug Evaluation III (CDER)

ODE IV (CDER)	Office of Drug Evaluation IV (CDER)
ODM	Operational Data Model (CDISC)
OE (ORA)	Office of Enforcement (ORA)
OECD	Organisation for Economic Co-Operation and Development
OEEODEM (OC)	Office of EEO and Diversity Management (OC)
OEI	Official Establishment inventory
OEL	Occupational Exposure Level
OEM	Original Equipment Manufacturer
OEO (OC)	Office of Executive Operations (OC)
OEP	Office of Emergency Preparedness (PHS)
OEP (CDER)	Office of Executive Programs (CDER)
OER (OC)	Office of External Relations (OC)
OES (OC)	Office of Executive Secretariat (OC)
OFACS	Office of Facilities, Acquisitions, and Central Services (FDA)
OFAS (CFSAN)	Office of Food Additive Safety (CFSAN)
OFDA	Office of foreign Disaster Assistance
OFDCER (CFSAN)	Office of Food Defense, Communication and Emergency Response (CFSAN)
OFFAS (OC)	Office of Field Financial and Acquisitions Services (OC)
OFM (OC)	Office of Financial Management (OC)
OFPA	Organic Foods Production Act of 1990
OFS (CFSAN)	Office of Food Safety (CFSAN)
OFS (OC)	Office of Financial Services (OC)
OFSDO (CFSAN)	Office of Food Safety, Defense and Outreach (CFSAN)
OGC	Office of the General Counsel (DHHS)
OGD (CDER)	Office of Generic Drugs (CDER)
OGE	Office of Government Ethics (U.S.)
OGUD (CDRH)	Obstetrics and Gynecology Devices Branch (CDRH)

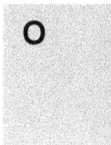

O

O

OHRMS	Office of Human Resources and Management Services (FDA)
OIA (OC)	Office of internal Affairs (OC)
OIASI (OC)	Office of international Activities and Strategic initiatives (OC)
OIG	Office of inspector General (DHHS)
OIM	Office of information Management (OC)
OIP (OC)	Office of international Programs (OC)
OIRA	Office of information and Regulatory Affairs (OMB)
OIT (CBER)	Office of information Technology (CBER)
OIT (CDER)	Office of information Technology (CDER)
OIT (CDRH)	Office of information Technology (CDRH)
OIT (CFSAN)	Office of information Technology (CFSAN)
OIT (CVM)	Office of information Technology (CVM)
OIT (NCTR)	Office of information Technology (NCTR)
OIT (OC)	Office of information Technology (OC)
OIT (ORA)	Office of information Technology (ORA)
OITSS (OC)	Office of information Technology Shared Services (OC)
OIVD (CDRH)	Office of in Vitro Diagnostic Device Evaluation and Safety (CDRH)
OJDB (CDRH)	Orthopedic Joint Devices Branch (CDRH)
OLA (OC)	Office of Legislative Affairs (OC)
OLE	Object Linking and Embedding (Microsoft)
OM (CBER)	Office of Management (CBER)
OM (CDER)	Office of Management (CDER)
OM (CVM)	Office of Management (CVM)
OM (OC)	Office of Management (OC)
OMB	Office of Management and Budget (U.S.)
OMB (NCTR)	Operations and Maintenance Branch (NCTR)
OMO (CDRH)	Office of Management Operations (CDRH)
OMP (CDER)	Office of Medical Policy (CDER)

OMP (OC)	Office of Management Programs (OC)
OMRF	Oklahoma Medical Research Foundation
OMS (CFSAN)	Office of Management Systems (CFSAN)
OMS (NCTR)	Office of Management Services (NCTR)
OMT	ORAI Mucosal Transudate
ONADE (CVM)	Office of New Animal Drug Evaluation (CVM)
ONC	Office of the National Coordinator for Health information Technology (DHHS)
ONCHIT	Office of the National Coordinator for Health information Technology (DHHS)
OND (CDER)	Office of New Drugs (CDER)
ONDQA (CDER)	Office of New Drug Quality Assessment (CDER)
ONLDS (CFSAN)	Office of Nutrition, Labeling and Dietary Supplements (CFSAN)
ONP (CDER)	Office of Nonprescription Products (CDER)
ONPLDS (CFSAN)	Office of Nutritional Products, Labeling and Dietary Supplements (CFSAN)
OO (CFSAN)	Office of Operations (CFSAN)
OO (OC)	Office of Operations (OC)
OO (OC)	Office of the Ombudsman (OC)
OOB	Out of Business
OODP (CDER)	Office of Oncology Drug Products (CDER)
OOP	Order of Predominance [in the ingredients Statement]
OOS	Out of Specification
OP (OC)	Office of Policy (OC)
OP 1 (OC)	Operations Team 1 (OC)
OP 2 (OC)	Operations Team 2 (OC)
OP 3 (OC)	Operations Team 3 (OC)
OP 4 (OC)	Operations Team 4 (OC)
OPA (OC)	Office of Public Affairs (OC)
OPB (ORA)	Operations and Policy Branch (ORA)

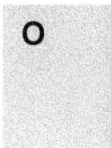

O

OPD (OC)	Office of Orphan Products Development (OC)
OPDFB (CFSAN)	Office of Plants, Dairy Foods and Beverages (CFSAN)
OPF	Official Personnel Folder
OPFIT (NCTR)	Office of Planning, Finance and information Technology (NCTR)
OPHEP	Office of Public Health Emergency Preparedness (HHS)
OPHEP	Office of Public Health Emergency Preparedness (HHS)
OPL (OC)	Office of Planning (OC)
OPM	Office of Personnel Management (U.S.)
OPMAD (CDRH)	Orthopedic Physical Medicine and Anesthesiology Devices Branch (CDRH)
OPO	Organ Procurement Organization
OPPL (OC)	Office of Policy, Planning and Legislation (OC)
OPS (CDER)	Office of Pharmaceutical Science (CDER)
OPT (OC)	Office of Pediatric Therapeutics (OC)
OPTN	Organ Procurement and Transplantation Network
OPV	ORAl Polio Vaccine
OQ	Operational Qualification
OR (CVM)	Office of Research (CVM)
ORA	Office of Regulatory Affairs (FDA)
ORA	Operations Research Analyst
ORADSS	Office of Regulatory Affairs Reporting, Analysis and Decision Support System
Orange Book	Approved Drug Products With therapeutic Equivalence Evaluations
ORI	Office of Research integrity (HHS)
ORISE	Oak Ridge institute for Science and Education
ORL-DO (ORA)	Orlando District Office (ORA)
ORM	Operational Risk Management
ORM	Operational Risk Management

ORM (ORA)	Office of Resource Management (ORA)
ORNL	Oak Ridge National Laboratory
ORO (ORA)	Office of Regional Operations (ORA)
ORP (CDER)	Office of Regulatory Policy (CDER)
ORP (CFSAN)	Office of Regulations and Policy (CFSAN)
ORPS (OC)	Office of Real Property Services (OC)
ORPSS (CFSAN)	Office of Regulations, Policy and Social Sciences (CFSAN)
ORS (CFSAN)	Office of Regulatory Science (CFSAN)
OS (CDER)	Operations Staff (CDER)
OS (CFSAN)	Office of Seafood (CFSAN)
OS (OC)	Operations Staff (OC)
OSAS (CFSAN)	Office of Scientific Analysis and Support (CFSAN)
OSB (CDRH)	Office of Surveillance and Biometrics (CDRH)
OSB (CFSAN)	Office Services Branch (CFSAN)
OSC (CVM)	Office of Surveillance and Compliance (CVM)
OSCAR	ORACLE System for Center Automation and Retrieval
OSCI (CFSAN)	Office of Science (CFSAN)
OSDB (CDRH)	Orthopedic Spine Devices Branch (CDRH)
OSD-HD	Office of the Secretary of Defense for Homeland Defense
OSE (CDER)	Office of Surveillance and Epidemiology (CDER)
OSEL (CDRH)	Office of Science and Engineering Laboratories (CDRH)
OSG	Office of the Surgeon General (PHS)
OSHA	Occupational Safety and Health Administration (U.S. Department of Labor)
OSHC (OC)	Office of Science and Health Coordination (OC)

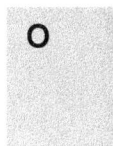

O

O

OSHC (OC)	Office of Science and Health Coordination (OC)
OSHI (OC)	Office of Special Health Issues (OC)
OSHRC	Occupational Safety and Health Review Commission (U.S.)
OSM	Office of Surface Mining (Department of the interior)
OSO (OC)	Office of Security Operations (OC)
OSS (OC)	Office of Shared Services (OC)
OST (CFSAN)	Office Services Team (CFSAN)
OSTP	Office of Science and Technology Policy (U.S.)
OTC	Over-the-Counter
OTC	Ornithine Transcarbamylase Deficiency
OTCDHFB (CDER)	OTC Drugs and Health Fraud Branch (CDER)
OTCOM (CDER)	Office of Training and Communications (CDER)
OTFP	Other Than a Food Processing Facility
OTR (CDER)	Office of Testing and Research (CDER)
OTRR (CBER)	Office of therapeutics Research and Review (CBER)
OTS (CDER)	Office of Translational Sciences (CDER)
OVI	organic Volatile Impurities
OVRR (CBER)	Office of Vaccines Research and Review (CBER)
OVST (CFSAN)	Operations and Veterinary Support Team (CFSAN)
OWH (OC)	Office of Women's Health (OC)

P

P & PC	Production and Process Controls
PA	Physical Activity
PAAB	Pharmaceutical Advertising Advisory Board (Canada)
PAB	Pharmaceutical Affairs Bureau (Japan)
PAB (CFSAN)	Product Adulteration Branch (CFSAN)
PAC	Post-Approval Changes
PAC	Program Assignment Code
PAC	Political Action Committee
PAC	Private Analytical Certificate Date (ORA AofC Code)
PACE	Patient-Centered Assessment and Counseling for Exercise
PAD	Pharmacologically Active Drug
PADE	Postmarketing Adverse Drug Experience
PAER	Preliminary Adverse Event Report Review (CDRH)
PAFA	Priority-Based Assessment of Food Additives (CFSAN)
PAG	Project Advisory Group
PAGE	Polyacrylimide Gel Electrophoresis
PAHO	Pan American Health organization (Who)
PAI	Pre-Approval inspection
PAIS (ORA)	Public Affairs and information Staff (ORA)
PAITS	Pre-Approval inspection Tracking System
PAL	Public Affairs Liaison
PAM	Pesticide Analytical Manual
PAMP	Post-Approval Monitoring System
PAO	Public Affairs Office
PAP	Patient Assistance Programs
PAR	Proven Acceptable Range
PARN	Problem/Action Request Notice

PARQ	Physical Activity Readiness Questionnaire
PARS (CDER)	Program Activities Review Staff (CDER)
PART	Program Assessment Rating tool
PAS	Public Affairs Specialist
PAS	Prior Approval Supplement
PAS (CDRH)	Premarket Approval Section (CDRH)
PAT	Process Analytical Technology initiative (CDER)
PB (CDRH)	Planning Branch (CDRH)
PBM	Pharmacy Benefits Management
PBPC	Peripheral Blood Progenitor Cell
PBSC	Peripheral Blood Stem Cell
PC	Personal Computer
PCB	Placental Cord Blood
PCBE	President's Council on Bioethics
PCBs	Polychlorinated Biphenyls
PCC	Poison Control Center
PCERT	Preclinical and Clinical Evaluation Review Template (Canada)
PCP	Pneumocystis Carinii Pneumonia
PCR	Polymerase Chain Reaction
PCS	Permanent Change of Station
PCT	Practical Clinical Trial
PCT	Photochemical Treatment
PD	Position Description
PD	Pharmacodynamics
PDA	Parenteral Drug Association
PDA	Prescription Drug Advertising
PDB (CDER)	Prescription Drugs Branch (CDER)
PDCS (OC)	Policy Development and Coordination Staff (OC)
PDE	Pediatric Exclusivity
PDE	Permitted Daily Exposure
PDF	Portable Document format
PDI	Post Donation information

PDLB (CDRH)	Pacing, Defibrillator and Leads Branch (CDRH)
PDMA	Prescription Drug Marketing Act of 1988
PDO	Protected Designation of origin
PDP	Principal Display Panel
PDP	Product Development Protocol
PDQ	Physician Data Query (NCI)
PDR	Physician's Desk Reference
PDR	Product Defect Reporting
PDS	Permanent Duty Station
PDS (CDER)	Project Development Staff (CDER)
PDUFA	Prescription Drug User Fee Act of 1992
PE	Pharmacoeconomics
PE	Physical Education
PEB (CBER)	Planning and Evaluation Branch (CBER)
PEB (CDRH)	Program Enforcement Branch (CDRH)
PEB (CFSAN)	Process Engineering Branch (CFSAN)
PEB (CFSAN)	Program and Enforcement Branch (CFSAN)
PEB (ORA)	Program Evaluation Branch (ORA)
PEB 1 (CDRH)	Postmarket Evaluation Branch 1 (CDRH)
PEB 2 (CDRH)	Postmarket Evaluation Branch 2 (CDRH)
PELT (CFSAN)	Product Evaluation and Labeling Team (CFSAN)
PEP	Performance Evaluation Plan
PER	Pharmaceutical Evaluation Reports (EMEA)
Per Diem	Per Day (total Allowance for Daily Travel Expenses)
PERI	Pharmaceutical Education and Research institute
PERT	Product-Enhanced Reverse Transcriptase
PERV	Porcine Endogenous Retrovirus
PET	Positron Emission tomography
PET	Polyethylene Terephthalate

P

PETA	People for the Ethical Treatment of Animals
PETG	Polyethylene Terephthalate G
PFGE	Pulsed-Field Gel Electrophoresis
PFI	Pet Food institute
PFL	Professional Flexible Labeling
PFO	Principal Federal official
PFS	Piper Fatigue Scale
PGB (CFSAN)	Policy Guidance Branch (CFSAN)
PHA	Public Health Advisory
PHI	Protected Health information
PHIN	Public Health information Network (CDC)
PHN	Population, Health and Nutrition (Center)
PHPPO	Public Health Practice Program Office (CDC)
PHPS	Public Health Prevention Service (CDC)
PhRMA	Pharmaceutical Research and Manufacturers of America
PHS	Public Health Service (DHHS)
PHSA	Public Health Service Act of 1944
PHTN	Public Health Training Network (CDC)
PI	Package insert (Approved Product Labeling)
PI	Principal investigator
PIB (CBER)	Program inspection Branch (CBER)
PIC/S	Pharmaceutical inspection Convention/Pharmaceutical inspection Co-Operation Scheme
PICNIC	Professionals & Citizens Network for integrated Care
PIFSI	Produce and Imported Foods Safety initiative (CFSAN)
PIM	Product information Management
PIN	Personal Identification Number
PIP	Plant-incorporated Protectant
PK	Pharmacokinetics
PKA	Prekallikrein Activator

PKI	Public Key infrastructure
PKLN	Parklawn Building
PKU	Phenylketonuria
PLA	Product License Application (CBER)
PLAS	Prior Label Approval System (Fsis)
PLF	Product Licensing Framework (Canada)
PLI	Pre-License inspection (CBER)
PLR	Physician Labeling Rule
PLS	Product License [Application] Supplement
PLS	Pending Logging System
PM	Post-Marketing
PM	Project Manager
PMA	Pharmaceutical Manufacturer's Association
PMA	Premarket Approval
PMA	Premarket Application
PMA	Device Premarket Approval Number (ORA AofC Code)
PMAA	Premarket Approval Application
PMB	Pharmacy Benefit Manager
PMC	Postmarketing Commitment
PMCC	Project Management Coordinating Committee (CDER)
PMF	Public Master File
PMHS (CDER)	Pediatric and Maternal Health Staff (CDER)
PMN	Premarket Notification
PMN	Device Premarket Notification Number (510k) (ORA AofC Code)
PMO	Pasteurized Milk ordinance
PMO	Project Management Officer
PMOA	Primary Mode of Action
PMP	Plant-Made Pharmaceutical
PMP	Performance Management Program
PMPRB	Patented Medicine Prices Review Board (Canada)

P

PMR	Premarket Report
PMR	Postmarketing Requirement
PMRI	Patient Medical Record information
PMRI	Preventive Medicine Research institute
PMS	Postmarketing Surveillance
PMS (CDRH)	Program Management Staff (CDRH)
PMS (OC)	Print Media Staff (OC)
PMSB	Pharmaceutical and Medical Safety Bureau (Japan)
PMSB (CBER)	Program Management Services Branch (CBER)
PMSB (CDER)	Program Management Services Branch (CDER)
PMSC	Pre-Market Surveillance and Compliance (CFSAN)
PN	Product Name
PNC (ORA)	Prior Notice Center (ORA)
PNNL	Pacific Northwest National Laboratory
PNR	Passenger Name Record
PNS	Peripheral Nervous System
PNS (CDRH)	Premarket Notification Section (CDRH)
PNSI	Prior Notice System interface
PO	Per Os (By Mouth)
POA	Privately Owned Automobile
POB (CBER)	Program Operations Branch (CBER)
POC	Point of Contact
PODS	Program oriented Data System
PODS	Project oriented Data System
POM	Prescription-only Medicine (UK)
POM	Program Objective Memorandum
POMS	Profile of Mood States
POS	Point of Sale
POS (CBER)	Program Operation Staff (CBER)
POS (CDRH)	Program Operations Staff (CDRH)
POV	Privately-Owned Vehicle

POWER	Petition Optical Workflow, Exchange and Retrieval (CFSAN's FARM System)
PP	Pay Period
PPA	Phenylpropanolamine
PPA	Poison Prevention Act
ppb	Parts Per Billion
PPB (CFSAN)	Plant Products Branch (CFSAN)
PPC	Production and Process Controls
PPE	Pay Period Ending
PPE	Personal Protective Equipment
PPI	Patient Package insert
PPI	Planned Product Improvements
PPIA	Poultry Products inspection Act
ppm	Parts Per Million
PPM	Planned Preventive Maintenance
PPP	Point-to-Point Protocol
PPQ	Plant Protection and Quarantine (USDA)
PPS (CBER)	Policy and Publications Staff (CBER)
PPSR	Proposal for Pediatric Studies Request
PPT	Plasma Preparation Tube
PPTA	Plasma Protein therapeutics Association
PPTP	Point-to-Point Tunneling Protocol (Microsoft)
PPV	Patient Profile Viewer
PPWMB (ORA)	Program Planning and Workforce Management Branch (ORA)
PQ	Performance Qualification
PQ	Process Qualification
PQAS	Pharmaceutical Quality Assessment System
PQG	Pharmaceutical Quality Group
PQLS (CBER)	Product Quality Laboratory Staff (CBER)
PQRI	Product Quality Research institute
PR	Public Relations
PR	Pulse Rate
PR (CBER)	Product Review Branch (CBER)

P

PRA	Paperwork Reduction Act of 1995
PRB	Performance Review Board
PRB (CBER)	Product Release Branch (CBER)
PRB (CFSAN)	Pathology Branch (CFSAN)
PREA	Pediatric Research Equity Act of 2003
PRIM & R	Public Responsibility in Medicine and Research
PRL-NW	Pacific Regional Laboratory - Northwest (ORA)
PRL-SW	Pacific Regional Laboratory - Southwest (ORA)
PRMB (CDER)	Program and Resources Management Branch (CDER)
PRN	As Needed
Prop 65	Proposition 65
PrP	Prion Protein
PRRB (OC)	Paperwork Reduction and Records Branch (OC)
PRRMS (OC)	Paperwork Reduction and Records Management Staff (OC)
PRS (OC)	Policy Research Staff (OC)
PRSB (CDRH)	Plastic and Reconstructive Surgery Devices Branch (CDRH)
PS	Particle Size
PS (CDER)	Planning Staff (OC)
PSA	Prostate Specific Antigen
PSA	Poultry Science Association
PSB (CBER)	Program Surveillance Branch (CBER)
PSC	Postmarket Strategies Committee
PSC	Program Support Center (DHHS)
PSD (OC)	Payment Services Division (OC)
PSI	Pharmaceutical Society of Ireland
PSNI	Pharmaceutical Society of Northern Ireland
PSP	Physician Special Pay
PSS (CDRH)	Patient Safety Staff (CDRH)

PSSB (CFSAN)	Program Support Services Branch (CFSAN)
PST	Porcine Somatotropin
PSUR	Periodic Safety Update Reports
PT	Part Time
PT	Preferred Term
PTB (CBER)	Pharmacology and toxicology Branch (CBER)
PTC	Points to Consider
PTC	Parklawn Training Center
PTCC	Pharmacology and toxicology Coordinating Committee (CDER)
PTE	Patent Term Extension
PTEI	Pittsburgh Tissue Engineering initiative
PTFE	Polytetrafluroethylene
PTK	Phototherapeutic Keratectomy
PTO	Patent and Trademark Office (U.S. Department of Commerce)
PTR	Platelet Transfusion Reaction
PTS (CBER)	Product Testing Section (CBER)
PTU	Propylthiouracil
PUD	Peptic Ulcer Disease
PUFI	Packed Under Federal inspection
PV	Process Validation
PVC	Polyvinyl Chloride
PVDB (CDRH)	Peripheral Vascular Devices Branch (CDRH)
PWS	Performance Work Statement

P

Q

Q & A	Questions and Answers
QA	Quality Assurance
QAO	Quality Assurance Officer
QAS (CBER)	Quality Assurance Staff (CBER)
QAS (CDER)	Quality Assurance Staff (CDER)
QAT (CBER)	Quality Assurance Team (CBER)
QAU (CFSAN)	Quality Assurance Unit (CFSAN)
QbD	Quality by Design
QbR	Question-Based Review
QC	Quality Control
QCP	Quality Control Program
QD	once Daily
QID	Four Times A Day
QIS-P	Quality information Summary Pharmaceuticals (Canada)
QL	Quality of Life
QMS	Quality Management System
QMS (CDER)	Quality Management Staff (CDER)
QNS	Quantity Not Sufficient
QOD	Every Other Day
QoL	Quality of Life
QOS	Quality Overall Summary (of CTD)
QP	Qualified Person (EU)
QS	Quality System
QSI	Quality Step increase
QSIT	Quality System inspection Technique (CDRH)
QSR	Quality System Regulation
QSR	Quality System Record
QSR	Quality System Representative
QTV	Qualified Through Verification (USDA)
QU	Quality Unit
QWL	Quality of Work Life

R

R & D	Research and Development
R & E	Recall and Emergency (ORA)
R & W	Recreation and Welfare
RA	Rheumatoid Arthritis
RAA	Research Across America
RAC	Raw Agricultural Commodity
RAC	Reviewer Affairs Committee (CDER) [Disbanded 2000]
RAC	Recombinant DNA Advisory Committee (NIH)
RACC	Reference Amount Customarily Consumed
RACT (CFSAN)	Risk Assessment Coordination Team (CFSAN)
RAD	Rapid Applications Development
RADAR	Risk Assessment of Drugs - Analysis and Response
RADAR	Radio Detecting and Ranging
RAE	Remedial Action Exemption
RAM	Random Access Memory
RAM	Reporting and Analysis Module (EASE)
RAMP	Remedial Action Management Program
RAPS	Regulatory Affairs Professionals Society
RBC	Red Blood Cells
RCC	Research Coordinating Committee
RCH	Remove Clinical Hold
RCHSA	Radiation Control for Health and Safety Act of 1968
RCS	Records Control Schedule
RCS (CFSAN)	Regulations Coordination Staff (CFSAN)
RCT	Randomized Clinical Trial
RCT (CFSAN)	Recall Team (CFSAN)
RD	Registration Dossier

R

R

RDA	Recommended Daily Allowance
RDB (CDRH)	Radiological Devices Branch (CDRH)
RDBMS	Relational Database Management System
RDE	Remote Data Entry
RDI	Reference Daily intake
rDNA	Recombinant Deoxyribonucleic
RDRC	Radioactive Drug Research Committee (CDER)
RDT	Rising Dose tolerance
RDTS	Reproductive and Developmental toxicology Subcommittee (CDER)
REDS-II	Retrovirus Epidemiology Donor Study
REE	Research, Education and Economics (USDA)
REG	Drug Registration Number (ORA AofC Code)
reg neg	Regulatory Negotiation
ReGo	Reinventing the United States Government
REIS	Regional Economic information System
REMS	Risk Evaluation and Mitigation Strategy
RES	Residence
RES	Recall Enterprise System (ORA)
RES (OC)	Regulations Editorial Section (OC)
RESNA	Rehabilitation Engineering & Assistive Technology Society of North America
RFA	Request for Application
RFC	Request for Contract
RFCPCS (CFAN)	Retail Food and Cooperative Programs Coordination Staff (CFSAN)
RFD	Request for Designation
RFDD	Regional Food and Drug Director
RFI	Request for information
RFID	Radio-Frequency Identification
RFP	Request for Proposal
RFPT (CFSAN)	Retail Food Protection Team (CFSAN)

RH	Responsible Head
RH	Relative Humidity
RIA	Radioimmunoassay
RIAS	Regulatory Impact Analysis Statement (Canada)
RIBA™	Recombinant Immunoblot Assay (Chiron ®)
RIC	Resident in Charge
RICHS	Rural information Center Health Service
RIF	Reduction-in-force
RIHSC	Research involving Human Subjects Committee (FDA)
RIM	Reference information Model (HL7)
RIMS	Regulatory information Management Staff
RIPA	Radioimunoprecipitation Assay
RIS	Regulatory information Specialist
RIS (CBER)	Retroviral Immunology Section (CBER)
RIT	Relocation income Tax
RKW1	Rockwall Building I
RKW2	Rockwall Building Ii
RL	Regulatory Letter (FDA Post-Audit Letter)
RLD	Reference Listed Drug
RM	Raw Material
RMAB (CDRH)	Risk Management and Analysis Branch (CDRH)
RMB (CBER)	Resource Management Branch (CBER)
RMCC	Review Management Coordinating Committee (CBER)
RMS	Reference Member State (Europe)
RMS	Regulatory Management System
RMS (CDER)	Review Management Staff (CDER)
RMS/BLA	Regulatory Management System for the Biologics License Application (CBER)
RMT (CFSAN)	Regulations Management Team (CFSAN)
RNA	Ribonucleic Acid

R

R

ROA	Read only Access
ROC	Receiver Operating Characteristic Curve
RODS	Real-Time Outbreak & Disease Surveillance System
ROI	Report of investigation
ROI	Return on investment
RP	Resident Post
RPB (CDRH)	Radiation Programs Branch (CDRH)
RPM	Regulatory Procedures Manual (ORA)
RPM	Regulatory Project Manager
RPMB (CBER)	Regulatory Project Management Branch (CBER)
RPMCC	Regulatory Project Management Coordinating Committee (CDER)
RPMS (OC)	Regulations Policy and Management Staff (OC)
RPS	Regulatory Product Submission
RPS (CDER)	Regulatory Policy Staff (CDER)
RPSGB	Royal Pharmaceutical Society of Great Britain
RR	Relative Risk
RR	Repeatedly Reactive
RR	Recall Recommendation
RRCC	Regional Response Coordination Center (FEMA)
RRHR	Regional Radiological Health Representative
RRS	Resource Reporting System (CBER)
RRSS (CDER)	Regulatory Review Support Staff (CDER)
RSB (CDER)	Review Support Branch (CDER)
RSGEMS (CFSAN)	Regulations and Special Government Employees Management Staff (CFSAN)
RSMB (CDRH)	Reporting Systems Monitoring Branch (CDRH)
RSNA	Radiological Society of North America
RSO	Radiation Safety Officer

RSOI	Reception, Staging, onward Movement, and integration
RSS	Really Simple Syndication
RSS	RDF (Resource Data Framework) Site Summary
RSS	Rich Site Summary
RSS (CDER)	Regulatory Support Staff (CDER)
RSV	Respiratory Syncytial Virus
RSVIG	Respiratory Synctial Virus Immune Globulin
RSVIGIV	Respiratory Synctial Virus Immune Globulin intravenous
RSVP	Resource Reporting System Via Projects (CFSAN)
RTA	Refusal-to-Accept
RTE	Ready-to-Eat
RTF	Refusal to File
RTF	Rich Text format
RTL (NCTR)	Reproductive toxicology Laboratory (NCTR)
RTM	Recall Team Member
RTR	Recall Termination Recommendation
RU-486	Roussel Uclaf (original Designer) Abortifacient Drug (Mifepristone)
RUG	Resource Utilization Group
RUO	Research Use only
RVIS	Residue Violation information System
Rx	Prescription

R

S

S & E	Safety and Effectiveness
S/C	Servings per Container
S/L	Sick Leave
S/NDS	Supplemental New Drug Submission (Canada)
SA	Sustained Action [Medication]
SAB	Science Advisory Board
SACD	Special Assistant to the Center Director
SACS	Scientific Advisors and Consultants Staff (CBER)
SACX	Secretary's Advisory Committee on Xenotransplantation (NIH)
SAD	Single Ascending Dose
SADR	Suspected Adverse Drug Reaction
SAE	Serious Adverse Event
SAER	Standard Adverse Event Report Review (CDRH)
SAF	State Access to FACTS
SAI	Single Active ingredient
SAL	Sterility Assurance Level
SAMHSA	Substance Abuse and Mental Heath Services Administration (DHHS)
SAN-DO	San Francisco District Office
SAP	Special Access Program
SAP	Scientific Advisory Panel
SAP	Service Access Point
SAPB (CFSAN)	Shellfish and Aquaculture Policy Branch (CFSAN)
SAR	Search and Rescue
SARS	Severe Acute Respiratory Syndrome
SAS	Symptom Assessment Scale
SAT (CFSAN)	Statistical Applications Team (CFSAN)
SB (ORA)	Systems Branch (ORA)

SBA	Summary Basis of Approval
SBA	Small Business Administration (U.S.)
SBIR	Small Business innovation Research
SBRS	Senior Biomedical Research Service
SC	Study Coordinator
SC	Subcutaneous
SC (CDRH)	Staff College (CDRH)
SC (CFSAN)	Staff College (CFSAN)
SCAW	Scientists Center for Animal Welfare
SCC	Sector Coordinating Council [for Food and Agriculture]
SCD	Service Computation Date
SCGD	Special Controls Guidance Documents
SCL	Symptom Checklist
SCLIR	Secondary Calibration Laboratories for Ionizing Radiation
SCOGS	Select Committee on GRAS Substances
SCR	System Change Request
SCRAG	Senior Civilian Representative of the Attorney General (Department of Homeland Security)
SCRRB (ORA)	Scientific Compliance and Regulatory Review Branch (ORA)
SCSB (CFSAN)	Scientific Computer Support Branch (CFSAN)
SCT	Society for Clinical Trials
SCVIR	Society for Cardiovascular and interventional Radiologists (Now SIR)
SD	Scientific Director
SD	Standard Deviation
SDAB (CDER)	Surveillance and Data Analysis Branch (CDER)
SDM	Submission Data Model (CDISC)
SDM	System Development Methodology
SDN	Screening Deficiency Notice (Canada)
SDO	Standards Development organization
SDS	Submission Data Standards (CDISC)

SDS-PAGE	Sodium DoDecyl Sulfate Polyacrylamide Gel Electrophoresis
SDTM	Study Data Tabulation Model (CDISC)
SDWA	Safe Drinking Water Act
SDWIS	Safe Drinking Water information System
SE	Salmonella Enteriditis
SE	Substantially Equivalent
SE	Standard Error
SEC	Securities and Exchange Commission (U.S.)
SEDS	Shared Establishment Data Service (FHA)
SEER	Surveillance, Epidemiology, and End Results (Registry of NCI)
SEIU	Service Employees international Union
SEND	Standards for Exchange of Nonclinical Data (Consortium)
SES	Senior Executive Service
SF	Standard form
SFB	Spore-forming Bacteria
SFLEO	Senior Federal Law Enforcement official
SG	Study Group
SGE	Special Government Employee
SGEMT (CFSAN)	Special Government Employees Management Team (CFSAN)
SGI	Summer Genetics institute
SGO	Surgeon General's Office
SHE	Safety, Health and Environment
SIA	Strip Immunoblot Assay
SIB (CDRH)	Special investigations Branch (CDRH)
SID	Schedule Identifier Number (ORA AofC Code)
SIDS	Sudden infant Death Syndrome
SIF	Seafood HACCP Importer form (ORA AofC Code)
SIG	Strategic Implementation Group
SIMCEN	National Exercise Simulation Center

SIMT	Scientific, internet/intranet and Middle Tier (CFSAN)
SIP	Summer internship Program in Biomedical Research
SIP	Sterilization in Place
SIR	Society of interventional Radiology (formerly SCVIR)
SIREN	Scientific information Retrieval and Exchange Network (CFSAN)
SIS	Streamlined inspection System (USDA)
SISTIR	Strategic information Systems Technical integration Resources
SITP (OC)	Strategic It Programs (OC)
SL	Signature (Address) Line
SLIP	Serial Line internet Protocol/Point-to-Point Protocol
SLK	Statens Legemiddel Kontroll (Norwegian Medicines Control Authorities)
SLO	State Liaison Officer
SLR	Supplement Labeling Revision
SM	Starting Material
SMART	Submission Management and Review Tracking
SMB (OC)	Space Management Branch (OC)
SMCC	Standards Management Coordinating Committee (CBER)
SMDA	Safe Medical Devices Act of 1990
SME	Significant Medical Event
SME	Subject Matter Expert
SMF	Site Master File
SMG	Staff Manual Guide
SMO	Site Management organization
SMPS (CDRH)	Standards Management Program Staff (CDRH)
SMS (CFSAN)	Safety Management Staff (CFSAN)
SMSB (CFSAN)	Spectroscopy and Mass Spectrometry Branch (CFSAN)

S

SMT (CFSAN)	Statistical Methodology Team (CFSAN)
SMTP	Simple Mail Transfer Protocol
SN/AEMS	Special Nutritional Adverse Events Monitoring System
sNDA	Supplemental New Drug Application
SNIP	Syndicat National De l'industrie Pharmaceutique
SNL	Sandia National Laboratories
SNOMED-RT	Systematized Nomenclature of Medicine Reference Terminology
SNRI	Serotonin-Norepinephrine Reuptake inhibitor
SNS	Strategic National Stockpile (CDC)
SOAB (OC)	Systems and Office Automation Branch (OC)
SOC	System organ Class
SOCRA	Society of Clinical Research Associates
SOM	Sensitivity of Method
SOP	Standard Operating Procedure
SoPA	Submission of Portion of Application
SOPP	Standard Operating Procedures and Policies
SORN	System of Records Notice
SOW	Statement of Work
SPAC	State Pharmaceutical Administration of China
SPC	Summary of Product Characteristics (EMEA)
SPCS (CDER)	Safety Policy and Communications Staff (CDER)
SPECT	Single-Photon Emission Computed tomography
SPIE	international Society for Optical Engineering
SPL	Structured Product Labeling
SPLAT	Structured Product Labeling Advisory Team

SPLIEP	Structured Product Labeling interagency Executive Panel	**S**
SPOTS	Special Products on-Line Tracking System (CDER)	
SPPA	Strategic Partnership Program Agroterrorism initiative	
SPR	System Problem Report	
SPRC	Seafood Products Research Center (CFSAN)	
SPS	Sanitary and Phytosanitary	
SPS (CFSAN)	Science and Policy Staff (CFSAN)	
SPTPB (CFSAN)	Seafood Processing and Technology Policy Branch (CFSAN)	
SQ	Subcutaneous	
SQA	Society of Quality Assurance	
SQL	Structured Query Language	
SR	Sustained Release [Medication]	
SR	Significant Risk	
SRAS	Secure Remote Access Service	
SRCS	Division of Surveillance, Research, and Communication Support (CDER)	
SRD	Single Rising Dose	
SRD	Significant Risk Device	
SRD	Swine Respiratory Disease	
SRD	System Requirements Document	
SRMs	Specified Risk Materials	
SRS	Substance Registration System	
SRS	Spontaneous Reporting System	
SRS (CDER)	Science and Research Staff (CDER)	
SS	Serving Size	
SSA	Social Security Administration (U.S.)	
SSA	Sector-Specific Agencies	
SSAST (CFSAN)	Senior Science Advisor's Staff (CFSAN)	
SSB (CDRH)	Systems Support Branch (CDRH)	
SSC	Special Search Category	
SSC	Systems Steering Committee (CBER)	

SSCT	Swedish Society for Clinical Trials
SSE	Summary of Safety and Effectiveness
SSED	Summary of Safety and Effectiveness Data
SSM	Skin Surface Microscopy
SSN	Social Security Number
SSOP	Sanitation Standard Operating Procedures
SSP	Sector-Specific Plan
SSRCR	Suggested State Regulations for Control of Radiation
SSRI	Selective Serotonin Reuptake inhibitor
STA	Special Temporary Authority
STAI	Strait Anxiety inventory
STAMP	Systematic Technology Assessment of Medical Products (CDRH)
STARS	Submission Tracking and Reporting System
STB (ORA)	State Training Branch (ORA)
STCD	Sterile Connecting Device
STEPS	System for Thalidomide Education and Prescribing Safety
STN	Submission Tracking Number
STOP	Safe Tables Our Priority
STS (CBER)	Standards and Testing Staff (CBER)
STT	Short Term Tests
Subpart H	That Subpart of 21 CFR Part 314 Pertaining to Accelerated Approval of Drugs
SUD	Sudden Unexpected Death
SUD	Single-Use Device
SUPAC	Scale Up and Post-Approval Changes
SUPAC-IR	Scale-Up and Post-Approval Changes-- Immediate Release
SUSAR	Suspected Unexpected Serious Adverse Reaction
SVP	Small-Volume Parenteral

SWAT	Special Weapons and Tactics
SWDB (CDRH)	Software and Web Development Staff (CDRH)
SX	Symptoms

S

T

T

T&A	Time and Attendance
T/PT	Traceability/Product Tracing
ta	Travel Authorization
TA	Temporary Abeyance
TA	Technology Administration (U.S.)
TAA	Transfusion-Associated AIDS
TAB (OC)	Travel Audit Branch (OC)
TAB (CDRH)	Technical Assistance Branch (CDRH)
TAH	Transfusion-Associated Hepatitis
TAS (NCTR)	Technology Advancement Staff (NCTR)
TAV	Travel Authorizations and Vouchers
TAVC	total Aerobic Viable Count
TB	Tuberculosis
TBD	to Be Determined
TBLS	Team Biologics Liaison Staff (CBER)
TBP	therapeutic Biologic Product
TBSB (CBER)	therapeutics and Blood Safety Branch (CBER)
TBT	Technical Barriers to Trade
TCP/IP	Transmission Control Protocol/internet Protocol
TCS	Temporary Change of Station
TD	Target Date
TDD	Telecommunications Device for the Deaf
TDDB (CDRH)	Television Design and Development Branch (CDRH)
TDDS	Transdermal Drug Delivery System
TDI	tolerable Daily intake
TDS	total Diet Study (CFSAN)
TDY	Temporary Duty
TE	therapeutic Equivalence
TEB (CBER)	therapeutics Evaluation Branch (CBER)
TELECON	Telephone Conferencing

TEP	therapeutic Exchange Plasmapheresis
TEPRSSC	Technical Electronic Product Radiation Safety Standards Committee
TERMIS	Tissue Engineering and Regenerative Medicine international Society
TESS	toxic Exposure Surveillance System
TESS	Treatment Emergent Signs and Symptoms
TFM	Tentative Final Monograph
TFRB (CDER)	therapeutic Facilities Review Branch (CDER)
TGA	therapeutic Goods Administration (Australia)
TI	tolerable intake
TID	Three Times A Day
TIFF	Tagged Image File format
TIND	Treatment investigational New Drug
TK	toxicokinetics
TLC	Thin Layer Chromatography
TMJ	Temporomandibular Joint
TMO	Trial Management organization
TNTC	too Numerous to Count
TO	Transportation Officer
TO	Table of Oganization
TOA	total Obligation Authority
TOC	total organic Carbon
TOI	Trial Outcome index
TOL	total organic Carbon
TOPOFF	top officials [Terrorism Exercise]
TOPRA	the organisation for Professionals in Regulatory Affairs
TOR	Threshold of Regulation
TPCC	therapeutic Products Classification Committee (Canada)
TPD	therapeutic Products Directorate (Canada)

T

T

TPDS	Training and Professional Development Staff (CBER)
TPN	total Parenteral Nutrition
TPP	Target Product Profile
TQM	total Quality Management
TRAC	tolerance Reassessment Advisory Committee (EPA)
TRALI	Transfusion-Related Acute Lung injury
Trans Net	internet-Based Blood Shortage Reporting Program (FDA)
TRB	Technical Review Board
TRI	toxics Release inventory (EPA)
TRIMS	Tissue Residue information System
TRO	Temporary Restraining order
TRx	total (Number of) Prescriptions
TSA	Transportation Security Administration (Department of Homeland Security)
TSCA	toxic Substances Control Act of 1976
TSCSB (CFSAN)	Telecommunications and Scientific Computer Support Branch (CFSAN)
TSD (OC)	Travel Services Division (OC)
TSE	Transmissible Spongiform Encephalopathies
TSEAC	Transmissible Spongiform Encephalopathies Advisory Committee (CBER)
TSH	Thyroid Stimulating Hormone
TSOPs	Temperature Standard Operating Procedures
TSP	Thrift Savings Plan
TSS	Transfusion Safety Study
TSSRC	toxicology Study Selection and Review Committee (FDA-NIEHS)
TSSS (CDER)	Technology Support Services Staff (CDER)
TTTC	Take Time to Care [Program]
TTY	Teletypewriters or Text Telephones

Turbo EIR	Turbo Establishment inspection Report (ORA)
TV	Travel Voucher
TVA	Tennessee Valley Authority
TVBB (CBER)	Tumor Vaccines and Biotechnology Branch (CBER)
TVC	total Viable Count
TWG	Technical Working Group

T

U

U	Units
UA	Urinalysis
UADE	Unanticipated Adverse Device Event
UCB	Umbilical Cord Blood
UCBU	Umbilical Cord Blood Unit
UCUM	Unified Codes for Units of Measure (Regenstrief institute)
UDHQ	Uniform Donor Health Questionnaire
UDI	Unique Device Identification
UFC	Unacceptable to foreign Country (ORA AofC Code)
UFMS	Unified Financial Management System
UIN	Unique Identification Number
UK	United Kingdom
UKCCR	United Kingdom Coordinating Committee on Cancer Research
UL	Underwriters Laboratories
ULDB (CDRH)	Urology and Lithotripsy Devices Branch (CDRH)
ULN	Upper Limit of Normal
ULPA	Ultra-Low Penetration Air
UMCP	University of Maryland-College Park
UMDNS	Universal Medical Device Nomenclature System
UMLS	Unified Medical Language System (Nlm)
UMS	Unified Modeling Language (Object Management Group)
UN	United Nations
UN	Unacceptable
UNAIDS	Joint United Nations Program on HIV/AIDS
UNESCO	United Nations Educational, Scientific and Cultural organization
UNICEF	United Nations Children's Fund

UNOS	United Network for organ Sharing
URAA	Uruguay Round Agreements Act of 1994
URL	Uniform Resource Locator
URS	User Requirement Specification
US & R	Urban Search and Rescue
USA	United States Army
USACE	United States Army Corps of Engineers
USAHA	United States Animal Health Association
USAID	United States Agency for international Development
USAMRIID	U.S. Army Medical Research institute for infectious Diseases
USAN	United States Adopted Name
USBR	Bureau of Reclamation (U.S. Department of the interior)
USC	United States Code
USCA	U.S. Code Annotated
USCG	United States Coast Guard
USCS	United States Customs Service (U.S. Department of Homeland Security)
USDA	Department of Agriculture (U.S.)
USFDA	United States Food and Drug Administration
USFS	United States forest Service (U.S. Department of Agriculture)
USGS	United States Geological Survey
USHIK	United States Health information Knowledge Base
USIA	United States information Agency
USITC	United States international Trade Commission
USJFCOM	United States Joint forces Command
USMS	United States Marshals Service
USOPM	United States Office of Personnel Management
USP	U.S. Pharmacopeia
USPC	U.S. Pharmacopeial Convention

U

U

USP-DI	United States Pharmacopeia-Drug information
USPEA	U.S. Poultry and Egg Association
USP-NF	United States Pharmacopeia-National formulary
USPS	United States Postal Service
USPTO	United States Patent and Trademark Office (U.S. Department of Commerce)
USTFA	U.S. Trout Farmers Association
USTR	United States Trade Representative
USUHS	Uniformed Services University of the Health Sciences

V

V/V	Verification/Validation
VA	Department of Veterans Affairs (U.S.)
VADM	Vice Admiral
VAERS	Vaccine Adverse Event Reporting System
VAI	Voluntary Action indicated
VATS	Viral Activation Transfusion Study
VATS	Vacancy Announcement Tracking System (PHS)
VAX	Virtual Address Extension
VBPF	Vegetative Bacteria, Protozoa and Viruses
VCH	Travel Voucher Claim
vCJD	Variant Creutzfeldt Jakob Disease
VCOOL	Voluntary Country-of-origin Labeling
VCPR	Veterinarian/Client/Patient Relationship
VCRP	Voluntary Cosmetic Registration Program (CFSAN)
VCTB (CBER)	Vaccine Clinical Trials Branch (CBER)
VDB (CDRH)	Virology Devices Branch (CDRH)
VE	Vaccine Efficacy
VEB (CBER)	Vaccine Evaluation Branch (CBER)
VEDB (CDRH)	Vitreal and Extraocular Devices Branch (CDRH)
VEE	Venezuelan Equine Encephalomyelitis
VetTrade	Veterinarian Trading Post (Website)
VFD	Veterinary Feed Directive
VHA	Veterans Health Administration
VHSP	Viral Hepatitis Surveillance Program (CDC)
VICH	international Cooperation on Harmonisation of Technical Requirements for Registration of Veterinary Medicinal Products

VICH	Veterinary international Committee on Harmonisation
VIG	Vaccinia Immune Globulin
VISB (OC)	Visual information Services Branch (OC)
VMAC	Veterinary Medicine Advisory Committee (CVM)
VMB (CFSAN)	Virulence Mechanisms Branch (CFSAN)
VMD	Veterinariae Medicinae Doctoris
VMF	Veterinary Master File
VMO	Veterinary Medical Officer
VMP	Validation Master Plan
VMS	Virtual Memory System [Operating System]
VOAD	Volunteer organizations Active in A Disaster
VPN	Virtual Private Network
VRBPAC	Vaccines and Related Biological Products Advisory Committee (CBER)
VS	Visiting Scientist
VS (CBER)	Validation Staff (CBER)
VSB (CBER)	Vaccine Safety Branch (CBER)
VSD	Vaccine Safety Datalink [Project] (CDC)
VSOF	Visual Status of Funds
VSS (NCTR)	Veterinary Services Staff (NCTR)
VVB (CBER)	Viral Vaccines Branch (CBER)

W

W3C	World Wide Web Consortium
WAE	When-Actually-Employed
WAG	Widely Attended Gathering
WAN	Wide Area Network
WAT (CFSAN)	Worklife Analysis Team (CFSAN)
WBC	White Blood Cell
WBS	Work Breakdown Structure
WEAC	Winchester Engineering and Analytical Center
WebSDM	Web-Based Submission Data Manager
WEDA	Workforce Equity and Diversity Action
WEDI	Workgroup for Electronic Data interchange
WFH	World Federation of Hemophilia
WFI	Water for injection
WG	Wage Grade
WHO	World Health organisation
WHO-ART	World Health organisation Adverse Reaction Terminology
WIB	Western Immunoblot
WIC	[Special Supplemental Nutrition Program for] Women, infants, and Children (USDA)
WIGI	within-Grade increase
WISQARS	Web-Based injury Statistics Query and Reporting System (CDC)
WIT	Workflow Improvement Team
WITS	Washington interagency Telecommunications System
WL	Warning Letter
WLF	Washington Legal Foundation
WMS (OC)	Website Management Staff (OC)
WNET	Women's Network for Entrepreneurial Training (SBA)

W
X
Y

WNME	West Nile Meningoencephalitis
WNV	West Nile Virus
WO	White Oak Campus - FDA
WO (NCTR)	Washington Office (NCTR)
WOC I	Woodmont Office Complex I (North)
WOC II	Woodmont Office Complex II (South)
WONF	With Other Natural Flavors
WPADP	Working Party on Automation and Data Processing (international Society of Blood Transfusion)
WPC	Wordperfect Character [Mapping File]
WPS (OC)	Workforce Programs Staff (OC)
WRAIR	Walter Reed Army institute of Research
WRAMC	Walter Reed Army Medical Center
WSHSC	Water Soluble, Heat Stable Chemicals
WSL (CFSAN)	Washington Seafood Laboratory (CFSAN)
WTA	Withholding Tax Allowance
WWW	World Wide Web
WYSIWYG	What You See Is What You Get

X, Y

XDR-TB	Extensively Drug-Resistant Tuberculosis
XML	Extensible Markup Language
X-SCID	X-Linked Severe Combined Immunodeficiency Disorder
Y2K	Year 2000
YTD	Year to Date

Part II
Terminology

Combined Glossary

30-day Premarket Approval Application (PMA) Supplement

A supplemental application to an approved PMA in accordance with 814.39(e). [21 CFR § 814]

505(b)(2) Application

An application submitted under section 505(b)(1) of the act for a drug for which the investigations described in section 505(b)(1)(A) of the act and relied upon by the applicant for approval of the application were not conducted by or for the applicant and for which the applicant has not obtained a right of reference or use from the person by or for whom the investigations were conducted. [21 CFR § 312]

510(k) Statement

A statement, made under section 513(i) of the act, asserting that all information in a premarket notification submission regarding safety and effectiveness will be made available within 30 days of request by any person if the device described in the premarket notification submission is determined to be substantially equivalent. The information to be made available will be a duplicate of the premarket notification submission, including any adverse safety and effectiveness information, but excluding all patient identifiers, and trade secret or confidential commercial information, as defined in 20.61 of this chapter. [21 CFR § 807]

510(k) Summary (summary of any information respecting safety and effectiveness)

A summary, submitted under section 513(i) of the act, of the safety and effectiveness information contained in a premarket notification submission upon which a determination of substantial equivalence can be based. Safety and effectiveness information refers to safety and effectiveness data and information supporting a finding of substantial equivalence, including all adverse safety and effectiveness information. [21 CFR § 807]

A

Abbreviated Application

Applies to an abbreviated new drug application and an abbreviated new animal drug application. [21 CFR § 25]

Abbreviated Application

The application described under 314.94, including all amendments and supplements to the application. "Abbreviated application" applies to both an abbreviated new drug application and an abbreviated antibiotic application. [21 CFR § 314]

Acceptance Criteria

The product specifications and acceptance/rejection criteria, such as acceptable quality level and unacceptable quality level, with an associated sampling plan, that are necessary for making a decision to accept or reject a lot or batch (or any other convenient subgroups of manufactured units). [21 CFR § 210]

Acceptance Number

The maximum number of defective sample units permitted in the sample in order to consider the lot as meeting the specified requirements. [21 CFR § 145]

Acceptable Quality Level (AQL)

> The maximum percent of defective sample units permitted in a lot that will be accepted approximately 95 percent of the time. [21 CFR § 145]

Accidental Radiation Occurrence

> A single event or series of events that has/have resulted in injurious or potentially injurious exposure of any person to electronic product radiation as a result of the manufacturing, testing, or use of an electronic product. [21 CFR § 1000]

Accreditation Body or Body

> An entity that has been approved by FDA under 900.3(d) to accredit mammography facilities. [21 CFR § 900]

Acid Foods or Acidified Foods

> Foods that have an equilibrium pH of 4.6 or below. [21 CFR § 110]

Acknowledgment Letter

> A written communication provided to a distributor by a consignee who is not the ultimate user of medicated feed containing a VFD drug. An acknowledgment letter affirms that the consignee will not ship such medicated animal feed to an animal production facility that does not have a VFD, and will not ship such feed to another distributor without receiving a similar written acknowledgment letter. [21 CFR § 558]

Act

The Federal Food, Drug, and Cosmetic Act approved
June 25, 1938, except as otherwise provided. [21 CFR
§ 11]

Action Limits or Action Levels

The minimum and maximum values of a quality
assurance measurement that can be interpreted as
representing acceptable performance with respect to
the parameter being tested. Values less than the
minimum or greater than the maximum action limit
or level indicate that corrective action must be taken
by the facility. Action limits or levels are also
sometimes called control limits or levels. [21 CFR §
900]

Active Ingredient

Any component that is intended to furnish
pharmacological activity or other direct effect in the
diagnosis, cure, mitigation, treatment, or prevention
of disease, or to affect the structure or any function of
the body of man or other animals. The term includes
those components that may undergo chemical change
in the manufacture of the drug product and be
present in the drug product in a modified form
intended to furnish the specified activity or effect. [21
CFR § 210]

Active Moiety

The molecule or ion, excluding those appended
portions of the molecule that cause the drug to be an
ester, salt (including a salt with hydrogen or

coordination bonds), or other noncovalent derivative (such as a complex chelate or clathrate) of the molecule responsible for the physiological or pharmacological action of the drug substance. [21 CFR § 25]

Actual Yield

The quantity that is actually produced at any appropriate phase of manufacture, processing, or packing of a particular drug product. [21 CFR § 210]

Adequate

That which is needed to accomplish the intended purpose in keeping with good public health practice. [21 CFR § 110]

Administrative Action

Includes every act, including the refusal or failure to act, involved in the administration of any law by the Commissioner, except that it does not include the referral of apparent violations to U.S. attorneys for the institution of civil or criminal proceedings or an act in preparation of a referral. [21 CFR § 10]

Administrative File

The file or files containing all documents pertaining to a particular administrative action, including internal working memoranda, and recommendations. [21 CFR § 10]

Administrative Record

The documents in the administrative file of a particular administrative action on which the Commissioner relies to support the action. [21 CFR § 10]

Advanced Prepared Food

Food that was prepared on location at the food service establishment prior to arrival of the Lead Investigator. [IOM Chapter 3]

Adverse Drug Experience

Any adverse event associated with the use of a new animal drug, whether or not considered to be drug related, and whether or not the new animal drug was used in accordance with the approved labeling (i.e., used according to label directions or used in an extralabel manner, including but not limited to different route of administration, different species, different indications, or other than labeled dosage). Adverse drug experience includes, but is not limited to:

(1) An adverse event occurring in animals in the course of the use of an animal drug product by a veterinarian or by a livestock producer or other animal owner or caretaker.

(2) Failure of a new animal drug to produce its expected pharmacological or clinical effect (lack of expected effectiveness).

---

(3) An adverse event occurring in humans from exposure during manufacture, testing, handling, or use of a new animal drug. [21 CFR § 514]

Adverse Event

An undesirable experience associated with mammography activities within the scope of 42 U.S.C. 263b. Adverse events include but are not limited to:

(1) Poor image quality;

(2) Failure to send mammography reports within 30 days to the referring physician or in a timely manner to the self-referred patient; and

(3) Use of personnel that do not meet the applicable requirements of 900.12(a). [21 CFR § 900]

Adverse Experience

Any adverse event associated with the use of a biological product in humans, whether or not considered product related, including the following: An adverse event occurring in the course of the use of a biological product in professional practice; an adverse event occurring from overdose of the product whether accidental or intentional; an adverse event occurring from abuse of the product; an adverse event occurring from withdrawal of the product; and any failure of expected pharmacological action. [21 CFR § 600]

Life-threatening Adverse Experience

Any adverse experience that places the patient, in the view of the initial reporter, at immediate risk of death from the adverse experience as it occurred, i.e., it does not include an adverse experience that, had it occurred in a more severe form, might have caused death. [21 CFR § 600]

Serious Adverse Experience

Any adverse experience occurring at any dose that results in any of the following outcomes: Death, a life-threatening adverse experience, inpatient hospitalization or prolongation of existing hospitalization, a persistent or significant disability/incapacity, or a congenital anomaly/birth defect. Important medical events that may not result in death, be life-threatening, or require hospitalization may be considered a serious adverse experience when, based upon appropriate medical judgment, they may jeopardize the patient or subject and may require medical or surgical intervention to prevent one of the outcomes listed in this definition. Examples of such medical events include allergic bronchospasm requiring intensive treatment in an emergency room or at home, blood dyscrasias or convulsions that do not result in inpatient hospitalization, or the development of drug dependency or drug abuse. [21 CFR § 600]

Unexpected Adverse Experience

Any adverse experience that is not listed in the current labeling for the biological product. This includes events that may be symptomatically and pathophysiologically related to an event listed in the labeling, but differ from the event because of greater severity or specificity. For example, under this definition, hepatic necrosis would be unexpected (by virtue of greater severity) if the labeling only referred to elevated hepatic enzymes or hepatitis. Similarly, cerebral thromboembolism and cerebral vasculitis would be unexpected (by virtue of greater specificity) if the labeling only listed cerebral vascular accidents. "Unexpected," as used in this definition, refers to an adverse experience that has not been previously observed (i.e., included in the labeling) rather than from the perspective of such experience not being anticipated from the pharmacological properties of the pharmaceutical product. [21 CFR § 600]

Advertising and Labeling

Include the promotional material described in 202.1(l) (1) and (2) respectively. [21 CFR § 207]

Agency

The Food and Drug Administration. [21 CFR § 11]

Agency component

the Center for Biologics Evaluation and Research, the Center for Devices and Radiological Health, the Center for Drug Evaluation and Research, or alternative organizational component of the agency. [21 CFR § 3]

Air Kerma

Kerma in a given mass of air. The unit used to measure the quantity of air kerma is the Gray (Gy). For X-rays with energies less than 300 kiloelectron volts (keV), 1 Gy = 100 rad. In air, 1 Gy of absorbed dose is delivered by 114 roentgens (R) of exposure. [21 CFR § 900]

Alcohol

The substance known as ethanol, ethyl alcohol, or Alcohol, USP. [21 CFR § 328]

All Business Trading Names Used by the Establishment

Any name which is used on a cosmetic product label and owned by the cosmetic product manufacturer or packer, but is different from the principal name under which the cosmetic product manufacturer or packer is registered. [21 CFR § 700]

Alumina

A suspension in water of precipitated aluminum hydroxide. [21 CFR § 82]

Amendment

The submission of information to a pending license application or supplement, to revise or modify the application as originally submitted. [21 CFR § 600]

Analytical Unit

The portion(s) of food taken from a subsample of a sample for the purpose of analysis. [21 CFR § 165]

ANADA

An abbreviated new animal drug application including all amendments and supplements. [21 CFR § 514]

Animal Drug Product

The active ingredient of a new animal drug (as that term is used in the Act) that is not primarily manufactured using recombinant deoxyribonucleic acid (DNA), recombinant ribonucleic acid (RNA), hybridoma technology, or other processes involving site-specific genetic manipulation techniques, including any salt or ester of the active ingredient, as a single entity or in combination with another active ingredient. [21 CFR § 60]

Animal Production Facility

A location where animals are raised for any purpose, but does not include the specific location where medicated feed is made. [21 CFR § 558]

Annual Review

An evaluation, conducted at least annually, that assesses the quality standards of each drug product to determine the need for changes in drug product specifications or manufacturing or control procedures. [source: Quality Systems Guidance]

Antitoxin

A product containing the soluble substance in serum or other body fluid of an immunized animal which specifically neutralizes the toxin against which the animal is immune. [21 CFR § 600]

A product is analogous to a toxin or antitoxin, if intended, irrespective of its source of origin, to be applicable to the prevention, treatment, or cure of disease or injuries of man through a specific immune process.

Any Material Change

Includes but is not limited to any change in the name of the drug, any change in the identity or quantity of the active ingredient(s), any change in the identity or quantity of the inactive ingredient(s) where quantitative listing of all ingredients is required by 207.31(a)(2), any significant change in the labeling of a prescription drug, and any significant change in the label or package insert of an over-the-counter drug. Changes that are not significant include changes in arrangement or printing or changes of an editorial nature. [21 CFR § 207]

Applicant

Any person who submits or plans to submit an application to the Food and Drug Administration for premarket review. For purposes of this section, the terms "sponsor" and "applicant" have the same meaning. [21 CFR § 3]

Applicant

A person or entity who owns or holds on behalf of the owner the approval for an NADA or an ANADA, and is responsible for compliance with applicable provisions of the act and regulations. [21 CFR § 514]

Applicable Product

A product is deemed applicable to the prevention, treatment, or cure of diseases or injuries of man irrespective of the mode of administration or application recommended, including use when intended through administration or application to a person as an aid in diagnosis, or in evaluating the degree of susceptibility or immunity possessed by a person, and including also any other use for purposes of diagnosis if the diagnostic substance so used is prepared from or with the aid of a biological product. [21 CFR § 600]

Applicant

Any person who submits an application or an amendment or supplement to an application under 35 U.S.C. 156 seeking patent term restoration. [21 CFR § 60]

Applicant

Any person who submits an application or abbreviated application or an amendment or supplement to them under this part to obtain FDA approval of a new drug or an antibiotic drug and any person who owns an approved application or abbreviated application. [21 CFR § 314]

Application

An application for patent term restoration submitted under 35 U.S.C. 156. [21 CFR § 60]

Application

The application described under 314.50, including all amendments and supplements to the application. [21 CFR § 314]

Application for research or marketing permit includes:

(1) A color additive petition, described in part 71.
(2) A food additive petition, described in parts 171 and 571.
(3) Data and information about a substance submitted as part of the procedures for establishing that the substance is generally recognized as safe for use that results or may reasonably be expected to result, directly or indirectly, in its becoming a component or otherwise affecting the characteristics of any food, described in 170.30 and 570.30.
(4) Data and information about a food additive submitted as part of the procedures for food additives permitted to be used on an interim basis pending additional study, described in 180.1.
(5) Data and information about a substance submitted as part of the procedures for establishing a tolerance for unavoidable contaminants in food and food-packaging materials, described in section 406 of the act.
(6) An investigational new drug application, described in part 312 of this chapter.
(7) A new drug application, described in part 314.
(8) Data and information about the bioavailability or

bioequivalence of drugs for human use submitted as part of the procedures for issuing, amending, or repealing a bioequivalence requirement, described in part 320.

(9) Data and information about an over-the-counter drug for human use submitted as part of the procedures for classifying these drugs as generally recognized as safe and effective and not misbranded, described in part 330.

(10) Data and information about a prescription drug for human use submitted as part of the procedures for classifying these drugs as generally recognized as safe and effective and not misbranded, described in this chapter.

(11) [Reserved]

(12) An application for a biologics license, described in part 601 of this chapter.

(13) Data and information about a biological product submitted as part of the procedures for determining that licensed biological products are safe and effective and not misbranded, described in part 601.

(14) Data and information about an in vitro diagnostic product submitted as part of the procedures for establishing, amending, or repealing a standard for these products, described in part 809.

(15) AnApplication for an Investigational Device Exemption, described in part 812.

(16) Data and information about a medical device submitted as part of the procedures for classifying these devices, described in section 513.

(17) Data and information about a medical device submitted as part of the procedures for establishing, amending, or repealing a standard for these devices, described in section 514.

(18) An application for premarket approval of a

medical device, described in section 515.

(19) A product development protocol for a medical device, described in section 515.

(20) Data and information about an electronic product submitted as part of the procedures for establishing, amending, or repealing a standard for these products, described in section 358 of the Public Health Service Act.

(21) Data and information about an electronic product submitted as part of the procedures for obtaining a variance from any electronic product performance standard, as described in 1010.4.

(22) Data and information about an electronic product submitted as part of the procedures for granting, amending, or extending an exemption from a radiation safety performance standard, as described in 1010.5.

(23) Data and information about a clinical study of an infant formula when submitted as part of an infant formula notification under section 412(c) of the Federal Food, Drug, and Cosmetic Act.

(24) Data and information submitted in a petition for a nutrient content claim, described in 101.69 of this chapter, or for a health claim, described in 101.70 of this chapter.

(25) Data and information from investigations involving children submitted in a new dietary ingredient notification, described in 190.6 of this chapter. [21 CFR § 50]

Appraised Value

The estimated domestic price at the time of seizure at which such or similar property is freely offered for sale. [21 CFR § 1316]

A

Approval Letter

A written communication to an applicant from FDA approving an application or an abbreviated application. [21 CFR § 314]

Area of the Eye

The area enclosed with in the circumference of the supra-orbital ridge and the infra-orbital ridge, including the eyebrow, the skin below the eyebrow, the eyelids and the eyelashes, and conjunctival sac of the eye, the eyeball, and the soft areolar tissue that lies within the perimeter of the infra-orbital ridge. [21 CFR § 70]

Assent

A child's affirmative agreement to participate in a clinical investigation. Mere failure to object may not, absent affirmative agreement, be construed as assent. [21 CFR § 50]

Assess the Effects of the Change

To evaluate the effects of a manufacturing change on the identity, strength, quality, purity, and potency of a drug product as these factors may relate to the safety or effectiveness of the drug product. [21 CFR § 314]

Assess the Effects of the Change

As used in 601.12 of this chapter, means to evaluate the effects of a manufacturing change on the identity, strength, quality, purity, and potency of a product as these factors may relate to the safety or effectiveness of the product. [21 CFR § 600]

Authorization

Obtaining approval from FDA to utilize new or changed State regulations or procedures during the issuance, maintenance, and withdrawal of certificates by the certification agency. [21 CFR § 900]

Authorized Dispenser

An individual licensed, registered, or otherwise permitted by the jurisdiction in which the individual practices to provide drug products on prescription in the course of professional practice. [21 CFR § 208]

Authorized Distributor of Record

A distributor with whom a manufacturer has established an ongoing relationship to distribute such manufacturer's products. [21 CFR § 203]

Automated Dispensing System

A mechanical system that performs operations or activities, other than compounding or administration, relative to the storage, packaging, counting, labeling, and dispensing of medications, and which collects, controls, and maintains all transaction information. [21 CFR § 1300]

Available for Distribution

The HCT/P has been determined to meet all release criteria. [21 CFR § 1271]

A

Bactericidal Treatment

The application of a method or substance for the destruction of pathogens and other organisms as set forth in 1240.10. [21 CFR § 1240]

Bacteriological Samples

During inspections of firms producing products susceptible to microbial contamination (e.g., frozen precooked; ready to eat seafood, creme filled goods, breaded items, egg rolls, prepared salads, etc.), proof of adulteration, with fecal organisms, or elevated levels of non-pathogenic microorganisms, must be established. Sampling of raw materials, in-line and finished product is warranted. Follow instructions under IOM 4.3.7.7 - Products Susceptible to Contamination with Pathogenic Microorganisms, Sampling During Inspection. [IOM Chapter 4]

Batch

A specific quantity or lot of a test or control article that has been characterized according to 58.105(a). [21 CFR § 58]

Batch

A homogeneous lot of color additive or color additive mixture produced by an identified production operation, which is set apart and held as a unit for the purpose of obtaining certification of such quantity. [21 CFR § 70]

Batch

A specific quantity of a drug or other material that is intended to have uniform character and quality, within specified limits, and is produced according to a single manufacturing order during the same cycle of manufacture. [21 CFR § 210]

Batch Number

The number assigned to a batch by the person who requests certification thereof. [21 CFR § 70]

Batter

A semifluid substance, usually composed of flour and other ingredients, into which principal components of food are dipped or with which they are coated, or which may be used directly to form bakery foods. [21 CFR § 110]

Bioavailability

The rate and extent to which the active ingredient or active moiety is absorbed from a drug product and becomes available at the site of action. For drug products that are not intended to be absorbed into the bloodstream, bioavailability may be assessed by measurements intended to reflect the rate and extent to which the active ingredient or active moiety becomes available at the site of action. [21 CFR § 320]

Bioequivalence

The absence of a significant difference in the rate and extent to which the active ingredient or active moiety in pharmaceutical equivalents or pharmaceutical alternatives becomes available at the site of drug action when administered at the same molar dose under similar conditions in an appropriately designed study. Where there is an intentional difference in rate (e.g., in certain extended release dosage forms), certain pharmaceutical equivalents or alternatives may be considered bioequivalent if there is no significant difference in the extent to which the active ingredient or moiety from each product becomes available at the site of drug action. This applies only if the difference in the rate at which the active ingredient or moiety becomes available at the site of drug action is intentional and is reflected in the proposed labeling, is not essential to the attainment of effective body drug concentrations on chronic use, and is considered medically insignificant for the drug. [21 CFR § 320]

Bioequivalence Requirement

A requirement imposed by the Food and Drug Administration for in vitro and/or in vivo testing of specified drug products which must be satisfied as a condition of marketing. [21 CFR § 320]

Biohazard Legend

Appears on the label as follows and is used to mark HCT/Ps that present a known or suspected relevant communicable disease risk. [21 CFR § 1271]

B

Biological Product

Any virus, therapeutic serum, toxin, antitoxin, or analogous product applicable to the prevention, treatment or cure of diseases or injuries of man. [21 CFR § 600]

A product is analogous to a virus if prepared from or with a virus or agent actually or potentially infectious, without regard to the degree of virulence or toxicogenicity of the specific strain used.

Biological Product

A virus, therapeutic serum, toxin, antitoxin, vaccine, blood, blood component or derivative, allergenic product, or analogous product, or arsphenamine or derivative of arsphenamine (or any other trivalent organic arsenic compound), applicable to the prevention, treatment, or cure of a disease or condition of human beings (Public Health Service Act Sec. 351(i)). Additional interpretation of the statutory language is found in 21 CFR 600.3. Biological products also meet the definition of either a drug or device under Sections 201(g) and (h) of the Federal Food, Drug, and Cosmetic Act (FD&C Act).

Veterinary biologicals are subject to the animal Virus, Serum, and Toxin Act which is enforced by USDA (21 U.S.C. 151-158). [IOM Chapter 5]

Biometric Authentication

Authentication based on measurement of the individual's physical features or repeatable actions

---

where those features or actions are both unique to the individual and measurable. [21 CFR § 1311]

Biometrics

A method of verifying an individual's identity based on measurement of the individual's physical feature(s) or repeatable action(s) where those features and/or actions are both unique to that individual and measurable. [21 CFR § 11]

Blanc Fixe

A suspension in water of precipitated barium sulfate. [21 CFR § 82]

Blanching

Except for tree nuts and peanuts, means a prepackaging heat treatment of foodstuffs for a sufficient time and at a sufficient temperature to partially or completely inactivate the naturally occurring enzymes and to effect other physical or biochemical changes in the food. [21 CFR § 110]

Blood

Whole blood collected from a single donor and processed either for transfusion or further manufacturing. [21 CFR § 203]

Blood Component

That part of a single-donor unit of blood separated by physical or mechanical means. [21 CFR § 203]

Blood Component

> As defined in 606.3(c) of this chapter. [21 CFR §
> 600]

Blood Component

> Any part of a single-donor unit of blood separated by
> physical or mechanical means. [21 CFR § 1270]

Bulk Drug Substance

> Any substance that is represented for use in a drug
> and that, when used in the manufacturing, processing,
> or packaging of a drug, becomes an active ingredient
> or a finished dosage form of the drug, but the term
> does not include intermediates used in the synthesis of
> such substances. [21 CFR § 207]

C

Cache

To download and store information on a local server or hard drive. [21 CFR § 1311]

Calendar Quarter

Any one of the following time periods during a given year: January 1 through March 31, April 1 through June 30, July 1 through September 30, or October 1 through December 31. [21 CFR § 900]

CAPA

Corrective and preventive action: A systematic approach that includes actions needed to correct ("correction"), prevent recurrence ("corrective action"), and eliminate the cause of potential nonconforming product and other quality problems (preventive action) (21CFR 820.100) [source: Quality Systems Guidance]

Category I

Medical educational activities that have been designated as Category I by the Accreditation Council for Continuing Medical Education (ACCME), the American Osteopathic Association (AOA), a state medical society, or an equivalent organization. [21 CFR § 900]

C

Cease Distribution and Notification Strategy or Mandatory Recall Strategy

A planned, specific course of action to be taken by the person named in a cease distribution and notification order or in a mandatory recall order, which addresses the extent of the notification or recall, the need for public warnings, and the extent of effectiveness checks to be conducted. [21 CFR § 810]

Center for Biologics Evaluation and Research

Center for Biologics Evaluation and Research of the Food and Drug Administration. [21 CFR § 600]

Central Fill Pharmacy

A pharmacy which is permitted by the state in which it is located to prepare controlled substances orders for dispensing pursuant to a valid prescription transmitted to it by a registered retail pharmacy and to return the labeled and filled prescriptions to the retail pharmacy for delivery to the ultimate user. Such central fill pharmacy shall be deemed "authorized" to fill prescriptions on behalf of a retail pharmacy only if the retail pharmacy and central fill pharmacy have a contractual relationship providing for such activities or share a common owner. [21 CFR § 1300]

Certificate

The certificate described in 900.11(a). [21 CFR § 900]

Certificate Policy

A named set of rules that sets forth the applicability of the specific digital certificate to a particular community or class of application with common security requirements. [21 CFR § 1311]

Certificate Revocation List (CRL)

A list of revoked, but unexpired certificates issued by a Certification Authority. [21 CFR § 1311]

Certification

The process of approval of a facility by FDA or a certification agency to provide mammography services. [21 CFR § 900]

Certification Agency

A State that has been approved by FDA under 900.21 to certify mammography facilities. [21 CFR § 900]

Certification Authority (CA)

An organization that is responsible for verifying the identity of applicants, authorizing and issuing a digital certificate, maintaining a directory of public keys, and maintaining a Certificate Revocation List. [21 CFR § 1311]

Certification Number

A unique combination of letters and numbers assigned by a shellfish control authority to a molluscan shellfish processor. [21 CFR § 1240]

Charitable Institution or Charitable Organization

A nonprofit hospital, health care entity, organization, institution, foundation, association, or corporation that has been granted an exemption under section 501(c)(3) of the Internal Revenue Code of 1954, as amended. [21 CFR § 203]

Chassis Family

A group of one or more models with all of the following common characteristics:

(1) The same circuitry in the high voltage, horizontal oscillator, and power supply sections;

(2) The same worst component failures;

(3) The same type of high voltage hold-down or safety circuits; and

(4) The same design and installation. [21 CFR § 1000]

Chemical Description

A concise definition of the chemical composition using standard chemical nomenclature so that the chemical structure or structures of the components of the ingredient would be clear to a practicing chemist. When the composition cannot be described chemically, the substance shall be described in terms of its source and processing. [21 CFR § 700]

Chief Counsel

> The Chief Counsel of the Food and Drug
> Administration. [21 CFR § 10]

Children

> Persons who have not attained the legal age for
> consent to treatments or procedures involved in
> clinical investigations, under the applicable law of the
> jurisdiction in which the clinical investigation will be
> conducted. [21 CFR § 50]

Citation (Cite)

> The section 305 Notice is a statutory requirement of
> the FD&C Act. It provides a respondent with an
> opportunity to show cause why he should not be
> prosecuted for an alleged violation. Response to the
> notice may be by letter, personal appearance, or an
> attorney(s). [IOM Chapter 2]

Civil Number

> A docket number used by US district courts to
> identify civil cases (seizure and injunction). [IOM
> Chapter 2]

Clarified Juice

> The liquid expressed wholly or in part from fruit
> peelings, fruit shells, fruit cores, or from the fruit flesh
> or parts thereof, which is clarified and may be further
> refined or concentrated. [21 CFR § 145]

Class 1 Resubmission

The resubmission of an application or efficacy supplement, following receipt of a complete response letter, that contains one or more of the following: Final printed labeling, draft labeling, certain safety updates, stability updates to support provisional or final dating periods, commitments to perform postmarketing studies (including proposals for such studies), assay validation data, final release testing on the last lots used to support approval, minor reanalyses of previously submitted data, and other comparatively minor information. [21 CFR § 314]

Class 2 Resubmission

The resubmission of an application or efficacy supplement, following receipt of a complete response letter, that includes any item not specified in the definition of "Class 1 resubmission," including any item that would require presentation to an advisory committee. [21 CFR § 314]

Class III Certification

A certification that the submitter of the 510(k) has conducted a reasonable search of all known information about the class III device and other similar, legally marketed devices. [21 CFR § 807]

Class III Summary

A summary of the types of safety and effectiveness problems associated with the type of device being compared and a citation to the information upon which the summary is based. The summary must be

comprehensive and describe the problems to which
the type of device is susceptible and the causes of such
problems. [21 CFR § 807]

Classification Name

The term used by the Food and Drug Administration
and its classification panels to describe a device or
class of devices for purposes of classifying devices
under section 513 of the act. [21 CFR § 807]

Classification Panel

One of the several advisory committees established by
the Commissioner under section 513 of the act and
part 14 of this chapter for the purpose of making
recommendations to the Commissioner on the
classification and reclassification of devices and for
other purposes prescribed by the act or by the
Commissioner. [21 CFR § 860]

Classification Questionnaire

A specific series of questions prepared by the
Commissioner for use as guidelines by classification
panels preparing recommendations to the
Commissioner regarding classification and by
petitioners submitting petitions for reclassification.
The questions relate to the safety and effectiveness
characteristics of a device and the answers are designed
to help the Commissioner determine the proper
classification of the device. [21 CFR § 860]

Clinical Image

A mammogram. [21 CFR § 900]

Clinical Investigation

> Any experiment that involves a test article and one or more human subjects, and that either must meet the requirements for prior submission to the Food and Drug Administration under section 505(i) or 520(g) of the act, or need not meet the requirements for prior submission to the Food and Drug Administration under these sections of the act, but the results of which are intended to be later submitted to, or held for inspection by, the Food and Drug Administration as part of an application for a research or marketing permit. The term does not include experiments that must meet the provisions of part 58, regarding nonclinical laboratory studies. The terms *research, clinical research, clinical study, study,* and *clinical investigation* are deemed to be synonymous for purposes of this part. [21 CFR § 56]

Clinical Investigation

> An investigation in humans that tests a specific clinical hypothesis. [21 CFR § 99]

Clinical Investigation

> Any experiment in which a drug is administered or dispensed to, or used involving, one or more human subjects. For the purposes of this part, an experiment is any use of a drug except for the use of a marketed drug in the course of medical practice. [21 CFR § 312]

Clinical Investigation or Study

> Any experiment that involves a test article and one or more subjects and that is either subject to requirements for prior submission to the Food and Drug Administration under section 505(i), 512(j), or 520(g) of the Federal Food, Drug, and Cosmetic Act, or is not subject to the requirements for prior submission to FDA under those sections of the Federal Food, Drug, and Cosmetic Act, but the results of which are intended to be submitted later to, or held for inspection by, FDA as part of an application for a research or marketing permit. The term does not include experiments that are subject to the provisions of part 58 regarding nonclinical laboratory studies. [21 CFR § 60]

Clinically Superior

> That a drug is shown to provide a significant therapeutic advantage over and above that provided by an approved orphan drug (that is otherwise the same drug) in one or more of the following ways:

> (i) Greater effectiveness than an approved orphan drug (as assessed by effect on a clinically meaningful endpoint in adequate and well controlled clinical trials). Generally, this would represent the same kind of evidence needed to support a comparative effectiveness claim for two different drugs; in most cases, direct comparative clinical trials would be necessary; or

> (ii) Greater safety in a substantial portion of the target populations, for example, by the elimination of an

ingredient or contaminant that is associated with
relatively frequent adverse effects. In some cases, direct
comparative clinical trials will be necessary; or

(iii) In unusual cases, where neither greater safety nor
greater effectiveness has been shown, a demonstration
that the drug otherwise makes a major contribution to
patient care. [21 CFR § 316]

Closed System

An environment in which system access is controlled
by persons who are responsible for the content of
electronic records that are on the system. [21 CFR §
11]

Colloid

A protein or polysaccharide solution that can be used
to increase or maintain osmotic (oncotic) pressure in
the intravascular compartment such as albumin,
dextran, hetastarch; or certain blood components,
such as plasma and platelets. [21 CFR § 1270]

Color Additive

Any substance that meets the definition in section
201(t) of the Act and which is subject to premarketing
approval under section 721 of the Act. [21 CFR § 60]

Color Additive

Any material, not exempted under section 201(t) of
the act, that is a dye, pigment, or other substance
made by a process of synthesis or similar artifice, or
extracted, isolated, or otherwise derived, with or

without intermediate or final change of identity, from a vegetable, animal, mineral, or other source and that, when added or applied to a food, drug, or cosmetic or to the human body or any part thereof, is capable (alone or through reaction with another substance) of imparting a color thereto. Substances capable of imparting a color to a container for foods, drugs, or cosmetics are not color additives unless the customary or reasonably foreseeable handling or use of the container may reasonably be expected to result in the transmittal of the color to the contents of the package or any part thereof. Food ingredients such as cherries, green or red peppers, chocolate, and orange juice which contribute their own natural color when mixed with other foods are not regarded as *color additives* ; but where a food substance such as beet juice is deliberately used as a color, as in pink lemonade, it is a *color additive.* Food ingredients as authorized by a definitions and standard of identity prescribed by regulations pursuant to section 401 of the act are *color additives,* where the ingredients are specifically designated in the definitions and standards of identity as permitted for use for coloring purposes. An ingredient of an animal feed whose intended function is to impart, through the biological processes of the animal, a color to the meat, milk, or eggs of the animal is a color additive and is not exempt from the requirements of the statute. This definition shall apply whether or not such ingredient has nutritive or other functions in addition to the property of imparting color. An ingested drug the intended function of which is to impart color to the human body is a *color additive.* For the purposes of this part, the term *color* includes black, white, and intermediate grays, but substances including migrants from packaging materials which do not contribute any color apparent to the naked eye are not *color additives*.

(1) For a material otherwise meeting the definition of*color additive* to be exempt from section 721 of the act, on the basis that it is used (or intended to be used) solely for a purpose or purposes other than coloring, the material must be used in a way that any color imparted is clearly unimportant insofar as the appearance, value, marketability, or consumer acceptability is concerned. (It is not enough to warrant exemption if conditions are such that the primary purpose of the material is other than to impart color.)

(2) The exemption that applies to a pesticide chemical, soil or plant nutrient, or other agricultural chemical, where its coloring effect results solely from its aiding, retarding, or otherwise affecting directly or indirectly, the growth or other natural physiological processes of produce of the soil, applies only to color developed in such product through natural physiological processes such as enzymatic action. If the pesticide chemical, soil or plant nutrient, or other agricultural chemical itself acts as a color or carries as an ingredient a color, and because of this property colors the produce of the soil, it is a color additive and is not exempt. [21 CFR § 70]

Color Certification Branch

The unit established within the Food and Drug Administration located in the Center for Food Safety and Applied Nutrition, charged with the responsibility for the mechanics of the certification procedure hereinafter described, and including the examination of samples of color additives subject to certification. [21 CFR § 70]

Combination Product

Includes:

(1) A product comprised of two or more regulated components, i.e., drug/device, biologic/device, drug/biologic, or drug/device/biologic, that are physically, chemically, or otherwise combined or mixed and produced as a single entity;

(2) Two or more separate products packaged together in a single package or as a unit and comprised of drug and device products, device and biological products, or biological and drug products;

(3) A drug, device, or biological product packaged separately that according to its investigational plan or proposed labeling is intended for use only with an approved individually specified drug, device, or biological product where both are required to achieve the intended use, indication, or effect and where upon approval of the proposed product the labeling of the approved product would need to be changed, e.g., to reflect a change in intended use, dosage form, strength, route of administration, or significant change in dose; or

(4) Any investigational drug, device, or biological product packaged separately that according to its proposed labeling is for use only with another individually specified investigational drug, device, or

biological product where both are required to achieve the intended use, indication, or effect. [21 CFR § 3]

Commerce

(1) Commerce between any place in any State and any place outside thereof, and

(2) Commerce wholly within the District of Columbia. [21 CFR § 1000]

Commercial Container

Any bottle, jar, tube, ampule, or other receptacle in which a substance is held for distribution or dispensing to an ultimate user, and in addition, any box or package in which the receptacle is held for distribution or dispensing to an ultimate user. The term commercial container does not include any package liner, package insert or other material kept with or within a commercial container, nor any carton, crate, drum, or other package in which commercial containers are stored or are used for shipment of controlled substances. [21 CFR § 1300]

Commercial Distribution

Any distribution of a human drug except for investigational use under part 312 of this chapter, and any distribution of an animal drug or animal feed bearing or containing an animal drug for noninvestigational uses, but the term does not include internal or interplant transfer of a bulk drug substance between registered establishments within the same parent, subsidiary, and/or affiliate company. For foreign establishments, the term "commercial distribution" shall have the same meaning except that the term shall not include distribution of any drug that is neither imported nor offered for import into the United States. [21 CFR § 207]

Commercial Distribution

Of a cosmetic product means annual gross sales in excess of $1,000 for that product. [21 CFR § 700]

Commercial Distribution

Any distribution of a device intended for human use which is held or offered for sale but does not include the following: [21 CFR § 807]

(1) Internal or interplant transfer of a device between establishments within the same parent, subsidiary, and/or affiliate company;

(2) Any distribution of a device intended for human use which has in effect an approved exemption for investigational use under section 520(g) of the act and part 812 of this chapter;

(3) Any distribution of a device, before the effective date of part 812 of this chapter, that was not introduced or delivered for introduction into interstate commerce for commercial distribution before May 28, 1976, and that is classified into class III under section 513(f) of the act:Provided, That the device is intended solely for investigational use, and under section 501(f)(2)(A) of the act the device is not required to have an approved premarket approval application as provided in section 515 of the act; or

(4) For foreign establishments, the distribution of any device that is neither imported nor offered for import into the United States.

Commercial Fishing Industry Vessel

(1) Commercially engages in the catching, taking, or harvesting of fish or an activity that can reasonably be expected to result in the catching, taking, or harvesting of fish;

(2) Commercially prepares fish or fish products other than by gutting, decapitating, gilling, skinning, shucking, icing, freezing, or brine chilling; or

(3) Commercially supplies, stores, refrigerates, or transports fish, fish products, or materials directly related to fishing or the preparation of fish to or from a fishing, fish processing, or fish tender vessel or fish processing facility. [21 CFR § 1316]

Commercial-use Request

A request from or on behalf of one who seeks information for a cause or purpose that furthers the commercial, trade or profit interests of the requester or the person or institution on whose behalf the request is made. In determining whether a requester properly belongs in this category, ONDCP will consider the intended use of the information. [21 CFR § 1401]

Commissioner

The Commissioner of Food and Drugs, Food and Drug Administration, U.S. Department of Health

and Human Services, or the Commissioner's designee.
[21 CFR § 10]

Commissioner of Food and Drugs

The Commissioner of the Food and Drug
Administration. [21 CFR § 600]

Common Control

The power to direct or cause the direction of the
management and policies of a person or an
organization, whether by ownership of stock, voting
rights, by contract, or otherwise. [21 CFR § 203]

Common Use in Food

A substantial history of consumption of a substance
for food use by a significant number of consumers.
[21 CFR § 170]

Communicable Diseases

Illnesses due to infectious agents or their toxic
products, which may be transmitted from a reservoir
to a susceptible host either directly as from an infected
person or animal or indirectly through the agency of
an intermediate plant or animal host, vector, or the
inanimate environment. [21 CFR § 1240]

Communicable Period

The period or periods during which the etiologic
agent may be transferred directly or indirectly from
the body of the infected person or animal to the body
of another. [21 CFR § 1240]

C

Compatibility Testing

The procedures performed to establish the matching of a donor's blood or blood components with that of a potential recipient. [21 CFR § 606]

Compelling Local Conditions

Includes any factors, considerations, or circumstances prevailing in, or characteristic of, the geographic area or population of the State or political subdivision that justify exemption from preemption. [21 CFR § 808]

Complaint

Any written, electronic, or oral communication that alleges deficiencies related to the identity, quality, durability, reliability, safety, effectiveness, or performance of a device after it is released for distribution. [21 CFR § 820]

Complaint

Any written, oral, or electronic communication about a distributed HCT/P that alleges:

(1) That an HCT/P has transmitted or may have transmitted a communicable disease to the recipient of the HCT/P; or

(2) Any other problem with an HCT/P relating to the potential for transmission of communicable disease, such as the failure to comply with current good tissue practice. [21 CFR § 1271]

Complaint for Forfeiture

A document furnished to the U.S. attorney for filing with the clerk of the court to initiate a seizure. [IOM Chapter 2]

Complaint Samples, Certain

Injury and illness investigation samples from certain complaints where there is no Federal jurisdiction, or where the alleged violation offers no basis for subsequent regulatory action. Complaint samples from lots for which Federal jurisdiction is clear should be submitted as Official Samples. [IOM Chapter 4]

Complete Response Letter

A written communication to an applicant from FDA usually describing all of the deficiencies that the agency has identified in an application or abbreviated application that must be satisfactorily addressed before it can be approved. [21 CFR § 314]

Complete Response Letter

A written communication to an applicant from FDA usually describing all of the deficiencies that the agency has identified in a biologics license application or supplement that must be satisfactorily addressed before it can be approved. [21 CFR § 600]

Component

Any ingredient intended for use in the manufacture of a drug product, including those that may not appear in such drug product. [21 CFR § 210]

Component

That part of a single-donor's blood separated by physical or mechanical means. [21 CFR § 606]

Component

Any raw material, substance, piece, part, software, firmware, labeling, or assembly which is intended to be included as part of the finished, packaged, and labeled device. [21 CFR § 820]

Component

For the purposes of this part, means an essential functional part of a subassembly or of an assembled electronic product, and which may affect the quantity, quality, direction, or radiation emission of the finished product. [21 CFR § 1000]

Compounder

Any person engaging in maintenance or detoxification treatment who also mixes, prepares, packages or changes the dosage form of a narcotic drug listed in Schedules II, III, IV or V for use in maintenance or detoxification treatment by another narcotic treatment program. [21 CFR § 1300]

Comprehensive Inspection

Directs coverage to everything in the firm subject to FDA jurisdiction to determine the firms compliance status. [IOM Chapter 5]

Consignee

> Anyone who received, purchased, or used the product being recalled. [21 CFR § 7]

Consignee

> Any person or firm that has received, purchased, or used a device subject to correction or removal. [21 CFR § 806]

Consignee

> Any person or firm that has received, purchased, or used a device that is subject to a cease distribution and notification order or a mandatory recall order. Consignee does not mean lay individuals or patients, i.e., nonhealth professionals. [21 CFR § 810]

Consumer

> An individual who chooses to comment or complain in reference to a mammography examination, including the patient or representative of the patient (e.g., family member or referring physician). [21 CFR § 900]

Contact Hour

> An hour of training received through direct instruction. [21 CFR § 900]

Container (referred to also as "final container")

> The immediate unit, bottle, vial, ampule, tube, or other receptacle containing the product as distributed for sale, barter, or exchange. [21 CFR § 600]

Contamination

> The presence of a certain amount of undesirable substance or material, which may contain pathogenic microorganisms. [21 CFR § 1240]

Continued

> The word, as applied to the safety, purity and potency of products is interpreted to apply to the dating period. [21 CFR § 600]

Continuing Education Unit or Continuing Education Credit

> One contact hour of training. [21 CFR § 900]

Contract Research Organization

> A person that assumes, as an independent contractor with the sponsor, one or more of the obligations of a sponsor, e.g., design of a protocol, selection or monitoring of investigations, evaluation of reports, and preparation of materials to be submitted to the Food and Drug Administration. [21 CFR § 312]

Contract Services

> Those functions pertaining to the recovery, screening, testing, processing, storage, or distribution of human

tissue that another establishment agrees to perform for a tissue establishment. [21 CFR § 1270]

Control

Having responsibility for maintaining the continued safety, purity, and potency of the product and for compliance with applicable product and establishment standards, and for compliance with current good manufacturing practices. [21 CFR § 600]

Control Article

Any food additive, color additive, drug, biological product, electronic product, medical device for human use, or any article other than a test article, feed, or water that is administered to the test system in the course of a nonclinical laboratory study for the purpose of establishing a basis for comparison with the test article. [21 CFR § 58]

Control Number

Any distinctive symbols, such as a distinctive combination of letters or numbers, or both, from which the history of the manufacturing, packaging, labeling, and distribution of a unit, lot, or batch of finished devices can be determined. [21 CFR § 820]

Controlled Premises

(1) Places where original or other records or documents required under the Act are kept or required to be kept, and

(2) Places, including factories, warehouses, or other establishments and conveyances, where persons registered under the Act or exempted from registration under the Act, or regulated persons may lawfully hold, manufacture, or distribute, dispense, administer, or otherwise dispose of controlled substances or listed chemicals or where records relating to those activities are maintained. [21 CFR § 1316]

Continual Improvement

Ongoing activities to evaluate and positively change products, processes, and the quality system to increase effectiveness [source: Quality Systems Guidance]

Conveyance

Conveyance means any land or air carrier, or any vessel as defined in paragraph (n) of this section. [21 CFR § 1240]

Corn Sirup

A clarified, concentrated aqueous solution of the products obtained by the incomplete hydrolysis of cornstarch, and includes dried corn sirup. The solids of corn sirup and of dried corn sirup contain not less than 40 percent by weight of reducing sugars calculated as anhydrous dextrose. [21 CFR § 145]

Correction

Repair, modification, adjustment, relabeling, destruction, or inspection (including patient monitoring) of a product without its physical removal to some other location. [21 CFR § 7]

Correction

Repair, rework, or adjustment relating to the disposition of an existing discrepancy [source: Quality Systems Guidance]

Correction or Removal Report Number

The number that uniquely identifies each report submitted. [21 CFR § 806]

Corrective Action

Action taken to eliminate the causes of an existing discrepancy or other undesirable situation to prevent recurrence [source: Quality Systems Guidance]

Corrective and Preventive Action (CAPA)

A systematic approach that includes actions needed to correct ("correction"), prevent recurrence ("corrective action"), and eliminate the cause of potential nonconforming product and other quality problems (preventive action) (21CFR 820.100) [source: Quality Systems Guidance]

Cosmetic Product

A finished cosmetic the manufacture of which has been completed. Any cosmetic product which is also a drug or device or component thereof is also subject to the requirements of Chapter V of the act. [21 CFR § 700]

Cosmetic Raw Material

Any ingredient, including an ingredient that is a mixture, which is used in the manufacture of a cosmetic product for commercial distribution and is supplied to a cosmetic product manufacturer, packer, or distributor by a cosmetic raw material manufacturer or supplier. [21 CFR § 700]

Cream

The liquid milk product high in fat separated from milk, which may have been adjusted by adding thereto: Milk, concentrated milk, dry whole milk, skim milk, concentrated skim milk, or nonfat dry milk. Cream contains not less than 18 percent milkfat. [21 CFR § 131]

Criminal Number

A docket number used by the US district courts to identify criminal cases (prosecutions). [IOM Chapter 2]

Critical Control Point

A point in a food process where there is a high probability that improper control may cause, allow, or contribute to a hazard or to filth in the final food or decomposition of the final food. [21 CFR § 110]

Crystalloid

A balanced salt and/or glucose solution used for electrolyte replacement or to increase intravascular volume such as saline, Ringer's lactate solution, or 5 percent dextrose in water. [21 CFR § 1270]

Custom Device

A device that:

(1) Necessarily deviates from devices generally available or from an applicable performance standard or premarket approval requirement in order to comply with the order of an individual physician or dentist;

(2) Is not generally available to, or generally used by, other physicians or dentists;

(3) Is not generally available in finished form for purchase or for dispensing upon prescription;

(4) Is not offered for commercial distribution through labeling or advertising; and

(5) Is intended for use by an individual patient named in the order of a physician or dentist, and is to be made in a specific form for that patient, or is intended to meet the special needs of the physician or dentist in the course of professional practice. [21 CFR § 812]

Customer

A person or organization (internal or external) that receives a product or service anywhere along the product's life cycle [source: Quality Systems Guidance]

C

Customs Territory of the United States

The several States, the District of Columbia, and Puerto Rico. [21 CFR § 1300]

D

Dating Period

The period beyond which the product cannot be
expected beyond reasonable doubt to yield its specific
results. [21 CFR § 600]

Dealer

For sample collection purposes, the dealer is the
person, firm (which could include the manufacturer),
institution or other party, who has possession of a
particular lot of goods. The dealer does not have to be
a firm or company, which is in the business of buying
or selling goods. The dealer might be a housewife in
her home, a physician, or a public agency; these
dealers obtain products to use but not to sell. The
dealer may be a party who does not own the goods,
but has possession of them, such as a public storage
warehouse or transportation agency. [IOM Chapter
4]

Dealer

A person engaged in the business of offering electronic
products for sale to purchasers, without regard to
whether such person is or has been primarily engaged
in such business, and includes persons who offer such
products for lease or as prizes or awards. [21 CFR §
1000]

D

Debossed

Imprinted with a mark below the dosage form surface. [21 CFR § 206]

Defective

For the purposes of interpreting 21 U.S.C. 333(g)(1)(B)(iii), includes any defect in performance, manufacture, construction, components, materials, specifications, design, installation, maintenance, or service of a device, or any defect in mechanical, physical, or chemical properties of a device. [21 CFR § 17]

Defective

Any sample unit shall be regarded as defective when the sample unit does not meet the criteria set forth in the standards. [21 CFR § 145]

Denaturing

Decharacterization of a product, whereby it is made unusable for its originally intended purpose. [IOM Chapter 2]

Department

The U.S. Department of Health and Human Services. [21 CFR § 10]

Departmental Appeals Board (DAB)

The Departmental Appeals Board of the Department of Health and Human Services. [21 CFR § 17]

Design History File (DHF)

A compilation of records which describes the design history of a finished device. [21 CFR § 820]

Design Input

The physical and performance requirements of a device that are used as a basis for device design. [21 CFR § 820]

Design Output

The results of a design effort at each design phase and at the end of the total design effort. The finished design output is the basis for the device master record. The total finished design output consists of the device, its packaging and labeling, and the device master record. [21 CFR § 820]

Design Review

A documented, comprehensive, systematic examination of a design to evaluate the adequacy of the design requirements, to evaluate the capability of the design to meet these requirements, and to identify problems. [21 CFR § 820]

Destruction

The procedures involved in rendering a product unsalvageable. Destruction may be accomplished by burning, burial, etc. [IOM Chapter 2]

Detoxification Treatment

The dispensing, for a period of time as specified below, of a narcotic drug or narcotic drugs in decreasing doses to an individual to alleviate adverse physiological or psychological effects incident to withdrawal from the continuous or sustained use of a narcotic drug and as a method of bringing the individual to a narcotic drug-free state within such period of time. There are two types of detoxification treatment: Short-term detoxification treatment and long-term detoxification treatment.

(i) Short-term detoxification treatment is for a period not in excess of 30 days.

(ii) Long-term detoxification treatment is for a period more than 30 days but not in excess of 180 days. [21 CFR § 1300]

Device

Section 201(h) of the FD&C Act [21 U.S.C. 321 (h)] defines a device as follows: "The term "device" *** means an instrument, apparatus, implement, machine, contrivance, implant, in-vitro reagent, or other similar or related article, including any component, part, or accessory, which is: [IOM Chapter 2]

1. Recognized in the official National Formulary, or the United States Pharmacopoeia, or any supplement to them,

2. Intended for use in the diagnosis of disease or other conditions, or in the cure, mitigation,

treatment, or prevention of disease, in man or other animals, or

3. Intended to affect the structure or any function of the body of man or other animals, and which does not achieve its primary intended purposes through chemical action within or on the body of man or other animals and which is not dependent upon being metabolized for the achievement of any primary intended purposes."

Device Failure

The failure of a device to perform or function as intended, including any deviations from the device's performance specifications or intended use. [21 CFR § 821]

Device History Record (DHR)

A compilation of records containing the production history of a finished device. [21 CFR § 820]

Device intended to be implanted in the human body for more than 1 year

A device that is intended to be placed into a surgically or naturally formed cavity of the human body for more than 1 year to continuously assist, restore, or replace the function of an organ system or structure of the human body throughout the useful life of the device. The term does not include a device that is intended and used only for temporary purposes or that is intended for explantation in 1 year or less. [21 CFR § 821]

Device Master Record (DMR)

A compilation of records containing the procedures and specifications for a finished device. [21 CFR § 820]

Device User Facility

A hospital, ambulatory surgical facility, nursing home, or outpatient treatment or diagnostic facility that is not a physician's office. [21 CFR § 810]

Dextrose

The hydrated or anhydrous, refined monosaccharide obtained from hydrolyzed starch. [21 CFR § 145]

Diluent

Any component of a color additive mixture that is not of itself a color additive and has been intentionally mixed therein to facilitate the use of the mixture in coloring foods, drugs, or cosmetics or in coloring the human body. The diluent may serve another functional purpose in the foods, drugs, or cosmetics, as for example sweetening, flavoring, emulsifying, or stabilizing, or may be a functional component of an article intended for coloring the human body. [21 CFR § 70]

Digital Certificate

A data record that, at a minimum:

(1) Identifies the certification authority issuing it;

(2) Names or otherwise identifies the certificate holder;

(3) Contains a public key that corresponds to a private key under the sole control of the certificate holder;

(4) Identifies the operational period; and

(5) Contains a serial number and is digitally signed by the Certification Authority issuing it. [21 CFR § 1311]

Digital Signature

An electronic signature based upon cryptographic methods of originator authentication, computed by using a set of rules and a set of parameters such that the identity of the signer and the integrity of the data can be verified. [21 CFR § 11]

Digital Signature

A record created when a file is algorithmically transformed into a fixed length digest that is then encrypted using an asymmetric cryptographic private key associated with a digital certificate. The combination of the encryption and algorithm transformation ensure that the signer's identity and the integrity of the file can be confirmed. [21 CFR § 1311]

Direct Costs

The expense actually expended to search, review, or duplicate in response to a FOIA request. For example, direct costs include 116% of the salary of the

---

employee performing work and the actual costs incurred while operating equipment. [21 CFR § 1401]

Direct Instruction

1) Face-to-face interaction between instructor(s) and student(s), as when the instructor provides a lecture, conducts demonstrations, or reviews student performance; or

(2) The administration and correction of student examinations by an instructor(s) with subsequent feedback to the student(s). [21 CFR § 900]

Direct Supervision

(1) During joint interpretation of mammograms, the supervising interpreting physician reviews, discusses, and confirms the diagnosis of the physician being supervised and signs the resulting report before it is entered into the patient's records; or

(2) During the performance of a mammography examination or survey of the facility's equipment and quality assurance program, the supervisor is present to observe and correct, as needed, the performance of the individual being supervised who is performing the examination or conducting the survey. [21 CFR § 900]

Directed Inspection

Directs coverage to specific areas to the depth described in the program, assignment, or as instructed by your supervisor. [IOM Chapter 5]

Directed Reproductive Donor

A donor of reproductive cells or tissue (including semen, oocytes, and embryos to which the donor contributed the spermatozoa or oocyte) to a specific recipient, and who knows and is known by the recipient before donation. The term directed reproductive donor does not include a sexually intimate partner under 1271.90. [21 CFR § 1271]

Disability

A substantial disruption of a person's ability to conduct normal life functions. [21 CFR § 600]

Discrepancy

Datum or result outside of the expected range; an unfulfilled requirement; may be called non-conformity, defect, deviation, out-of-specification, out-of-limit, out-of-trend [source: Quality Systems Guidance]

Dispense to Patients

The act of delivering a prescription drug product to a patient or an agent of the patient either:

(1) By a licensed practitioner or an agent of a licensed practitioner, either directly or indirectly, for self-administration by the patient, or the patient's agent, or outside the licensed practitioner's direct supervision; or

(2) By an authorized dispenser or an agent of an authorized dispenser under a lawful prescription of a licensed practitioner. [21 CFR § 208]

Dispenser

An individual practitioner, institutional practitioner, pharmacy or pharmacist who dispenses a controlled substance. [21 CFR § 1300]

Distribute

To sell, offer to sell, deliver, or offer to deliver a drug to a recipient, except that the term "distribute" does not include:

(1) Delivering or offering to deliver a drug by a common carrier in the usual course of business as a common carrier; or

(2) Providing of a drug sample to a patient by:

(i) A practitioner licensed to prescribe such drug;

(ii) A health care professional acting at the direction and under the supervision of such a practitioner; or

(iii) The pharmacy of a hospital or of another health care entity that is acting at the direction of such a practitioner and that received such sample in accordance with the act and regulations. [21 CFR § 203]

Distribute

The act of delivering, other than by dispensing, a drug product to any person. [21 CFR § 208]

Distributed

The biological product has left the control of the licensed manufacturer. [21 CFR § 600]

Distributes

Any distribution of a tracked device, including the charitable distribution of a tracked device. This term does not include the distribution of a device under an effective investigational device exemption in accordance with section 520(g) of the act and part 812 of this chapter or the distribution of a device for teaching, law enforcement, research, or analysis as specified in 801.125 of this chapter. [21 CFR § 821]

Distribution

Any conveyance or shipment (including importation and exportation) of an HCT/P that has been determined to meet all release criteria, whether or not such conveyance or shipment is entirely intrastate. If an entity does not take physical possession of an HCT/P, the entity is not considered a distributor. [21 CFR § 1271]

Distributor

A person who distributes a drug product. [21 CFR § 208]

Distributor

Any person who furthers the distribution of a device from the original place of manufacture to the person who makes delivery or sale to the ultimate user, i.e., the final or multiple distributor, but who does not repackage or otherwise change the container, wrapper, or labeling of the device or device package. [21 CFR § 821]

Distributor

A person engaged in the business of offering electronic products for sale to dealers, without regard to whether such person is or has been primarily or customarily engaged in such business. [21 CFR § 1000]

District Contact

The Director, Investigations Branch. [IOM Chapter 3]

Division of Dockets Management

The Division of Dockets Management, Office of Management and Operations of the Food and Drug Administration, U.S. Department of Health and Human Services, 5630 Fishers Lane, rm. 1061, Rockville, MD 20852. [21 CFR § 10]

Document

Official records which are considered to be U.S. Government property regardless of the media e.g. Regulatory notes (electronic and hardcopy), memoranda, inspection reports, e-mails, and official government forms (e.g. SF-71, FDA-482, FDA-483, etc.) [IOM Chapter 1]

Donor

A human being, living or dead, who is the source of tissue for transplantation. [21 CFR § 1270]

Donor Medical History Interview

A documented dialogue with an individual or individuals who would be knowledgeable of the donor's relevant medical history and social behavior; such as the donor if living, the next of kin, the nearest available relative, a member of the donor's household, other individual with an affinity relationship, and/or the primary treating physician. The relevant social history includes questions to elicit whether or not the donor met certain descriptions or engaged in certain activities or behaviors considered to place such an individual at increased risk for HIV and hepatitis. [21 CFR § 1270]

Dried Glucose Sirup

The product obtained by drying "glucose sirup." [21 CFR § 145]

Drug Coupon

A form that may be redeemed, at no cost or at reduced cost, for a drug that is prescribed in accordance with section 503(b) of the act. [21 CFR § 203]

Drug Product

> A finished dosage form, for example, tablet, capsule, solution, etc., that contains an active drug ingredient generally, but not necessarily, in association with inactive ingredients. The term also includes a finished dosage form that does not contain an active ingredient but is intended to be used as a placebo. [21 CFR § 210]

Drug Product

> A finished dosage form, e.g., a tablet or capsule that contains a drug substance, generally, but not necessarily, in association with one or more other ingredients. [21 CFR § 206]

Drug Product

> A finished dosage form, e.g., tablet, capsule, or solution, that contains an active drug ingredient, generally, but not necessarily, in association with inactive ingredients. For purposes of this part, drug product also means biological product within the meaning of section 351(a) of the Public Health Service Act. [21 CFR § 208]

Drug Product Salvaging

> The act of segregating drug products that may have been subjected to improper storage conditions, such as extremes in temperature, humidity, smoke, fumes, pressure, age, or radiation, for the purpose of returning some or all of the products to the marketplace. [21 CFR § 207]

Drug-Related Offense

> Any proscribed offense which involves the possession, distribution, manufacture, cultivation, sale, transfer, or the attempt or conspiracy to possess, distribute, manufacture, cultivate, sell or transfer any substance the possession of which is prohibited by Title 21, U.S.C. [21 CFR § 1316]

Drug Sample

> A unit of a prescription drug that is not intended to be sold and is intended to promote the sale of the drug. [21 CFR § 203]

Drug Substance

> An active ingredient that is intended to furnish pharmacological activity or other direct effect in the diagnosis, cure, mitigation, treatment, or prevention of disease or to affect the structure or any function of the human body, but does not include intermediates use in the synthesis of such ingredient. [21 CFR § 314]

Due Diligence Petition

> A petition submitted under 60.30(a). [21 CFR § 60]

Duplicate

> The process of making a copy of a document. Such copies may take the form of paper, microform, audio-visual materials, or machine-readable documentation. ONDCP will provide a copy of the material in a form that is usable by the requester. [21 CFR § 1401]

E

Edible Organic Acid and Edible Organic Salt

Refer to any edible organic acid and any edible organic salt added for the purpose of flavor enhancement that either is not a food additive as defined in section 201(s) of the Federal Food, Drug, and Cosmetic Act or, if it is a food additive as so defined, is used in conformity with regulations established pursuant to section 409 of the act. [21 CFR § 145]

Educational Institution

Preschool, a public or private elementary or secondary school, an institution of undergraduate higher education, an institution of graduate higher education, an institution of professional education, or an institution of vocational education that operates a program or programs of scholarly research. [21 CFR § 1401]

Efficacy Supplement

A supplement to an approved application proposing to make one or more related changes from among the following changes to product labeling:

(1) Add or modify an indication or claim;

(2) Revise the dose or dose regimen;

(3) Provide for a new route of administration;

(4) Make a comparative efficacy claim naming another drug product;

(5) Significantly alter the intended patient population;

(6) Change the marketing status from prescription to over-the-counter use;

(7) Provide for, or provide evidence of effectiveness necessary for, the traditional approval of a product originally approved under subpart H of part 314; or

(8) Incorporate other information based on at least one adequate and well-controlled clinical study. [21 CFR § 314]

Egg and Egg Products (Dual Jurisdiction)

The term "egg" means the shell egg of the domesticated chicken, turkey, duck, goose, or guinea.

The term "egg product" means any dried, frozen, or liquid eggs, with or without added ingredients, excepting products which contain eggs only in relatively small proportion or historically have not been, in the judgment of the Secretary, considered by consumers as products of the egg food industry, and which may be exempted by the Secretary under such conditions as he may prescribe to assure the egg ingredients are not adulterated and such products are not represented as egg products. This would be done on a case by case basis by USDA. [IOM Chapter 2]

Electromagnetic Radiation

Includes the entire electromagnetic spectrum of radiation of any wavelength. The electromagnetic spectrum illustrated in figure 1 includes, but is not limited to, gamma rays, x-rays, ultra-violet, visible, infrared, microwave, radiowave, and low frequency radiation. [21 CFR § 1000]

Electronic Product

(1) Any manufactured or assembled product which, when in operation:

(i) Contains or acts as part of an electronic circuit and

(ii) Emits (or in the absence of effective shielding or other controls would emit) electronic product radiation, or

(2) Any manufactured or assembled article that is intended for use as a component, part, or accessory of a product described in paragraph (j)(1) of this section and which, when in operation, emits (or in the absence of effective shielding or other controls would emit) such radiation. [21 CFR § 1000]

Electronic Product Radiation

(1) Any ionizing or nonionizing electromagnetic or particulate radiation, or

(2) Any sonic, infrasonic, or ultrasonic wave that is emitted from an electronic product as the result of the operation of an electronic circuit in such product.

Electronic Record

> Any combination of text, graphics, data, audio, pictorial, or other information representation in digital form that is created, modified, maintained, archived, retrieved, or distributed by a computer system. [21 CFR § 11]

Electronic Signature

> A computer data compilation of any symbol or series of symbols executed, adopted, or authorized by an individual to be the legally binding equivalent of the individual's handwritten signature. [21 CFR § 11]

Electronic Signature

> A method of signing an electronic message that identifies a particular person as the source of the message and indicates the person's approval of the information contained in the message. [21 CFR § 1311]

Embossed

> Imprinted with a mark raised above the dosage form surface. [21 CFR § 206]

Emergency Medical Reasons

> Include, but are not limited to, transfers of a prescription drug between health care entities or from a health care entity to a retail pharmacy to alleviate a temporary shortage of a prescription drug arising from delays in or interruption of regular distribution schedules; sales to nearby emergency medical services,

i.e., ambulance companies and fire fighting
organizations in the same State or same marketing or
service area, or nearby licensed practitioners, of drugs
for use in the treatment of acutely ill or injured
persons; provision of minimal emergency supplies of
drugs to nearby nursing homes for use in emergencies
or during hours of the day when necessary drugs
cannot be obtained; and transfers of prescription
drugs by a retail pharmacy to another retail pharmacy
to alleviate a temporary shortage; but do not include
regular and systematic sales to licensed practitioners of
prescription drugs that will be used for routine office
procedures. [21 CFR § 203]

Emergency Use

The use of a test article on a human subject in a life-
threatening situation in which no standard acceptable
treatment is available, and in which there is not
sufficient time to obtain IRB approval. [21 CFR § 56]

Enforcement

Action taken by an authority to protect the public
from products of suspect quality, safety, and
effectiveness or to assure that products are
manufactured in compliance with appropriate laws,
regulations, standards, and commitments made as part
of the approval to market a product. [21 CFR § 26]

Engraved

Imprinted with a code that is cut into the dosage form
surface after it has been completed. [21 CFR § 206]

Essential Nutrients

Compounds that are found in the tissues of untreated, healthy target animals and not produced in sufficient quantity to support the animal's growth, development, function, or reproduction, e.g., vitamins, *essential* minerals, *essential* amino acids, and *essential* fatty acids. These compounds must be supplied from external sources. [21 CFR § 500]

Establish

Define, document (in writing or electronically), and implement. [21 CFR § 820]

Establish and Maintain

Define, document (in writing or electronically), and implement; then follow, review, and, as needed, revise on an ongoing basis. [21 CFR § 1271]

Established Operating Level

The value of a particular quality assurance parameter that has been established as an acceptable normal level by the facility's quality assurance program. [21 CFR § 900]

Establishment

A place of business under one management at one general physical location. The term includes, among others, independent laboratories that engage in control activities for a registered drug establishment (e.g., consulting laboratories), manufacturers of medicated feeds and of vitamin products that are drugs in accordance with section 201(g) of the act, human blood donor centers, and animal facilities used for the production or control testing of licensed biologicals, and establishments engaged in drug product salvaging. [21 CFR § 207]

Establishment

Has the same meaning as "facility" in section 351 of the Public Health Service Act and includes all locations. [21 CFR § 600]

Establishment

A place of business under one management at one general physical location at which a device is manufactured, assembled, or otherwise processed. [21 CFR § 807]

Establishment

Any facility under one management including all locations, that engages in the recovery, screening, testing, processing, storage, or distribution of human tissue intended for transplantation. [21 CFR § 1270]

Ethylene Oxide (EO)

EO is a colorless gas or volatile liquid with a characteristic ether-like odor above 500 ppm. Unmonitored and inadequate ventilation will allow EO buildup of extremely high concentrations, especially in facilities utilizing malfunctioning or leaking equipment. [IOM Chapter 1]

Equivalence of the Regulatory Systems

The systems are sufficiently comparable to assure that the process of inspection and the ensuing inspection reports will provide adequate information to determine whether respective statutory and regulatory requirements of the authorities have been fulfilled. Equivalence does not require that the respective regulatory systems have identical procedures. [21 CFR § 26]

Ex Parte Communication

An oral or written communication not on the public record for which reasonable prior notice to all parties is not given, but does not include requests for status reports on a matter. [21 CFR § 10]

Exhibits

Filth exhibits and other articles taken for exhibit purposes during inspections to demonstrate manufacturing or storage conditions, employee practices, and the like. Typically filth exhibits submitted as part of an INV sample are not tied to any specific lot of product, but are meant to illustrate the conditions at a firm. An example of an INV filth sample would be rodent excreta pellets, apparent nesting or other rodent gnawed material, and other evidence of rodent activity collected from the perimeter and at multiple locations throughout a manufacturing facility or warehouse in order to document widespread rodent infestation. [IOM Chapter 4]

E

Existing Vessel

Any vessel the construction of which was started prior to the effective date of the regulations in this part. [21 CFR § 1250]

Expiration Date

The calendar month and year, and where applicable, the day and hour, that the dating period ends. [21 CFR § 600]

Export

With respect to any article, any taking out or removal of such article from the jurisdiction of the United States (whether or not such taking out or removal constitutes an exportation within the meaning of the customs and related laws of the United States). [21 CFR § 1300]

Exporter

Includes every person who exports, or who acts as an export broker for exportation of, controlled substances listed in any schedule. [21 CFR § 1300]

Externally Applied Drugs and Externally Applied Cosmetics

Drugs or cosmetics applied only to external parts of the body and not to the lips or any body surface covered by mucous membrane. [21 CFR § 70]

Extralabel Use

Actual use or intended use of a drug in an animal in a manner that is not in accordance with the approved labeling. This includes, but is not limited to, use in species not listed in the labeling, use for indications (disease or other conditions) not listed in the labeling, use at dosage levels, frequencies, or routes of administration other than those stated in the labeling, and deviation from the labeled withdrawal time based on these different uses. [21 CFR § 530]

F

F

Facilities

Any area used for the collection, processing, compatibility testing, storage or distribution of blood and blood components. [21 CFR § 606]

Facility

A hospital, outpatient department, clinic, radiology practice, mobile unit, office of a physician, or other facility that conducts mammography activities, including the following: Operation of equipment to produce a mammogram, processing of the mammogram, initial interpretation of the mammogram, and maintaining viewing conditions for that interpretation. This term does not include a facility of the Department of Veterans Affairs. [21 CFR § 900]

Factory Samples

Raw materials, in-process and finished products to demonstrate manufacturing conditions. Note: Photographs taken in a firm are not samples. They are exhibits except when they are part of a DOC Sample. See IOM 4.5.2.4, 5.3.3, and 5.3.4. [IOM Chapter 4]

Family Member

Any one of the following legally competent persons: Spouse; parents; children (including adopted children); brothers, sisters, and spouses of brothers and sisters; and any individual related by blood or affinity whose close association with the subject is the equivalent of a family relationship. [21 CFR § 50]

FDC and INJ Numbers

The number used by the Chief Counsel's office to identify FDA cases. [IOM Chapter 2]

Federal Information Processing Standards (FIPS)

These Federal standards, as incorporated by reference in 1311.08, prescribe specific performance requirements, practices, formats, communications protocols, etc., for hardware, software, data, etc.

FIPS 140-2, as incorporated by reference in 1311.08, means a Federal standard for security requirements for cryptographic modules.

FIPS 180-2, as incorporated by reference in 1311.08, means a Federal secure hash standard.

FIPS 186-2, as incorporated by reference in 1311.08, means a Federal standard for applications used to generate and rely upon digital signatures. [21 CFR § 1311]

Federal Standard

A performance standard issued pursuant to section 534 of the Federal Food, Drug, and Cosmetic Act. [21 CFR § 1000]

Fiber

Any particulate contaminant with a length at least three times greater than its width. [21 CFR § 210]

Filed Screening Procedure

A procedure that is:

(1) On file with the Food and Drug Administration and subject to public inspection;

(2) Designed to determine that there is a reasonable basis for concluding that an alleged injury did not occur in conjunction with the use of the cosmetic product; and

(3) Which is subject, upon request by the Food and Drug Administration, to an audit conducted by the Food and Drug Administration at reasonable times and, where an audit is conducted, such audit shows that the procedure is consistently being applied and that the procedure is not disregarding reportable information. [21 CFR § 700]

Filling, "a Filling"

Refers to a group of final containers identical in all respects, which have been filled with the same product from the same bulk lot without any change that will affect the integrity of the filling assembly. [21 CFR § 600]

Final Distributor

>Any person who distributes a tracked device intended for use by a single patient over the useful life of the device to the patient. This term includes, but is not limited to, licensed practitioners, retail pharmacies, hospitals, and other types of device user facilities. [21 CFR § 821]

Finished Device

>Any device or accessory to any device that is suitable for use or capable of functioning, whether or not it is packaged, labeled, or sterilized. [21 CFR § 820]

First Allowable Time

>The earliest time a resident physician is eligible to take the diagnostic radiology boards from an FDA-designated certifying body. The "first allowable time" may vary with the certifying body. [21 CFR § 900]

Flavor

>Any natural or synthetic substance or substances used solely to impart a taste to a cosmetic product. [21 CFR § 700]

Fragrance

>Any natural or synthetic substance or substances used solely to impart an odor to a cosmetic product. [21 CFR § 700]

F

Food

For the purpose of detention of food under section 304(h) of the FD&C Act, see section 201(f) of the FD&C Act, which defines food as follows: "(1) articles used for food or drink for man or other animals, (2) chewing gum, and (3) articles used for components of any such article."

Examples of food include, but are not limited to, fruits, vegetables, fish, dairy products, eggs, raw agricultural commodities for use as food or components of food, animal feed, including pet food, food and feed ingredients and additives, including substances that migrate into food from food packaging and other articles that contact food, dietary supplements and dietary ingredients, infant formula, beverages, including alcoholic beverages and bottled water, live food animals, bakery goods, snack foods, candy, and canned foods. [IOM Chapter 2]

Food

Food as defined in section 201(f) of the act and includes raw materials and ingredients. [21 CFR § 110]

Food-contact Surfaces

Those surfaces that contact human food and those surfaces from which drainage onto the food or onto surfaces that contact the food ordinarily occurs during the normal course of operations. "Food-contact surfaces" includes utensils and food-contact surfaces of equipment. [21 CFR § 110]

Food Additive

Any substance that meets the definition in section 201(s) of the Act and which is subject to premarketing approval under section 409 of the Act. [21 CFR § 60]

Food Additives

Includes all substances not exempted by section 201(s) of the act, the intended use of which results or may reasonably be expected to result, directly or indirectly, either in their becoming a component of food or otherwise affecting the characteristics of food. A material used in the production of containers and packages is subject to the definition if it may reasonably be expected to become a component, or to affect the characteristics, directly or indirectly, of food packed in the container.*Affecting the characteristics of food* does not include such physical effects, as protecting contents of packages, preserving shape, and preventing moisture loss. If there is no migration of a packaging component from the package to the food, it does not become a component of the food and thus is not a food additive. A substance that does not become a component of food, but that is used, for example, in preparing an ingredient of the food to give a different flavor, texture, or other characteristic in the food, may be a food additive. [21 CFR § 570]

Food Contact Substance

Any substance that is intended for use as a component of materials used in manufacturing, packing, packaging, transporting, or holding food if such use is not intended to have any technical effect in such food. [21 CFR § 170]

Food Service Function

A public event where food will be provided to a protectee. [IOM Chapter 3]

Formal Evidentiary Public Hearing

A hearing conducted under part 12. [21 CFR § 10]

Freight Forwarding Facility

A separate facility operated by a distributing registrant through which sealed, packaged controlled substances in unmarked shipping containers (i.e., the containers do not indicate that the contents include controlled substances) are, in the course of delivery to, or return from, customers, transferred in less than 24 hours. A distributing registrant who operates a freight forwarding facility may use the facility to transfer controlled substances from any location the distributing registrant operates that is registered with the Administration to manufacture, distribute, or import controlled substances, or, with respect to returns, registered to dispense controlled substances, provided that the notice required by 1301.12(b)(4) of Part 1301 of this chapter has been submitted and approved. For purposes of this definition, a distributing registrant is a person who is registered with the Administration as a manufacturer, distributor, and/or importer. [21 CFR § 1300]

Fruit Juice(s)

Single strength expressed juice(s) of sound, mature fruit(s). It may be fresh, frozen, canned, or made from concentrate(s). However, if it is made from concentrate(s), the juice(s) shall be reconstituted with water to not less than the soluble solids that such fruit juice had before concentration. Fruit juice(s) may be used singly or in combination. If a fruit juice(s) is used which is regulated by a standard of identity of this chapter, it shall conform to the compositional requirements prescribed by such standard prior to the addition of any sweetener which may be used. [21 CFR § 145]

Fruit Juice(s) and Water

Any mixture of fruit juice as herein defined and water, including any water contributed by the use of liquid nutritive carbohydrate sweeteners, in which the fruit juice(s) is 50 percent, or more, of such mixture except that water used in preparing equivalent single strength juice(s) from concentrate(s) shall not be considered to be a mixture of fruit juice and water. [21 CFR § 145]

G

Gang-printed Labeling

Labeling derived from a sheet of material on which more than one item of labeling is printed. [21 CFR § 210]

Garbage

(1) The solid animal and vegetable waste, together with the natural moisture content, resulting from the handling, preparation, or consumption of foods in houses, restaurants, hotels, kitchens, and similar establishments, or (2) any other food waste containing pork. [21 CFR § 1240]

Generic Type of Device

A grouping of devices that do not differ significantly in purpose, design, materials, energy source, function, or any other feature related to safety and effectiveness, and for which similar regulatory controls are sufficient to provide reasonable assurance of safety and effectiveness. [21 CFR § 860]

Gloss White

A suspension in water of co-precipitated aluminum hydroxide and barium sulfate. [21 CFR § 82]

Glucose Sirup

A clarified, concentrated, aqueous solution of the
products obtained by the incomplete hydrolysis of any
edible starch. The solids of glucose sirup contain not
less than 40 percent by weight of reducing sugars
calculated as anhydrous dextrose. [21 CFR § 145]

Good Manufacturing Practices (GMP's).

[The United States has clarified its interpretation that
under the MRA, paragraph (c)(1) of this section has
to be understood as the U.S. definition and paragraph
(c)(2) as the EC definition.] [21 CFR § 26]

(1) GMP's mean the requirements found in the
legislations, regulations, and administrative
provisions for methods to be used in, and the
facilities or controls to be used for, the
manufacturing, processing, packing, and/or
holding of a drug to assure that such drug meets
the requirements as to safety, and has the identity
and strength, and meets the quality and purity
characteristics that it purports or is represented to
possess.

(2) GMP's are that part of quality assurance which
ensures that products are consistently produced
and controlled to quality standards. For the
purpose of this subpart, GMP's include, therefore,
the system whereby the manufacturer receives
the specifications of the product and/or process
from the marketing authorization/product
authorization or license holder or applicant and
ensures the product is made in compliance with
its specifications (qualified person certification in
the EC).

G

Group Health Plan

An employee welfare benefit plan (as defined in section 3(1) of the Employee Retirement Income Security Act of 1974 (29 U.S.C. 1002(1))) to the extent that the plan provides medical care (as defined in paragraphs (c)(1) through (c)(3) of this section and including items and services paid for as medical care) to employees or their dependents (as defined under the terms of the plan) directly or through insurance, reimbursement, or otherwise. [21 CFR § 99]

Group Purchasing Organization

Any entity established, maintained, and operated for the purchase of prescription drugs for distribution exclusively to its members with such membership consisting solely of hospitals and health care entities bound by written contract with the entity. [21 CFR § 203]

Guardian

An individual who is authorized under applicable State or local law to consent on behalf of a child to general medical care when general medical care includes participation in research. For purposes of subpart D of this part, a guardian also means an individual who is authorized to consent on behalf of a child to participate in research. [21 CFR § 50]

H

Handwritten Signature

The scripted name or legal mark of an individual handwritten by that individual and executed or adopted with the present intention to authenticate a writing in a permanent form. The act of signing with a writing or marking instrument such as a pen or stylus is preserved. The scripted name or legal mark, while conventionally applied to paper, may also be applied to other devices that capture the name or mark. [21 CFR § 11]

Harm

Damage to health, including the damage that can occur from the loss of product quality or availability [source: Quality Systems Guidance]

HCT/P Deviation

An event:

(1) That represents a deviation from applicable regulations in this part or from applicable standards or established specifications that relate to the prevention of communicable disease transmission or HCT/P contamination; or

(2) That is an unexpected or unforeseeable event that may relate to the transmission or potential transmission of a communicable disease or may lead to HCT/P contamination.

Health Care Entity

> Any person that provides diagnostic, medical, surgical, or dental treatment, or chronic or rehabilitative care, but does not include any retail pharmacy or any wholesale distributor. Except as provided in 203.22(h) and (i), a person cannot simultaneously be a "health care entity" and a retail pharmacy or wholesale distributor. [21 CFR § 203]

Health Care Practitioner

> A physician or other individual who is a health care provider and licensed under State law to prescribe drugs or devices. [21 CFR § 99]

Health Insurance Issuer

> An insurance company, insurance service, or insurance organization (including a health maintenance organization, as defined in paragraph (e)(2) of this section) which is licensed to engage in the business of insurance in a State and which is subject to State law which regulates insurance (within the meaning of section 514(b)(2) of the Employee Retirement Income Security Act of 1974 (29 U.S.C. 1144(b)(2))). [21 CFR § 99]

> (1) Such term does not include a group health plan.

> (2) For purposes of this part, the term *health maintenance organization* means:

> (i) A Federally qualified health maintenance organization (as defined in section 1301(a) of the Public Health Service Act (42 U.S.C. 300e(a)));

(ii) An organization recognized under State law as a health maintenance organization; or

(iii) A similar organization regulated under State law for solvency in the same manner and to the same extent as such a health maintenance organization.

Health Maintenance Organization

(1) A Federally qualified health maintenance organization (as defined in section 1301(a) of the Public Health Service Act (42 U.S.C. 300e(a)));

(2) An organization recognized under State law as a health maintenance organization; or

(3) A similar organization regulated under State law for solvency in the same manner and to the same extent as such a health maintenance organization. [21 CFR § 99]

Health Professionals

Practitioners, including physicians, nurses, pharmacists, dentists, respiratory therapists, physical therapists, technologists, or any other practitioners or allied health professionals that have a role in using a device for human use. [21 CFR § 810]

Hearing

(i) In part 1301 of this chapter, any hearing held for the granting, denial, revocation, or suspension of a registration pursuant to sections 303, 304, and 1008 of the Act (21 U.S.C. 823, 824 and 958).

(ii) In part 1303 of this chapter, any hearing held regarding the determination of aggregate production quota or the issuance, adjustment, suspension, or denial of a procurement quota or an individual manufacturing quota.

(iii) In part 1308 of this chapter, any hearing held for the issuance, amendment, or repeal of any rule issuable pursuant to section 201 of the Act (21 U.S.C. 811). [21 CFR § 1300]

Holder

The sponsor in whose name an orphan drug is designated and approved. [21 CFR § 316]

Home District

The Home District is the district in whose territory the alleged violation of the Act occurs, or in whose territory the firm or individual responsible for the alleged violation is physically located. The original point from which the article was shipped, or offered for shipment, as shown by the interstate records, is usually considered the point where the violation occurred; and the shipper of such article, as shown by such records, may be considered to be the alleged violator.

Where actions against a firm are based on goods which became violative after interstate shipment was made, or after reaching its destination (such as 301(k) violations), the dealer in whose possession the goods are sampled may be considered the violator, and the location of this dealer determines the "Home District". [IOM Chapter 2]

Human Drug Product

The active ingredient of a new drug or human biologic product (as those terms are used in the Act and the Public Health Service Act), including any salt or ester of the active ingredient, as a single entity or in combination with another active ingredient. [21 CFR § 60]

Human Subject

An individual who is or becomes a participant in research, either as a recipient of the test article or as a control. A subject may be either a healthy human or a patient. [21 CFR § 50]

Human Tissue

For the purpose of this part means any tissue derived from a human body and recovered before May 25, 2005, which:

(1) Is intended for transplantation to another human for the diagnosis, cure, mitigation, treatment, or prevention of any condition or disease;

(2) Is recovered, processed, stored, or distributed by methods that do not change tissue function or characteristics;

(3) Is not currently regulated as a human drug, biological product, or medical device;

(4) Excludes kidney, liver, heart, lung, pancreas, or any other vascularized human organ; and

(5) Excludes semen or other reproductive tissue, human milk, and bone marrow.

Humanitarian Device Exemption (HDE)

A premarket approval application submitted pursuant to this subpart seeking a humanitarian device exemption from the effectiveness requirements of sections 514 and 515 of the act as authorized by section 520(m)(2) of the act. [21 CFR § 814]

Humanitarian Use Device (HUD)

A medical device intended to benefit patients in the treatment or diagnosis of a disease or condition that affects or is manifested in fewer than 4,000 individuals in the United States per year. [21 CFR § 814]

I, J, K

Immediately

Within 20 days of the filing of a petition for expedited release by an owner. [21 CFR § 1316]

Implant

A device that is placed into a surgically or naturally formed cavity of the human body if it is intended to remain there for a period of 30 days or more. FDA may, in order to protect public health, determine that devices placed in subjects for shorter periods are also "implants" for purposes of this part. [21 CFR § 812]

Import

With respect to any article, any bringing in or introduction of such article into either the jurisdiction of the United States or the customs territory of the United States, and from the jurisdiction of the United States into the customs territory of the United States (whether or not such bringing in or introduction constitutes an importation within the meaning of the tariff laws of the United States). [21 CFR § 1300]

Importer

For the purposes of this part, any person who imports a device into the United States. [21 CFR § 806]

Importer

Includes every person who imports, or who acts as an import broker for importation of, controlled substances listed in any schedule. [21 CFR § 1300]

Importer of Record

The person, establishment or their representative responsible for making entry of imported goods in accordance with all laws affecting such importation. [21 CFR § 1270]

Imprinted

Marked with an identification code by means of embossing, debossing, engraving, or printing with ink. [21 CFR § 206]

In Vitro Diagnostic Products

Those reagents, instruments, and systems intended for use in the diagnosis of disease or other conditions, including a determination of the state of health, in order to cure, mitigate, treat, or prevent disease or its sequelae. Such products are intended for use in the collection, preparation, and examination of specimens taken from the human body. These products are devices as defined in section 201(h) of the Federal Food, Drug, and Cosmetic Act (the act), and may also be biological products subject to section 351 of the Public Health Service Act. [21 CFR § 809]

In-process Material

Any material fabricated, compounded, blended, or derived by chemical reaction that is produced for, and used in, the preparation of the drug product. [21 CFR § 210]

Inactive Ingredient

Any component of a product other than an active ingredient as defined in 210.3(b)(7) of this chapter. [21 CFR § 328]

Increased Frequency of Adverse Drug Experience

An increased rate of occurrence of a particular serious adverse drug event, expected or unexpected, after appropriate adjustment for drug exposure. [21 CFR § 514]

Increased Use

Of a drug or biologic product may occur if the drug will be administered at higher dosage levels, for longer duration or for different indications than were previously in effect, or if the drug is a new molecular entity. The term "use" also encompasses disposal of FDA-regulated articles by consumers. [21 CFR § 25]

Incubation Period

The period between the implanting of disease organisms in a susceptible person and the appearance of clinical manifestation of the disease. [21 CFR § 1240]

Independent Ethics Committee (IEC)

A review panel that is responsible for ensuring the
protection of the rights, safety, and well-being of
human subjects involved in a clinical investigation
and is adequately constituted to provide assurance of
that protection. An institutional review board (IRB),
as defined in 56.102(g) of this chapter and subject to
the requirements of part 56 of this chapter, is one type
of IEC. [21 CFR § 312]

Individual

A natural living person who is a citizen of the United
States or an alien lawfully admitted for permanent
residence. Individual does not include sole
proprietorships, partnerships, or corporations engaged
in the production or distribution of products
regulated by the Food and Drug Administration or
with which the Food and Drug Administration has
business dealings. Any such business enterprise that is
identified by the name of one or more individuals is
not an individual within the meaning of this part.
Employees of regulated business enterprises are
considered individuals. Accordingly, physicians and
other health professionals who are engaged in business
as proprietors of establishments regulated by the Food
and Drug Administration are not considered
individuals; however, physicians and other health
professionals who are engaged in clinical
investigations, employed by regulated enterprises, or
the subjects of records concerning their own health,
e.g., exposure to excessive radiation, are considered
individuals. Food and Drug Administration
employees, consultants, and advisory committee

members, State and local officials, and consumers are considered individuals. [21 CFR § 21]

Individual Practitioner

A physician, dentist, veterinarian, or other individual licensed, registered, or otherwise permitted, by the United States or the jurisdiction in which he/she practices, to dispense a controlled substance in the course of professional practice, but does not include a pharmacist, a pharmacy, or an institutional practitioner. [21 CFR § 1300]

Infrasonic, Sonic (or Audible) and Ultrasonic Waves

Refer to energy transmitted as an alteration (pressure, particle displacement or density) in a property of an elastic medium (gas, liquid or solid) that can be detected by an instrument or listener. [21 CFR § 1000]

Ingredient

Any single chemical entity or mixture used as a component in the manufacture of a cosmetic product. [21 CFR § 700]

Initial Importer

Any importer who furthers the marketing of a device from a foreign manufacturer to the person who makes the final delivery or sale of the device to the ultimate consumer or user, but does not repackage, or otherwise change the container, wrapper, or labeling of the device or device package. [21 CFR § 807]

Inspection

An onsite evaluation of a manufacturing facility to
determine whether such manufacturing facility is
operating in compliance with GMP's and/or
commitments made as part of the approval to market
a product. [21 CFR § 26]

Inspection Report

The written observations and GMP's compliance
assessment completed by an authority listed in
Appendix B of this subpart. [21 CFR § 26]

Inspector

An officer or employee of the Administration
authorized by the Administrator to make inspections
under the Act. [21 CFR § 1316]

Institution

Any public or private entity or agency (including
Federal, State, and other agencies). The word *facility*
as used in section 520(g) of the act is deemed to be
synonymous with the term *institution* for purposes of
this part. [21 CFR § 50]

Institution

A person, other than an individual, who engages in
the conduct of research on subjects or in the delivery
of medical services to individuals as a primary activity
or as an adjunct to providing residential or custodial
care to humans. The term includes, for example, a
hospital, retirement home, confinement facility,

academic establishment, and device manufacturer. The term has the same meaning as "facility" in section 520(g) of the act. [21 CFR § 812]

Institutional Practitioner

A hospital or other person (other than an individual) licensed, registered, or otherwise permitted, by the United States or the jurisdiction in which it practices, to dispense a controlled substance in the course of professional practice, but does not include a pharmacy. [21 CFR § 1300]

Institutional Review Board (IRB)

Any board, committee, or other group formally designated by an institution to review biomedical research involving humans as subjects, to approve the initiation of and conduct periodic review of such research. The term has the same meaning as the phrase *institutional review committee* as used in section 520(g) of the act. [21 CFR § 50]

Interested Party

One who was in legal possession of the property at the time of seizure and is entitled to legal possession at the time of the granting of the petition for expedited release. This includes a lienholder (to the extent of his interest in the property) whose claim is in writing (except for a maritime lien which need not be in writing), unless the collateral is in the posession of the secured party. The agreement securing such lien must create or provide for a security interest in the collateral, describe the collateral, and be signed by the debtor. [21 CFR § 1316]

Interested Person

Any person adversely affected or aggrieved by any rule or proposed rule issuable pursuant to section 201 of the Act (21 U.S.C. 811). [21 CFR § 1300]

Interested Person or Any Person who will be Adversely Affected

A person who submits a petition or comment or objection or otherwise asks to participate in an informal or formal administrative proceeding or court action. [21 CFR § 10]

Interpreting Physician

A licensed physician who interprets mammograms and who meets the requirements set forth in 900.12(a)(1). [21 CFR § 900]

Interstate Traffic

(1) The movement of any conveyance or the transportation of persons or property, including any portion of such movement or transportation which is entirely within a State or possession,

(i) From a point of origin in any State or possession to a point of destination in any other State or possession, or

(ii) Between a point of origin and a point of destination in the same State or possession but through any other State, possession, or contiguous foreign country.

(2) Interstate traffic does not include the following:

(i) The movement of any conveyance which is solely for the purpose of unloading persons or property transported from a foreign country, or loading persons or property for transportation to a foreign country.

(ii) The movement of any conveyance which is solely for the purpose of effecting its repair, reconstruction, rehabilitation, or storage. [21 CFR § 1240]

Inventory

All factory and branch stocks in finished form of a basic class of controlled substance manufactured or otherwise acquired by a registrant, whether in bulk, commercial containers, or contained in pharmaceutical preparations in the possession of the registrant (including stocks held by the registrant under separate registration as a manufacturer, importer, exporter, or distributor). [21 CFR § 1300]

Invert Sugar Sirup

An aqueous solution of inverted or partly inverted, refined or partly refined sucrose, the solids of which contain not more than 0.3 percent by weight of ash, and which is colorless, odorless, and flavorless, except for sweetness. [21 CFR § 145]

Investigation

A clinical investigation or research involving one or more subjects to determine the safety or effectiveness of a device. [21 CFR § 812]

Investigator

An individual who actually conducts a clinical investigation, i.e., under whose immediate direction the test article is administered or dispensed to, or used involving, a subject, or, in the event of an investigation conducted by a team of individuals, is the responsible leader of that team. [21 CFR § 812]

Investigational Device

A device, including a transitional device, that is the object of an investigation. [21 CFR § 812]

Investigational Device Exemption (IDE)

An approved or considered approved investigational device exemption under section 520(g) of the act and parts 812 and 813. [21 CFR § 814]

Investigational New Drug

A new drug or biological drug that is used in a clinical investigation. The term also includes a biological product that is used in vitro for diagnostic purposes. The terms "investigational drug" and "investigational new drug" are deemed to be synonymous for purposes of this part. [21 CFR § 312]

Investigational New Drug Application

For purposes of this part, "IND" is synonymous with "Notice of Claimed Investigational Exemption for a New Drug." [21 CFR § 312]

Investigator

An individual who actually conducts a clinical
investigation, i.e., under whose immediate direction
the test article is administered or dispensed to, or used
involving, a subject, or, in the event of an
investigation conducted by a team of individuals, is
the responsible leader of that team. [21 CFR § 50]

Investigator

An individual who actually conducts a clinical
investigation (*i.e.*, under whose immediate direction
the drug is administered or dispensed to a subject). In
the event an investigation is conducted by a team of
individuals, the investigator is the responsible leader
of the team. "Subinvestigator" includes any other
individual member of that team. [21 CFR § 312]

IRB Approval

The determination of the IRB that the clinical
investigation has been reviewed and may be
conducted at an institution within the constraints set
forth by the IRB and by other institutional and
Federal requirements. [21 CFR § 56]

Jurisdiction of the United States

The customs territory of the United States, the Virgin
Islands, the Canal Zone, Guam, American Samoa,
and the Trust Territories of the Pacific Islands. [21
CFR § 1300]

Kerma

The sum of the initial energies of all the charged particles liberated by uncharged ionizing particles in a material of given mass. [21 CFR § 900]

Key Pair

Two mathematically related keys having the properties that:

(1) One key can be used to encrypt a message that can only be decrypted using the other key; and

(2) Even knowing one key, it is computationally infeasible to discover the other key. [21 CFR § 1311]

Knowing Departure

For the purposes of interpreting 21 U.S.C. 333(g)(1)(B)(i), means a departure from a requirement taken: (a) With actual knowledge that the action is such a departure, or (b) in deliberate ignorance of a requirement, or (c) in reckless disregard of a requirement. [21 CFR § 17]

L

Label

Any written, printed, or graphic matter on the container or package or any such matter clearly visible through the immediate carton, receptacle, or wrapper. [21 CFR § 600]

Label

Any display of written, printed, or graphic matter placed upon the commercial container of any controlled substance by any manufacturer of such substance. [21 CFR § 1300]

Labeling

All labels and other written, printed, or graphic matter:

(i) Upon any controlled substance or any of its commercial containers or wrappers, or

(ii) Accompanying such controlled substance. [21 CFR § 1300]

Lake

A straight color extended on a substratum by adsorption, coprecipitation, or chemical combination that does not include any combination of ingredients made by simple mixing process. [21 CFR § 70]

L

Laterality

The designation of either the right or left breast. [21 CFR § 900]

Lead Advance Agent

The Secret Service Agent in charge of all security arrangements. This person is responsible for all sites to be visited by the protectee, and is a representative of the Office of Protective Operations (Secret Service Headquarters). [IOM Chapter 3]

Lead Interpreting Physician

The interpreting physician assigned the general responsibility for ensuring that a facility's quality assurance program meets all of the requirements of 900.12(d) through (f). The administrative title and other supervisory responsibilities of the individual, if any, are left to the discretion of the facility. [21 CFR § 900]

Lead Investigator

The FDA person designated by the FDA district/region to coordinate the investigational activities at the site of a food service function. [IOM Chapter 3]

Legal and Factual Basis of the Seizure

A statement of the applicable law under which the property is seized, and a statement of the circumstances of the seizure sufficiently precise to enable an owner or other interested party to identify the date, place, and use or acquisition which makes the property subject to forfeiture. [21 CFR § 1316]

Legally Authorized Representative

An individual or judicial or other body authorized under applicable law to consent on behalf of a prospective subject to the subject's participation in the procedure(s) involved in the research. [21 CFR § 50]

Legislative Consent

Relating to any of the laws of the various States that allow the medical examiner or coroner to procure corneal tissue in the absence of consent of the donor's next-of-kin. [21 CFR § 1270]

Letter of Designation

The written notice issued by the product jurisdiction officer specifying the agency component with primary jurisdiction for a combination product. [21 CFR § 3]

Letter of Request

An applicant's written submission to the product jurisdiction officer seeking the designation of the agency component with primary jurisdiction. [21 CFR § 3]

Leukapheresis

The procedure in which blood is removed from the donor, a leukocyte concentrate is separated, and the remaining formed elements and residual plasma are returned to the donor. [21 CFR § 606]

Licensed Practitioner

Any person licensed or authorized by State law to prescribe drugs. [21 CFR § 203]

Licensed Practitioner

An individual licensed, registered, or otherwise permitted by the jurisdiction in which the individual practices to prescribe drug products in the course of professional practice. [21 CFR § 208]

Life-supporting or life-sustaining device

A device that is essential to, or that yields information that is essential to, the restoration or continuation of a bodily function important to the continuation of human life. [21 CFR § 860]

Life-supporting or life-sustaining device used outside a device user facility

A device which is essential, or yields information that is essential, to the restoration or continuation of a bodily function important to the continuation of human life that is intended for use outside a hospital, nursing home, ambulatory surgical facility, or diagnostic or outpatient treatment facility. Physicians' offices are not device user facilities and, therefore, devices used therein are subject to tracking if they otherwise satisfy the statutory and regulatory criteria. [21 CFR § 821]

Life-threatening Adverse Experience

Any adverse experience that places the patient, in the view of the initial reporter, at immediate risk of death from the adverse experience as it occurred, i.e., it does not include an adverse experience that, had it occurred in a more severe form, might have caused death. [21 CFR § 600]

Limit of Detection (LOD)

The lowest concentration of analyte that can be confirmed by the approved regulatory method. [21 CFR § 500]

List, The

The list of drug products with effective approvals published in the current edition of FDA's publication "Approved Drug Products with Therapeutic Equivalence Evaluations" and any current supplement to the publication. [21 CFR § 314]

Listed Drug

A new drug product that has an effective approval under section 505(c) of the act for safety and effectiveness or under section 505(j) of the act, which has not been withdrawn or suspended under section 505(e)(1) through (e)(5) or (j)(5) of the act, and which has not been withdrawn from sale for what FDA has determined are reasons of safety or effectiveness. Listed drug status is evidenced by the drug product's identification as a drug with an effective approval in the current edition of FDA's "Approved Drug Products with Therapeutic

Equivalence Evaluations" (the list) or any current supplement thereto, as a drug with an effective approval. A drug product is deemed to be a listed drug on the date of effective approval of the application or abbreviated application for that drug product. [21 CFR § 314]

Locality or Political Subdivision

Any lawfully established local governmental unit within a State which unit has the authority to establish or continue in effect any requirement having the force and effect of law with respect to a device intended for human use. [21 CFR § 808]

Location

Includes all buildings, appurtenances, equipment and animals used, and personnel engaged by a manufacturer within a particular area designated by an address adequate for identification. [21 CFR § 600]

Long Term Care Facility (LTCF)

A nursing home, retirement care, mental care or other facility or institution which provides extended health care to resident patients. [21 CFR § 1300]

Lot

The food produced during a period of time indicated by a specific code. [21 CFR § 110]

Lot

A collection of primary containers or units of the same size, type, and style manufactured or packed under similar conditions and handled as a single unit of trade. [21 CFR § 145]

Lot

Means a batch, or a specific identified portion of a batch, having uniform character and quality within specified limits; or, in the case of a drug product produced by continuous process, it is a specific identified amount produced in a unit of time or quantity in a manner that assures its having uniform character and quality within specified limits. [21 CFR § 210]

Lot

That quantity of uniform material identified by the manufacturer as having been thoroughly mixed in a single vessel. [21 CFR § 600]

Lot or Batch

One or more components or finished devices that consist of a single type, model, class, size, composition, or software version that are manufactured under essentially the same conditions and that are intended to have uniform characteristics and quality within specified limits. [21 CFR § 820]

L

Lot Number

An identifying number or symbol assigned to a batch by the Food and Drug Administration. [21 CFR § 70]

Lot Number, Control Number, or Batch Number

Any distinctive combination of letters, numbers, or symbols, or any combination of them, from which the complete history of the manufacture, processing, packing, holding, and distribution of a batch or lot of drug product or other material can be determined. [21 CFR § 210]

Lot Size

The number of primary containers or units in the lot. [21 CFR § 145]

Maintenance Treatment

The dispensing for a period in excess of twenty-one days, of a narcotic drug or narcotic drugs in the treatment of an individual for dependence upon heroin or other morphine-like drug. [21 CFR § 1300]

Mammographic Modality

A technology, within the scope of 42 U.S.C. 263b, for radiography of the breast. Examples are screen-film mammography and xeromammography. [21 CFR § 900]

Mammography Equipment Evaluation

An onsite assessment of mammography unit or image processor performance by a medical physicist for the purpose of making a preliminary determination as to whether the equipment meets all of the applicable standards in 900.12(b) and (e). [21 CFR § 900]

Mammography Medical Outcomes Audit

A systematic collection of mammography results and the comparison of those results with outcomes data. [21 CFR § 900]

Mammography Unit or Units

An assemblage of components for the production of X-rays for use during mammography, including, at a minimum: An X-ray generator, an X-ray control, a tube housing assembly, a beam limiting device, and the supporting structures for these components. [21 CFR § 900]

Management with Executive Responsibility

Those senior employees of a manufacturer who have the authority to establish or make changes to the manufacturer's quality policy and quality system. [21 CFR § 820]

Mandatory Recall Strategy or Cease Distribution and Notification Strategy

A planned, specific course of action to be taken by the person named in a cease distribution and notification order or in a mandatory recall order, which addresses the extent of the notification or recall, the need for public warnings, and the extent of effectiveness checks to be conducted. [21 CFR § 810]

Manufacture

All steps in propagation or manufacture and preparation of products and includes but is not limited to filling, testing, labeling, packaging, and storage by the manufacturer. [21 CFR § 600]

Manufacture, preparation, propagation, compounding, assembly, or processing of a device

The making by chemical, physical, biological, or other procedures of any article that meets the definition of device in section 201(h) of the act. These terms include the following activities: [21 CFR § 807]

(1) Repackaging or otherwise changing the container, wrapper, or labeling of any device package in furtherance of the distribution of the device from the original place of manufacture to the person who makes final delivery or sale to the ultimate consumer;

(2) Initial importation of devices manufactured in foreign establishments; or

(3) Initiation of specifications for devices that are manufactured by a second party for subsequent commercial distribution by the person initiating specifications.

Manufacture, processing, packing, or holding of a drug product

Includes packaging and labeling operations, testing, and quality control of drug products [21 CFR § 210]

Manufacturer

A person who manufactures a drug or device or who is licensed by such person to distribute or market the drug or device. For purposes of this part, the term may also include the sponsor of the approved, licensed, or cleared drug or device. [21 CFR § 99]

Manufacturer

For a drug product that is not also a biological product, both the manufacturer as described in 201.1 and the applicant as described in 314.3(b) of this chapter, and for a drug product that is also a biological product, the manufacturer as described in 600.3(t) of this chapter. [21 CFR § 208]

Manufacturer

> Any legal person or entity engaged in the manufacture
> of a product subject to license under the act;
> "Manufacturer" also includes any legal person or
> entity who is an applicant for a license where the
> applicant assumes responsibility for compliance with
> the applicable product and establishment standards.
> [21 CFR § 600]

Manufacturer

> Any person who designs, manufactures, fabricates,
> assembles, or processes a finished device.
> Manufacturer includes but is not limited to those who
> perform the functions of contract sterilization,
> installation, relabeling, remanufacturing, repacking, or
> specification development, and initial distributors of
> foreign entities performing these functions. [21 CFR
> § 820]

Manufacturer

> Any person who manufactures, prepares, propagates,
> compounds, assembles, or processes a device by
> chemical, physical, biological, or other procedures.
> The term includes any person who:
>
> (1) Repackages or otherwise changes the container,
> wrapper, or labeling of a device in furtherance of the
> distribution of the device from the original place of
> manufacture to the person who makes final delivery or
> sale to the ultimate user or consumer;
>
> (2) Initiates specifications for devices that are
> manufactured by a second party for subsequent

distribution by the person initiating the specifications; or

(3) Manufactures components or accessories which are devices that are ready to be used and are intended to be commercially distributed and are intended to be used as is, or are processed by a licensed practitioner or other qualified person to meet the needs of a particular patient. [21 CFR § 806]

Manufacturing or Processing

The manufacture, preparation, propagation, compounding, or processing of a drug or drugs as used in section 510 of the act and is the making by chemical, physical, biological, or other procedures of any articles that meet the definition of drugs in section 201(g) of the act. The term includes manipulation, sampling, testing, or control procedures applied to the final product or to any part of the process. The term also includes repackaging or otherwise changing the container, wrapper, or labeling of any drug package to further the distribution of the drug from the original place of manufacture to the person who makes final delivery or sale to the ultimate consumer. [21 CFR § 207]

Manufacturing Material

Any material or substance used in or used to facilitate the manufacturing process, a concomitant constituent, or a byproduct constituent produced during the manufacturing process, which is present in or on the finished device as a residue or impurity not

by design or intent of the manufacturer. [21 CFR §
820]

Marker Residue

The residue selected for assay whose concentration is
in a known relationship to the concentration of the
residue of carcinogenic concern in the last tissue to
deplete to its Sm. [21 CFR § 500]

Market Withdrawal

A firm's removal or correction of a distributed
product which involves a minor violation that would
not be subject to legal action by the Food and Drug
Administration or which involves no violation, e.g.,
normal stock rotation practices, routine equipment
adjustments and repairs, etc. [21 CFR § 7]

Market Withdrawal

A correction or removal of a distributed device that
involves a minor violation of the act that would not be
subject to legal action by FDA or that involves no
violation of the act, e.g., normal stock rotation
practices. [21 CFR § 806]

Marketing Applicant

Any person who submits an application for
premarketing approval by FDA under:

(i) Section 505(b) of the Act or section 351 of the
Public Health Service Act (human drug products);

(ii) Section 515 of the Act (medical devices);

(iii) Section 409 or 721 of the Act (food and color additives); or

(iv) Section 512 of the Act (animal drug products). [21 CFR § 60]

Marketing Application

An application for:

(i) Human drug products submitted under section 505(b) of the Act or section 351 of the Public Health Service Act;

(ii) Medical devices submitted under section 515 of the Act;

(iii) Food and color additives submitted under section 409 or 721 of the Act; or

(iv) Animal drug products submitted under section 512 of the Act. [21 CFR § 60]

Marketing Application

An application for approval of a new drug filed under section 505(b) of the act or an application for a biologics license submitted under section 351 of the Public Health Service Act (42 U.S.C. 262). [21 CFR § 316]

Master File

A reference source that a person submits to FDA. A master file may contain detailed information on a specific manufacturing facility, process, methodology, or component used in the manufacture, processing, or packaging of a medical device. [21 CFR § 814]

Material Change

Includes but is not limited to any change in the name of the drug, any change in the identity or quantity of the active ingredient(s), any change in the identity or quantity of the inactive ingredient(s) where quantitative listing of all ingredients is required by 207.31(a)(2), any significant change in the labeling of a prescription drug, and any significant change in the label or package insert of an over-the-counter drug. Changes that are not significant include changes in arrangement or printing or changes of an editorial nature. [21 CFR § 207]

Material Change

Includes any change or modification in the labeling or advertisements that affects the identity or safety and effectiveness of the device. These changes may include, but are not limited to, changes in the common or usual or proprietary name, declared ingredients or components, intended use, contraindications, warnings, or instructions for use. Changes that are not material may include graphic layouts, grammar, or correction of typographical errors which do not change the content of the labeling, changes in lot number, and, for devices where the biological activity or known composition differs with each lot produced, the labeling containing the actual values for each lot. [21 CFR § 807]

May Proceed

Product may proceed without FDA examination. FDA has made no determination the product complies with all provisions of the Food, Drug, and Cosmetic Act, or other related acts. This message does not preclude action should the products later be found violative." (No compliance decision has been made.) [IOM Chapter 6]

Mean Optical Density

The average of the optical densities measured using phantom thicknesses of 2, 4, and 6 centimeters with values of kilovolt peak (kVp) clinically appropriate for those thicknesses. [21 CFR § 900]

Meat Products and Poultry Products (Dual Jurisdiction)

For FDA purposes, meat products and poultry products are defined as the carcasses of cattle, sheep, swine, goats, horses, mules, other equines, or domesticated birds, parts of such carcasses, and products made wholly or in part from such carcasses, except products exempted by U.S.D.A. because they contain a relatively small amount of meat or poultry products (e.g.; meat flavored sauces, pork and beans, etc.). Examine labels for USDA Shield or coding information to help determine if it is a USDA product. [IOM Chapter 2]

Medical Care

(1) Amounts paid for the diagnosis, cure, mitigation, treatment, or prevention of disease, or amounts paid

for the purpose of affecting any structure or function of the body;

(2) Amounts paid for transportation primarily for and essential to medical care referred to in paragraph (c)(1) of this section; and

(3) Amounts paid for insurance covering medical care referred to in paragraphs (c)(1) and (c)(2) of this section. [21 CFR § 99]

Medical Device

Any article that meets the definition in section 201(h) of the Act and which is subject to premarketing approval under section 515 of the Act. [21 CFR § 60]

Medical Device Notification

A communication issued by the manufacturer, distributor, or other responsible person in compliance with a Notification Order. It notifies health professionals and other appropriate persons of an unreasonable risk of substantial harm to the public health presented by a device in commercial distribution. [IOM Chapter 7]

Medical Device Notification Order

An order issued by FDA requiring notification under section 518(a) of the FD & C Act [21 U.S.C. 360h (a)]. The directive issues when FDA determines a device in commercial distribution, and intended for human use, presents an unreasonable risk of substantial harm to the public health. The notification is necessary to eliminate the unreasonable risk of such harm, and no more practicable means is available under the provisions of the Act to eliminate such risk. [IOM Chapter 7]

Medical Device Safety Alert

This is a communication voluntarily issued by a manufacturer, distributor, or other responsible person (including FDA). It informs health professionals and other appropriate persons of a situation which may present an unreasonable risk to the public health by a device in commercial distribution. [IOM Chapter 7]

Medical Physicist

A person trained in evaluating the performance of mammography equipment and facility quality assurance programs and who meets the qualifications for a medical physicist set forth in 900.12(a)(3). [21 CFR § 900]

Medicated Feed

Any Type B or Type C medicated feed as defined in 558.3 of this chapter. The feed contains one or more drugs as defined in section 201(g) of the act. The manufacture of medicated feeds is subject to the requirements of part 225 of this chapter. [21 CFR § 210]

Medicated Premix

A Type A medicated article as defined in 558.3 of this chapter. The article contains one or more drugs as defined in section 201(g) of the act. The manufacture of medicated premixes is subject to the requirements of part 226 of this chapter. [21 CFR § 210]

Medication Guide

FDA-approved patient labeling conforming to the specifications set forth in this part and other applicable regulations. [21 CFR § 208]

Meeting

Any oral discussion, whether by telephone or in person. [21 CFR § 10]

Microorganisms

Yeasts, molds, bacteria, and viruses and includes, but is not limited to, species having public health significance. The term "undesirable microorganisms" includes those microorganisms that are of public health significance, that subject food to decomposition, that indicate that food is contaminated with filth, or that otherwise may cause food to be adulterated within the meaning of the act. Occasionally in these regulations, FDA used the adjective "microbial" instead of using an adjectival phrase containing the word microorganism. [21 CFR § 110]

Mid-level Practitioner

An individual practitioner, other than a physician, dentist, veterinarian, or podiatrist, who is licensed, registered, or otherwise permitted by the United States or the jurisdiction in which he/she practices, to dispense a controlled substance in the course of professional practice. Examples of mid-level practitioners include, but are not limited to, health care providers such as nurse practitioners, nurse midwives, nurse anesthetists, clinical nurse specialists and physician assistants who are authorized to dispense controlled substances by the state in which they practice. [21 CFR § 1300]

Milk Products

Food products made exclusively or principally from the lacteal secretion obtained from one or more healthy milk-producing animals, e.g., cows, goats, sheep, and water buffalo, including, but not limited to, the following: lowfat milk, skim milk, cream, half and half, dry milk, nonfat dry milk, dry cream, condensed or concentrated milk products, cultured or acidified milk or milk products, kefir, eggnog, yogurt, butter, cheese (where not specifically exempted by regulation), whey, condensed or dry whey or whey products, ice cream, ice milk, other frozen dairy desserts and products obtained by modifying the chemical or physical characteristics of milk, cream, or whey by using enzymes, solvents, heat, pressure, cooling, vacuum, genetic engineering, fractionation, or other similar processes, and any such product made by the addition or subtraction of milkfat or the addition of safe and suitable optional ingredients for the protein, vitamin, or mineral fortification of the product. [21 CFR § 1240]

Minimal Manipulation

(1) For structural tissue, processing that does not alter the original relevant characteristics of the tissue

---

relating to the tissue's utility for reconstruction, repair, or replacement; and

(2) For cells or nonstructural tissues, processing that does not alter the relevant biological characteristics of cells or tissues. [21 CFR § 1271]

Minimal Risk

That the probability and magnitude of harm or discomfort anticipated in the research are not greater in and of themselves than those ordinarily encountered in daily life or during the performance of routine physical or psychological examinations or tests. [21 CFR § 50]

Minimum Heat Treatment

The causing of all particles in garbage to be heated to a boiling temperature and held at that temperature for a period of not less than 30 minutes. [21 CFR § 1240]

Minor Violations

For the purposes of interpreting 21 U.S.C. 333(g)(1)(B)(ii), means departures from requirements that do not rise to a level of a single major incident or a series of incidents that are collectively consequential. [21 CFR § 17]

Mixed Oxides

The sum of the quantities of aluminum, iron, calcium, and magnesium (in whatever combination they may exist in a coal-tar color) calculated as aluminum trioxide, ferric oxide, calcium oxide, and magnesium oxide. [21 CFR § 82]

Mixture

A color additive made by mixing two or more straight colors, or one or more straight colors and one or more diluents. [21 CFR § 70]

Mode of Action

The means by which a product achieves an intended therapeutic effect or action. For purposes of this definition, "therapeutic" action or effect includes any effect or action of the combination product intended to diagnose, cure, mitigate, treat, or prevent disease, or affect the structure or any function of the body. When making assignments of combination products under this part, the agency will consider three types of mode of action: The actions provided by a biological product, a device, and a drug. Because combination products are comprised of more than one type of regulated article (biological product, device, or drug), and each constituent part contributes a biological product, device, or drug mode of action, combination products will typically have more than one identifiable mode of action. [21 CFR § 3]

(1) A constituent part has a biological product mode of action if it acts by means of a virus, therapeutic serum, toxin, antitoxin, vaccine, blood, blood component or derivative, allergenic product, or analogous product applicable to the prevention, treatment, or cure of a disease or condition of human

beings, as described in section 351(i) of the Public Health Service Act.

(2) A constituent part has a device mode of action if it meets the definition of device contained in section 201(h)(1) to (h)(3) of the act, it does not have a biological product mode of action, and it does not achieve its primary intended purposes through chemical action within or on the body of man or other animals and is not dependent upon being metabolized for the achievement of its primary intended purposes.

(3) A constituent part has a drug mode of action if it meets the definition of drug contained in section 201(g)(1) of the act and it does not have a biological product or device mode of action.

Model

Any identifiable, unique electronic product design, and refers to products having the same structural and electrical design characteristics and to which the manufacturer has assigned a specific designation to differentiate between it and other products produced by that manufacturer. [21 CFR § 1000]

Model Family

Products having similar design and radiation characteristics but different manufacturer model numbers. [21 CFR § 1000]

Modified Model

A product that is redesigned so that actual or potential radiation emission, the manner of compliance with a standard, or the manner of radiation safety testing is affected. [21 CFR § 1000]

Mold Samples

During inspections of manufacturers such as canneries, bottling plants, milling operations, etc., it may be necessary to collect scrapings or swabs of slime or other material to verify the presence of mold. The sample should represent the conditions observed at the time of collection and consist of sufficient material to confirm and identify mold growth on the equipment. If possible, take photographs and obtain scrapings or bits of suspect material. Describe the area scraped or swabbed, e.g., material was scraped or swabbed from a 2" x 12" area. [IOM Chapter 4]

Molluscan Shellfish

Any edible species of fresh or frozen oysters, clams, mussels, and scallops or edible portions thereof, except when the product consists entirely of the shucked adductor muscle. [21 CFR § 1240]

Monitor

When used as a noun, means an individual designated by a sponsor or contract research organization to oversee the progress of an investigation. The monitor may be an employee of a sponsor or a consultant to the sponsor, or an employee of or consultant to a contract research organization. *Monitor,* when used as

a verb, means to oversee an investigation. [21 CFR §
812]

More Stringent

Refers to a requirement of greater restrictiveness or
one that is expected to afford to those who may be
exposed to a risk of injury from a device a higher
degree of protection than is afforded by a requirement
applicable to the device under the act. [21 CFR §
808]

Multi-reading

Two or more physicians, at least one of whom is an
interpreting physician, interpreting the same
mammogram. [21 CFR § 900]

Multiple Distributor

Any device user facility, rental company, or any other
entity that distributes a life-sustaining or life-
supporting device intended for use by more than one
patient over the useful life of the device. [21 CFR §
821]

NADA

A new animal drug application including all amendments and supplements. [21 CFR § 514]

Name

The official name, common or usual name, chemical name, or brand name of a substance. [21 CFR § 1300]

Narcotic Drug

Any of the following whether produced directly or indirectly by extraction from substances of vegetable origin or independently by means of chemical synthesis or by a combination of extraction and chemical synthesis:

(i) Opium, opiates, derivatives of opium and opiates, including their isomers, esters, ethers, salts, and salts of isomers, esters, and ethers whenever the existence of such isomers, esters, ethers and salts is possible within the specific chemical designation. Such term does not include the isoquinoline alkaloids of opium.

(ii) Poppy straw and concentrate of poppy straw.

(iii) Coca leaves, except coca leaves and extracts of coca leaves from which cocaine, ecgonine and derivatives of ecgonine or their salts have been removed.

(iv) Cocaine, its salts, optical and geometric isomers, and salts of isomers.

(v) Ecgonine, its derivatives, their salts, isomers and salts of isomers.

(vi) Any compound, mixture, or preparation which contains any quantity of any of the substances referred to in paragraphs (b)(31)(i) through (v) of this section. [21 CFR § 1300]

Narcotic Treatment Program

A program engaged in maintenance and/or detoxification treatment with narcotic drugs. [21 CFR § 1300]

Net Disposal

For a stated period, the quantity of a basic class of controlled substance distributed by the registrant to another person, plus the quantity of that basic class used by the registrant in the production of (or converted by the registrant into) another basic class of controlled substance or a noncontrolled substance, plus the quantity of that basic class otherwise disposed of by the registrant, less the quantity of that basic class returned to the registrant by any purchaser, and less the quantity of that basic class distributed by the registrant to another registered manufacturer of that basic class for purposes other than use in the production of, or conversion into, another basic class of controlled substance or a noncontrolled substance or in the manufacture of dosage forms of that basic class. [21 CFR § 1300]

New Animal Drugs

New animal drugs approved for use in animal feed are placed in two categories as follows:

(i) Category I--These drugs require no withdrawal period at the lowest use level in each species for which they are approved.

(ii) Category II--These drugs require a withdrawal period at the lowest use level for at least one species for which they are approved, or are regulated on a "no-residue" basis or with a zero tolerance because of a carcinogenic concern regardless of whether a withdrawal period is required, or are a veterinary feed directive drug. [21 CFR § 558]

New Drug Substance

Any substance that when used in the manufacture, processing, or packing of a drug, causes that drug to be a new drug, but does not include intermediates used in the synthesis of such substance. [21 CFR § 310]

The newness of a drug may arise by reason (among other reasons) of:

(1) The newness for drug use of any substance which composes such drug, in whole or in part, whether it be an active substance or a menstruum, excipient, carrier, coating, or other component.

(2) The newness for a drug use of a combination of two or more substances, none of which is a new drug.

(3) The newness for drug use of the proportion of a substance in a combination, even though such combination containing such substance in other proportion is not a new drug.

(4) The newness of use of such drug in diagnosing, curing, mitigating, treating, or preventing a disease, or to affect a structure or function of the body, even though such drug is not a new drug when used in another disease or to affect another structure or function of the body.

(5) The newness of a dosage, or method or duration of administration or application, or other condition of use prescribed, recommended, or suggested in the labeling of such drug, even though such drug when used in other dosage, or other method or duration of administration or application, or different condition, is not a new drug.

New Use

A use that is not included in the approved labeling of an approved drug or device, or a use that is not included in the statement of intended use for a cleared device. [21 CFR § 99]

Newly Acquired Information

Data, analyses, or other information not previously submitted to the agency, which may include (but are not limited to) data derived from new clinical studies, reports of adverse events, or new analyses of previously submitted data (e.g., meta-analyses) if the studies, events or analyses reveal risks of a different type or greater severity or frequency than previously included in submissions to FDA. [21 CFR § 314]

Nolle Prosequi (Nol-Pros)

The prosecutor or plaintiff in a legal matter will proceed no further in prosecuting the whole suit or specified counts. [IOM Chapter 2]

Nolo Contendere (Nolo)

A plea by a defendant in a criminal prosecution meaning "I will not contest it". [IOM Chapter 2]

Non-fiber-releasing Filter

Any filter, which after any appropriate pretreatment such as washing or flushing, will not release fibers into the component or drug product that is being filtered. All filters composed of asbestos are deemed to be fiber-releasing filters. [21 CFR § 210]

Nonapplicant

Any person other than the applicant whose name appears on the label and who is engaged in manufacturing, packing, distribution, or labeling of the product. [21 CFR § 514]

Nonclinical Laboratory Study

In vivo or in vitro experiments in which test articles are studied prospectively in test systems under laboratory conditions to determine their safety. The term does not include studies utilizing human subjects or clinical studies or field trials in animals. The term

does not include basic exploratory studies carried out
to determine whether a test article has any potential
utility or to determine physical or chemical
characteristics of a test article. [21 CFR § 58]

Noncommercial Scientific Institution

An institution that is not operated on a commercial
basis as that term is defined in this section, and that is
operated solely for the purpose of conducting
scientific research not intended to promote any
particular product or industry. [21 CFR § 1401]

Nonconformity

The nonfulfillment of a specified requirement. [21
CFR § 820]

Non-conformity

A deficiency in a characteristic, product specification,
process parameter, record, or procedure that renders
the quality of a product unacceptable, indeterminate,
or not according to specified requirements [source:
Quality Systems Guidance]

Noninvasive

When applied to a diagnostic device or procedure,
means one that does not by design or intention: (1)
Penetrate or pierce the skin or mucous membranes of
the body, the ocular cavity, or the urethra, or (2) enter
the ear beyond the external auditory canal, the nose
beyond the nares, the mouth beyond the pharynx, the
anal canal beyond the rectum, or the vagina beyond
the cervical os. For purposes of this part, blood

sampling that involves simple venipuncture is considered noninvasive, and the use of surplus samples of body fluids or tissues that are left over from samples taken for noninvestigational purposes is also considered noninvasive. [21 CFR § 812]

Nonperishable Processed Food

Any processed food not subject to rapid decay or deterioration that would render it unfit for consumption. Examples are flour, sugar, cereals, packaged cookies, and crackers. Not included are hermetically sealed foods or manufactured dairy products and other processed foods requiring refrigeration. [21 CFR § 170]

Nonprofit Affiliate

Any not-for-profit organization that is either associated with or a subsidiary of a charitable organization as defined in section 501(c)(3) of the Internal Revenue Code of 1954. [21 CFR § 203]

Normal and Customary Manner

that inquiry suggested by particular facts and circumstances which would customarily be undertaken by a reasonably prudent individual in a like or similar situation. Actual knowledge of such facts and circumstances is unnecessary, and implied, imputed, or constructive knowledge is sufficient. An established norm, standard, or custom is persuasive but not conclusive or controlling in determining whether an owner acted in a normal and customary manner to ascertain how property would be used by another legally in possession of the property. The failure to act in a normal and customary manner as defined herein will result in the denial of a petition for expedited release of the property and is intended to have the desirable effect of inducing owners of the property to exercise greater care in transferring possession of their property. [21 CFR § 1316]

O

Office of the Commissioner

Includes the offices of the Associate Commissioners but not the centers or the regional or district offices. [21 CFR § 10]

Official Correspondent

the person designated by the owner or operator of an establishment as responsible for the following: [21 CFR § 807]

(1) The annual registration of the establishment;

(2) Contact with the Food and Drug Administration for device listing;

(3) Maintenance and submission of a current list of officers and directors to the Food and Drug Administration upon the request of the Commissioner;

(4) The receipt of pertinent correspondence from the Food and Drug Administration directed to and involving the owner or operator and/or any of the firm's establishments; and

(5) The annual certification of medical device reports required by 804.30 of this chapter or forwarding the certification form to the person designated by the firm as responsible for the certification.

O

Official Sample

An Official Sample is one taken from a lot for which
Federal jurisdiction can be established. If violative, the
Official Sample provides a basis for administrative or
legal action. Official Samples generally, but not
always, consist of a physical portion of the lot
sampled. [IOM Chapter 4]

Official Name

With respect to a drug or ingredient thereof, the name
designated in this part 299 under section 508 of the
act as the official name. [21 CFR § 299]

Ongoing Relationship

An association that exists when a manufacturer and a
distributor enter into a written agreement under
which the distributor is authorized to distribute the
manufacturer's products for a period of time or for a
number of shipments. If the distributor is not
authorized to distribute a manufacturer's entire
product line, the agreement must identify the specific
drug products that the distributor is authorized to
distribute. [21 CFR § 203]

Open System

An environment in which system access is not
controlled by persons who are responsible for the
content of electronic records that are on the system.
[21 CFR § 11]

Order

The final agency disposition, other than the issuance of a regulation, in a proceeding concerning any matter and includes action on a new drug application, new animal drug application, or biological license. [21 CFR § 10]

Original Application

A pending application for which FDA has never issued a complete response letter or approval letter, or an application that was submitted again after FDA had refused to file it or after it was withdrawn without being approved. [21 CFR § 314]

Orphan Drug

A drug intended for use in a rare disease or condition as defined in section 526 of the act. [21 CFR § 316]

Orphan-drug Designation

FDA's act of granting a request for designation under section 526 of the act. [21 CFR § 316]

Orphan-drug Exclusive Approval or Exclusive Approval

Effective on the date of FDA approval as stated in the approval letter of a marketing application for a sponsor of a designated orphan drug, no approval will be given to a subsequent sponsor of the same drug product for the same indication for 7 years, except as otherwise provided by law or in this part. [21 CFR § 316]

O

Owner or Operator

> The corporation, subsidiary, affiliated company, partnership, or proprietor directly responsible for the activities of the registering establishment. [21 CFR § 807]

P

Package

> The immediate container in which a color additive or
> color additive mixture has been packed for shipment
> or delivery. If the package is then packed in a shipping
> carton or other protective container, such container
> shall not be considered to be the immediate container.
> In the case of color additive mixtures for household
> use containing less than 15 percent pure color, when
> two or more containers of 3 ounces each or less, each
> containing a different color, are distributed as a unit,
> the immediate container for such unit shall be
> considered to be the package as defined in this
> section. [21 CFR § 70]

Package

> The immediate carton, receptacle, or wrapper,
> including all labeling matter therein and thereon, and
> the contents of the one or more enclosed containers.
> If no package, as defined in the preceding sentence, is
> used, the container shall be deemed to be the package.
> [21 CFR § 600]

P

Packaging

> Of a cosmetic product means filling or labeling the
> product container, including changing the immediate
> container or label (but excluding changing other
> labeling) at any point in the distribution of the
> cosmetic product from the original place of

manufacture to the person who makes final delivery or sale to the ultimate consumer. [21 CFR § 700]

Packer

A person who packages a drug product. [21 CFR § 208]

Parent

A child's biological or adoptive parent. [21 CFR § 50]

Participant

Any person participating in any proceeding, including each party and any other interested person. [21 CFR § 10]

Particulate Radiation

(1) Charged particles, such as protons, electrons, alpha particles, or heavy particles, which have sufficient kinetic energy to produce ionization or atomic or electron excitation by collision, electrical attractions or electrical repulsion; or

(2) Uncharged particles, such as neutrons, which can initiate a nuclear transformation or liberate charged particles having sufficient kinetic energy to produce ionization or atomic or electron excitation. [21 CFR § 1000]

Party

The center of the Food and Drug Administration responsible for a matter involved and every person who either has exercised a right to request or has been granted the right by the Commissioner to have a hearing under part 12 or part 16 or who has waived the right to a hearing to obtain the establishment of a Public Board of Inquiry under part 13 and as a result of whose action a hearing or a Public Board of Inquiry has been established. [21 CFR § 10]

Pasteurized

when used to describe a dairy product means that every particle of such product shall have been heated in properly operated equipment to one of the temperatures specified in the table of this paragraph and held continuously at or above that temperature for the specified time (or other time/temperature relationship which has been demonstrated to be equivalent thereto in microbial destruction):

Temperature	Time
145 deg. F[1]	30 minutes
161 deg. F[1]	15 seconds
191 deg. F	1 second
204 deg. F	0.05 second
212 deg. F	0.01 second

[1]If the dairy ingredient has a fat content of 10 percent or more, or if it contains added sweeteners, the specified temperature shall be increased by 5 deg. F. [21 CFR § 131]

Patient

> Any individual with respect to whom a drug product is intended to be, or has been, used. [21 CFR § 208]

Percentage of Theoretical Yield

> The ratio of the actual yield (at any appropriate phase of manufacture, processing, or packing of a particular drug product) to the theoretical yield (at the same phase), stated as a percentage. [21 CFR § 210]

Performance Indicators

> The measures used to evaluate the certification agency's ability to conduct certification, inspection, and compliance activities. [21 CFR § 900]

Perishable Food

> For the purpose of detention of food under section 304(h) of the FD&C Act, the term "perishable food" means food that is not heat-treated; not frozen; and not otherwise preserved in a manner so as to prevent the quality of the food from being adversely affected if held longer than 7 calendar days under normal shipping and storage conditions. See 21 CFR 1.377. [IOM Chapter 2]

Permission

> The agreement of parent(s) or guardian to the participation of their child or ward in a clinical investigation. Permission must be obtained in compliance with subpart B of this part and must

include the elements of informed consent described in 50.25. [21 CFR § 50]

Person

Includes an individual, partnership, corporation, association, or other legal entity. [21 CFR § 10]

Person

Includes an individual, partnership, corporation, association, scientific or academic establishment, government agency, or organizational unit thereof, and any other legal entity. [21 CFR § 58]

Person

Includes any individual, partnership, corporation, or association. [21 CFR § 203]

Person-in-Charge

The available person in the food service establishment authorized to make necessary changes/decisions such as the general manager, executive chef, banquet manager, caterer's representative or other management person. [IOM Chapter 3]

Person or Respondent

Includes an individual, partnership, corporation, association, scientific or academic establishment, government agency or organizational unit thereof, or other legal entity, or as may be defined in the act or regulation pertinent to the civil penalty action being brought. [21 CFR § 17]

Personal Identifiers

Includes individual names, identifying numbers, symbols, or other identifying designations assigned to individuals.*Personal identifiers* does not include names, numbers, symbols, or other identifying designations that identify products, establishments, or actions. [21 CFR § 21]

Personal Use Quantities

Possession of controlled substances in circumstances where there is no other evidence of an intent to distribute, of to facilitate the manufacturing, compounding, processing, delivering, importing or exporting of any controlled substance. Evidence of personal use quantities shall not include sweepings or other evidence of possession of quantities of a controlled substance for other than personal use. [21 CFR § 1316]

(1) Such other evidence shall include:

(i) Evidence, such as drug scales, drug distribution paraphernalia, drug records, drug packaging material, method of drug packaging, drug "cutting" agents and other equipment, that indicates an intent to process, package or distribute a controlled substance;

(ii) Information from reliable sources indicating possession of a controlled substance with intent to distribute;

(iii) The arrest and/or conviction record of the person or persons in actual or constructive possession of the controlled substance for offenses under Federal, State or local law that indicates an intent to distribute a controlled substance;

(iv) The controlled substance is related to large amounts of cash or any amount of prerecorded government funds;

(v) The controlled substance is possessed under circumstances that indicate such a controlled substance is a sample intended for distribution in anticipation of a transaction involving large quantities, or is part of a larger delivery; or

(vi) Statements by the possessor, or otherwise attributable to the possessor, including statements of conspirators, that indicate possession with intent to distribute.

(2) Possession of a controlled substance shall be presumed to be for personal use when there are no indicia of illicit drug trafficking or distribution such as, but not limited to, the factors listed above and the amounts do not exceed the following quantities:

(i) One gram of a mixture of substance containing a detectable amount of heroin;

(ii) One gram of a mixture or substance containing a detectable amount of--

(A) Coca leaves, except coba leaves and extracts of coca leaves frol which cocaine, ecgonine, and derivations of ecgonine or their salts have been removed;

(B) Cocaine, its salts, optical and geometric isomers, and salts of isomers;

(C) Ecgonine, its derivatives, their salts, isomers, and salts of isomers; or

(D) Any compound, mixture or preparation which contains any quantity of any of the substances referred to in paragraphs (j)(2)(ii)(A) through (j)(2)(ii)(C) of this section;

(iii)1/10th gram of a mixture or substance described in paragraph (j)(2)(ii) of this section which contains cocaine base;

(iv)1/10th gram of a mixture or substance containing a detectable amount of phencyclidine (PCP);

(v) 500 micrograms of a mixture or substance containing a detectable amount of lysergic acid diethylamide (LSD);

(vi) One ounce of a mixture of substance containing a detectable amount of marihuana;

(vii) One gram of methamphetamine, its salts, isomers, and salts of its isomers, or one gram of a mixture or substance containing a detectable amount of methamphetamine, its salts, isomers, or salts of its isomers.

(3) The possession of a narcotic, a depressant, a stimulant, a hallucinogen or cannabis-controlled substance will be considered in excess of personal use quantities if the dosage unit amount possessed

---

provides the same or greater equivalent efficacy as described in paragraph (j)(2) of this section.

Personnel Records

Any personal information maintained in a Privacy Act Record System that is needed for personnel management programs or processes such as staffing, employee development, retirement, and grievances and appeals. [21 CFR § 21]

Pest

Any objectionable animals or insects including, but not limited to, birds, rodents, flies, and larvae. [21 CFR § 110]

Pesticide Episode

An "episode" is defined as a violative pesticide (or other chemical contaminant) finding and all samples collected in follow-up to that finding. All samples must be associated with one responsible firm (grower, pesticide applicator, etc.) and one specific time period (e.g. growing season). [IOM Chapter 4]

Petition

A petition, application, or other document requesting the Commissioner to establish, amend, or revoke a regulation or order, or to take or not to take any other form of administrative action, under the laws administered by the Food and Drug Administration. [21 CFR § 10]

Petition

A submission seeking reclassification of a device in accordance with 860.123. [21 CFR § 860]

Phantom

A test object used to simulate radiographic characteristics of compressed breast tissue and containing components that radiographically model aspects of breast disease and cancer. [21 CFR § 900]

Phantom Image

A radiographic image of a phantom. [21 CFR § 900]

Pharmaceutical Alternatives

Drug products that contain the identical therapeutic moiety, or its precursor, but not necessarily in the same amount or dosage form or as the same salt or ester. Each such drug product individually meets either the identical or its own respective compendial or other applicable standard of identity, strength, quality, and purity, including potency and, where applicable, content uniformity, disintegration times and/or dissolution rates. [21 CFR § 320]

Pharmaceutical Equivalents

Drug products in identical dosage forms that contain identical amounts of the identical active drug ingredient,*i.e.* , the same salt or ester of the same therapeutic moiety, or, in the case of modified release dosage forms that require a reservoir or overage or such forms as prefilled syringes where residual volume may vary, that deliver identical amounts of the active drug ingredient over the identical dosing period; do not necessarily contain the same inactive ingredients; and meet the identical compendial or other applicable standard of identity, strength, quality, and purity, including potency and, where applicable, content uniformity, disintegration times, and/or dissolution rates. [21 CFR § 320]

Pharmacist

Any pharmacist licensed by a State to dispense controlled substances, and shall include any other person (e.g., pharmacist intern) authorized by a State to dispense controlled substances under the supervision of a pharmacist licensed by such State. [21 CFR § 1300]

Pharmacy Benefit Manager

A person or entity that has, as its principal focus, the implementation of one or more device and/or prescription drug benefit programs. [21 CFR § 99]

Phototherapy Product

Any ultraviolet lamp, or product containing such lamp, that is intended for irradiation of any part of the living human body by light in the wavelength range of 200 to 400 nanometers, in order to perform a therapeutic function. [21 CFR § 1000]

Physical Assessment

A limited autopsy or recent antemortem or postmortem physical examination of the donor to assess for any signs of HIV and hepatitis infection or signs suggestive of any risk factor for such infections. [21 CFR § 1270]

Physical Assessment of a Cadaveric Donor

A limited autopsy or recent antemortem or postmortem physical examination of the donor to assess for signs of a relevant communicable disease and for signs suggestive of any risk factor for a relevant communicable disease. [21 CFR § 1271]

Physical Science

Physics, chemistry, radiation science (including medical physics and health physics), and engineering. [21 CFR § 900]

Plant

The building or facility or parts thereof, used for or in connection with the manufacturing, packaging, labeling, or holding of human food. [21 CFR § 110]

Plasma Dilution

A decrease in the concentration of the donor's plasma proteins and circulating antigens or antibodies resulting from the transfusion of blood or blood components and/or infusion of fluids. [21 CFR § 1270]

Plasma for Further Manufacturing

That liquid portion of blood separated and used as material to prepare another product. [21 CFR § 606]

Plasmapheresis

The procedure in which blood is removed from the donor, the plasma is separated from the formed elements and at least the red blood cells are returned to the donor. [21 CFR § 606]

Plateletpheresis

The procedure in which blood is removed from a donor, a platelet concentrate is separated, and the remaining formed elements are returned to the donor along with a portion of the residual plasma. [21 CFR § 606]

Prescription

An order for medication which is dispensed to or for an ultimate user but does not include an order for medication which is dispensed for immediate administration to the ultimate user. (e.g., an order to dispense a drug to a bed patient for immediate administration in a hospital is not a prescription.) [21 CFR § 1300]

Political Subdivision or Locality

Any lawfully established local governmental unit within a State which unit has the authority to establish or continue in effect any requirement having the force and effect of law with respect to a device intended for human use. [21 CFR § 808]

Positive Mammogram

A mammogram that has an overall assessment of findings that are either "suspicious" or "highly suggestive of malignancy." [21 CFR § 900]

Possession

Any of the possessions of the United States, including Puerto Rico and the Virgin Islands. [21 CFR § 1240]

Potable Water

Water which meets the standards prescribed in the Environmental Protection Agency's Primary Drinking Water Regulations as set forth in 40 CFR part 141 and the Food and Drug Administration's sanitation requirements as set forth in this part and part 1250 of this chapter. [21 CFR § 1240]

Potency

Interpreted to mean the specific ability or capacity of the product, as indicated by appropriate laboratory tests or by adequately controlled clinical data obtained through the administration of the product in the manner intended, to effect a given result. [21 CFR § 600]

Potential Applicant

Any person:

(1) Intending to investigate a new animal drug under section 512(j) of the Federal Food, Drug, and Cosmetic Act (the act),

(2) Investigating a new animal drug under section 512(j) of the act,

(3) Intending to file a new animal drug application (NADA) or supplemental NADA under section 512(b)(1) of the act, or

(4) Intending to file an abbreviated new animal drug application (ANADA) under section 512(b)(2) of the act. [21 CFR § 514]

Premarket Approval Application (PMA)

Any premarket approval application for a class III medical device, including all information submitted with or incorporated by reference therein. "PMA" includes a new drug application for a device under section 520(1) of the act. [21 CFR § 814]

Premarket Approval Application (PMA) Amendment

Information an applicant submits to FDA to modify a pending PMA or a pending PMA supplement. [21 CFR § 814]

Premarket Approval Application (PMA) Supplement

A supplemental application to an approved PMA for approval of a change or modification in a class III medical device, including all information submitted with or incorporated by reference therein. [21 CFR § 814]

*30-day Premarket Approval Application (PMA)
Supplement*

A supplemental application to an approved PMA in
accordance with 814.39(e). [21 CFR § 814]

Pre-prepared Food

Potentially hazardous food that was received at the
food service establishment in a prepared form.
Examples would include chicken salad, liver pate,
gefilte fish, hors d'oeuvres, etc. which were prepared
at another location, and then transported to the food
service establishment providing food for the event.
[IOM Chapter 3]

Prescription Drug

Any drug (including any biological product, except
for blood and blood components intended for
transfusion or biological products that are also
medical devices) required by Federal law (including
Federal regulation) to be dispensed only by a
prescription, including finished dosage forms and
bulk drug substances subject to section 503(b) of the
act. [21 CFR § 203]

Presubmission Conference

One or more conferences between a potential
applicant and FDA to reach a binding agreement
establishing a submission or investigational
requirement. [21 CFR § 514]

Presubmission Conference Agreement

That section of the memorandum of conference headed "Presubmission Conference Agreement" that records any agreement on the submission or investigational requirement reached by a potential applicant and FDA during the presubmission conference. [21 CFR § 514]

Premarket Review

Includes the examination of data and information in an application for premarket review described in sections 505, 510(k), 513(f), 515, or 520(g) or 520(l) of the act or section 351 of the Public Health Service Act of data and information contained in any investigational new drug (IND) application, investigational device exemption (IDE), new drug application (NDA), biologics license application, device premarket notification, device reclassification petition, and premarket approval application (PMA). [21 CFR § 3]

Presiding Officer

The Commissioner or the Commissioner's designee or an administrative law judge appointed as provided in 5 U.S.C. 3105. [21 CFR § 10]

Presiding Officer

An administrative law judge qualified under 5 U.S.C. 3105. [21 CFR § 17]

Preslaughter Withdrawal Period or Milk Discard Time

The time after cessation of administration of the sponsored compound at which no residue is detectable in the edible product using the approved regulatory method (i.e., the marker residue is below the LOD). [21 CFR § 500]

Preventive Action

Action taken to eliminate the cause of a potential discrepancy or other undesirable situation to prevent such an occurrence [source: Quality Systems Guidance]

Primary Mode of Action

The single mode of action of a combination product that provides the most important therapeutic action of the combination product. The most important therapeutic action is the mode of action expected to make the greatest contribution to the overall intended therapeutic effects of the combination product. [21 CFR § 3]

Prior Sanction

An explicit approval granted with respect to use of a substance in food prior to September 6, 1958, by the Food and Drug Administration or the United States Department of Agriculture pursuant to the Federal Food, Drug, and Cosmetic Act, the Poultry Products Inspection Act, or the Meat Inspection Act. [21 CFR § 170]

Privacy Act Record System

A system of records about individuals under the control of the Food and Drug Administration from which information is retrieved by individual names or other personal identifiers. The term includes such a system of records whether subject to a notice published by the Food and Drug Administration, the Department, or another agency. Where records are retrieved only by personal identifiers other than individual names, a system of records is not a Privacy Act Record System if the Food and Drug Administration cannot, by reference to information under its control, or by reference to records of contractors that are subject to this part under 21.30, ascertain the identity of individuals who are the subjects of the records. [21 CFR § 21]

Private Key

The key of a key pair that is used to create a digital signature. [21 CFR § 1311]

Proceeding

All actions taken for the issuance, amendment, or repeal of any rule issued pursuant to section 201 of the Act (21 U.S.C. 811), commencing with the publication by the Administrator of the proposed rule, amended rule, or repeal in theFederal Register. [21 CFR § 1300]

Proceeding and Administrative Proceeding

Any undertaking to issue, amend, or revoke a regulation or order, or to take or refrain from taking

any other form of administrative action. [21 CFR §
10]

Process

A manufacturing step that is performed on the
product itself which may affect its safety, purity or
potency, in contrast to such manufacturing steps
which do not affect intrinsically the safety, purity or
potency of the product. [21 CFR § 600]

Processing

Any procedure employed after collection, and before
or after compatibility testing of blood, and includes
the identification of a unit of donor blood, the
preparation of components from such unit of donor
blood, serological testing, labeling and associated
recordkeeping. [21 CFR § 606]

Processing

Any activity performed on tissue, other than tissue
recovery, including preparation, preservation for
storage, and/or removal from storage to assure the
quality and/or sterility of human tissue. Processing
includes steps to inactivate and remove adventitious
agents. [21 CFR § 1270]

Product

Any article that contains any drug as defined in
section 201(g)(1) of the act; any device as defined in
section 201(h) of the act; or any biologic as defined in
section 351(a) of the Public Health Service Act (42
U.S.C. 262(a)). [21 CFR § 3]

Product

> An article subject to the jurisdiction of the Food and Drug Administration, including any food, drug, and device intended for human or animal use, any cosmetic and biologic intended for human use, and any item subject to a quarantine regulation under part 1240 of this chapter. *Product* does not include an electronic product that emits radiation and is subject to parts 1003 and 1004 of this chapter. [21 CFR § 7]

Product

> Components, manufacturing materials, in- process devices, finished devices, and returned devices. [21 CFR § 820]

Product Class

> All those products intended for use for a particular determination or for a related group of determinations or products with common or related characteristics or those intended for common or related uses. A class may be further divided into subclasses when appropriate. [21 CFR § 809]

Product Defect / Manufacturing Defect

> The deviation of a distributed product from the standards specified in the approved application, or any significant chemical, physical, or other change, or deterioration in the distributed drug product, including any microbial or chemical contamination. A manufacturing defect is a product defect caused or aggravated by a manufacturing or related process. A manufacturing defect may occur from a single event

or from deficiencies inherent to the manufacturing process. These defects are generally associated with product contamination, product deterioration, manufacturing error, defective packaging, damage from disaster, or labeling error. For example, a labeling error may include any incident that causes a distributed product to be mistaken for, or its labeling applied to, another product. [21 CFR § 514]

Product Jurisdiction Officer

The person or persons responsible for designating the component of FDA with primary jurisdiction for the premarket review and regulation of a combination product or any product requiring a jurisdictional designation under this part. [21 CFR § 3]

Products

Includes biological products and trivalent organic arsenicals. [21 CFR § 600]

Product / Service

The intended results of activities or processes; products/services can be tangible or intangible [source: Quality Systems Guidance]

Proper Name

As applied to a product, means the name designated in the license for use upon each package of the product. [21 CFR § 600]

P

Property

Property subject to forfeiture under title 21, U.S.C., sections 881(a) (4), (6), and (7); title 19, U.S.C., section 1595a, and; title 49, U.S.C. App., section 782. [21 CFR § 1316]

Proprietary Ingredient

Any cosmetic product ingredient whose name, composition, or manufacturing process is protected from competition by secrecy, patent, or copyright. [21 CFR § 700]

Protectee

Any person eligible to receive the protection authorized by law. [IOM Chapter 3]

Protective Detail

A team of Secret Service agents responsible for security surrounding public events to be attended by a protectee during a trip. Protective details are assigned and coordinated by Secret Service Headquarters, but may include Secret Service field representatives. [IOM Chapter 3]

Public Advisory Committee or Advisory Committee

Any committee, board, commission, council, conference, panel, task force, or other similar group, or any subcommittee or other subgroup of an advisory committee, that is not composed wholly of full-time employees of the Federal Government and is established or utilized by the Food and Drug

Administration to obtain advice or recommendations. [21 CFR § 10]

Public Board of Inquiry or Board

An administrative law tribunal constituted under part 13. [21 CFR § 10]

Public Hearing before a Public Advisory Committee

A hearing conducted under part 14. [21 CFR § 10]

Public Hearing before a Public Board of Inquiry

A hearing conducted under part 13. [21 CFR § 10]

Public Hearing before the Commissioner

A hearing conducted under part 15. [21 CFR § 10]

Public Key

The key of a key pair that is used to verify a digital signature. The public key is made available to anyone who will receive digitally signed messages from the holder of the key pair. [21 CFR § 1311]

Public Key Infrastructure (PKI)

A structure under which a Certification Authority verifies the identity of applicants, issues, renews, and revokes digital certificates, maintains a registry of public keys, and maintains an up-to-date Certificate Revocation List. [21 CFR § 1311]

Purchaser

The first person who, for value, or as an award or prize, acquires an electronic product for purposes other than resale, and includes a person who leases an electronic product for purposes other than subleasing. [21 CFR § 1000]

Purchaser

Any registered person entitled to obtain and execute order forms pursuant to 1305.04 and 1305.06. [21 CFR § 1300]

Pure Color

The color contained in a color additive, exclusive of any intermediate or other component, or of any diluent or substratum contained therein. [21 CFR § 70]

Purity

Relative freedom from extraneous matter in the finished product, whether or not harmful to the recipient or deleterious to the product. Purity includes but is not limited to relative freedom from residual moisture or other volatile substances and pyrogenic substances. [21 CFR § 600]

Q

Qualified Instructor

An individual whose training and experience adequately prepares him or her to carry out specified training assignments. Interpreting physicians, radiologic technologists, or medical physicists who meet the requirements of 900.12(a) would be considered qualified instructors in their respective areas of mammography. Other examples of individuals who may be qualified instructors for the purpose of providing training to meet the regulations of this part include, but are not limited to, instructors in a post-high school training institution and manufacturer's representatives. [21 CFR § 900]

Quality

A measure of a product's or service's ability to satisfy the customer's stated or implied needs [source: Quality Systems Guidance]

Quality

The quality of a lot shall be considered acceptable when the number of defectives does not exceed the acceptance number in the sampling plans. [21 CFR § 145]

Quality

The totality of features and characteristics that bear on the ability of a device to satisfy fitness-for-use, including safety and performance. [21 CFR § 820]

Quality Assurance

Proactive and retrospective activities that provide confidence that requirements are fulfilled [source: Quality Systems Guidance]

Quality Assurance Unit

Any person or organizational element, except the study director, designated by testing facility management to perform the duties relating to quality assurance of nonclinical laboratory studies. [21 CFR § 58]

Quality Audit

A systematic, independent examination of a manufacturer's quality system that is performed at defined intervals and at sufficient frequency to determine whether both quality system activities and the results of such activities comply with quality system procedures, that these procedures are implemented effectively, and that these procedures are suitable to achieve quality system objectives. [21 CFR § 820]

Q

Quality Control

The steps taken during the generation of a product or service to ensure that it meets requirements and that the product or service is reproducible [source: Quality Systems Guidance]

Quality Control Operation

A planned and systematic procedure for taking all actions necessary to prevent food from being adulterated within the meaning of the act. [21 CFR § 110]

Quality Control Technologist

An individual meeting the requirements of 900.12(a)(2) who is responsible for those quality assurance responsibilities not assigned to the lead interpreting physician or to the medical physicist. [21 CFR § 900]

Quality Control Unit

Any person or organizational element designated by the firm to be responsible for the duties relating to quality control. [21 CFR § 210]

Quality Management

Accountability for the successful implementation of the quality system [source: Quality Systems Guidance]

Quality Objectives

Specific measurable activities or processes to meet the intentions and directions as defined in the quality policy [source: Quality Systems Guidance]

Q

Quality Plan

> The documented result of quality planning that is disseminated to all relevant levels of the organization [source: Quality Systems Guidance]

Quality Planning

> A management activity that sets quality objectives and defines the operational and/or quality system processes and the resources needed to fulfill the objectives [source: Quality Systems Guidance]

Quality Policy

> The overall intentions and direction of an organization with respect to quality, as established by management with executive responsibility. [21 CFR § 820]

Quality Policy

> A statement of intentions and direction issued by the highest level of the organization related to satisfying customer needs. It is similar to a strategic direction that communicates quality expectations that the organization is striving to achieve. [source: Quality Systems Guidance]

Q

Quality Program

> An organization's comprehensive system for manufacturing and tracking HCT/Ps in accordance with this part. A quality program is designed to prevent, detect, and correct deficiencies that may lead to circumstances that increase the risk of introduction,

transmission, or spread of communicable diseases. [21 CFR § 1271]

Quality System

The organizational structure, responsibilities, procedures, processes, and resources for implementing quality management. [21 CFR § 820]

Quality System

Formalized business practices that define management responsibilities for organizational structure, processes, procedures, and resources needed to fulfill product/service requirements, customer satisfaction, and continual improvement [source: Quality Systems Guidance]

Quality Unit

A group organized within an organization to promote quality in general practice [source: Quality Systems Guidance]

Quarantine

The identification of human tissue as not suitable for transplantation, including human tissue that has not yet been characterized as being suitable for transplantation. Quarantine includes the storage of such tissue in an area clearly identified for such use, or other procedures, such as automated designation, for prevention of release of such tissue for transplantation. [21 CFR § 1270]

Quarantine

The storage or identification of an HCT/P, to prevent improper release, in a physically separate area clearly identified for such use, or through use of other procedures, such as automated designation. [21 CFR § 1271]

Q

R

R

Radioactive Biological Product

A biological product which is labeled with a radionuclide or intended solely to be labeled with a radionuclide. [21 CFR § 600]

Radioactive Drug

Any substance defined as a drug in section 201(g)(1) of the Federal Food, Drug, and Cosmetic Act which exhibits spontaneous disintegration of unstable nuclei with the emission of nuclear particles or photons and includes any nonradioactive reagent kit or nuclide generator which is intended to be used in the preparation of any such substance but does not include drugs such as carbon-containing compounds or potassium-containing salts which contain trace quantities of naturally occurring radionuclides. The term "radioactive drug" includes a "radioactive biological product" as defined in 600.3(ee) of this chapter. [21 CFR § 310]

Radiographic Equipment

X-ray equipment used for the production of static X-ray images. [21 CFR § 900]

Radiologic Technologist

An individual specifically trained in the use of radiographic equipment and the positioning of patients for radiographic examinations and who meets the requirements set forth in 900.12(a)(2). [21 CFR § 900]

Raw Data

Any laboratory worksheets, records, memoranda, notes, or exact copies thereof, that are the result of original observations and activities of a nonclinical laboratory study and are necessary for the reconstruction and evaluation of the report of that study. In the event that exact transcripts of raw data have been prepared (e.g., tapes which have been transcribed verbatim, dated, and verified accurate by signature), the exact copy or exact transcript may be substituted for the original source as raw data. *Raw data* may include photographs, microfilm or microfiche copies, computer printouts, magnetic media, including dictated observations, and recorded data from automated instruments. [21 CFR § 58]

Readily Retrievable

That certain records are kept by automatic data processing systems or other electronic or mechanized recordkeeping systems in such a manner that they can be separated out from all other records in a reasonable time and/or records are kept on which certain items are asterisked, redlined, or in some other manner visually identifiable apart from other items appearing on the records. [21 CFR § 1300]

Reasonable Probability

That it is more likely than not that an event will occur. [21 CFR § 810]

R

Recall

A Recall is a firm's removal or correction of a marketed product that FDA considers to be in violation of the laws it administers, and against which the Agency would initiate legal action (e.g., seizure). Recall does not include a market withdrawal or a stock recovery. See the Agency recall policy outlined in 21 CFR 7.1/7.59 - Enforcement Policy - General Provisions, Recalls (Including Product Corrections) - Guidance on Policy, Procedures, and Industry Responsibilities. [IOM Chapter 7]

Recall

The correction or removal of a device for human use where FDA finds that there is a reasonable probability that the device would cause serious, adverse health consequences or death. [21 CFR § 810]

Recall Audit Check

A personal visit, telephone call, letter, or a combination thereof, to a consignee of a recalling firm, or a user or consumer in the chain of distribution. It is made to verify all consignees at the recall depth specified by the strategy have received notification about the recall and have taken appropriate action. [IOM Chapter 7]

Recall Classification

Means the numerical designation, i.e., I, II, or III, assigned by the FDA to a particular product recall to indicate the relative degree of health hazard presented by the product being recalled. [IOM Chapter 7]

Class I Recall

A situation in which there is a reasonable probability that the use of, or exposure to, a violative product will cause serious adverse health consequences or death.

Class II Recall

A situation in which use of, or exposure to, a violative product may cause temporary or medically reversible adverse health consequences or where the probability of serious adverse health consequences is remote.

Class III Recall

A situation in which use of, or exposure to, a violative product is not likely to cause adverse health consequences.

Recall Completed

For monitoring purposes, the FDA classifies a recall action "Completed" when all outstanding product, which could reasonably be expected is recovered, impounded, or corrected. [IOM Chapter 7]

Recall, Depth of

Depending on the product's degree of hazard and extent of distribution, the recall strategy will specify the level in the distribution chain to which the recall is to extend, i.e., wholesaler, retailer, user/consumer. [IOM Chapter 7]

R

R

Recall Number

Number assigned by a responsible Center for each re-called product they initiate. This number consists first of a letter designating the responsible Center (see letter Codes below), a 3-digit sequential number indicating the number of recalls initiated by that Center during the fiscal year, and a 1-digit number (the Center for Devices and Radiological Health (CDRH) uses 2-digit numbers) indicating the fiscal year the recall was initiated. For example: F-100-2 identifies the 100th recall initiated by the Center for Food Safety and Applied Nutrition (CFSAN) in FY-2002. [IOM Chapter 7]

Recall Strategy

A planned specific course of action to be taken in conducting a specific recall, which addresses the depth of recall, need for public warnings, and extent of effectiveness checks for the recall. [IOM Chapter 7]

Recall Terminated

A recall will be terminated when the FDA determines that all reasonable efforts have been made to remove or correct the violative product in accordance with the recall strategy, and when it is reasonable to assume that the product subject to the recall has been removed and proper disposition or correction has been made commensurate with the degree of hazard of the recalled product. Written notification that a recall is terminated will be issued by the appropriate District office to the recalling firm. [IOM Chapter 7]

Recall Type

A designation based on whether the recall is Voluntary, FDA Requested (at the request of the Commissioner or his designee), or ordered under section 518(e) of the FD & C Act [21 U.S.C 360h (e)]. [IOM Chapter 7]

Recalling Firm

The firm that initiates a recall or, in the case of a Food and Drug Administration-requested recall, the firm that has primary responsibility for the manufacture and marketing of the product to be recalled. [21 CFR § 7]

Reconditioning

The reworking, relabeling, segregation, or other manipulation which brings a product into compliance with the law, whether or not for its original intended use. [IOM Chapter 2]

Reconditioning Samples

These are taken from lots reconditioned under a Decree or other agreement to bring the lots into compliance with the law. The sample is taken to determine if reconditioning was satisfactorily performed. These samples should be submitted as Official Samples, rather than INV. [IOM Chapter 4]

Reconstituted Blood

The extracorporeal resuspension of a blood unit labeled as "Red Blood Cells" by the addition of colloids and/or crystalloids to produce a hematocrit in the normal range. [21 CFR § 1270]

Records about Individuals

Items, collections, or groupings of information about individuals contained in Privacy Act Record Systems, including, but not limited to education, financial transactions, medical history, criminal history, or employment history, that contain names or personal identifiers. [21 CFR § 21]

Recovery

The obtaining from a donor of tissue that is intended for use in human transplantation. [21 CFR § 1270]

Reference Listed Drug

The listed drug identified by FDA as the drug product upon which an applicant relies in seeking approval of its abbreviated application. [21 CFR § 314]

Reference Publication

A publication that:

(1) Has not been written, edited, excerpted, or published specifically for, or at the request of, a drug or device manufacturer;

(2) Has not been edited or significantly influenced by such a manufacturer;

(3) Is not solely distributed through such a manufacturer, but is generally available in bookstores

---

or other distribution channels where medical textbooks are sold;

(4) Does not focus on any particular drug or device of a manufacturer that disseminates information under this part and does not have a primary focus on new uses of drugs or devices that are marketed or are under investigation by a manufacturer supporting the dissemination of information; and

(5) Does not present materials that are false or misleading. [21 CFR § 99]

Register and Registration

Refer only to registration required and permitted by sections 303 or 1007 of the Act (21 U.S.C. 823 or 957). [21 CFR § 1300]

Registrant

Any person who is registered pursuant to either section 303 or section 1008 of the Act (21 U.S.C. 823 or 958). [21 CFR § 1300]

Regulations

An agency rule of general or particular applicability and future effect issued under a law administered by the Commissioner or relating to administrative practices and procedures. In accordance with 10.90(a), each agency regulation will be published in the Federal Register and codified in the Code of Federal Regulations. [21 CFR § 10]

R

R

Regulatory Hearing before the Food and Drug Administration

A hearing conducted under part 16. [21 CFR § 10]

Regulatory Method

The aggregate of all experimental procedures for measuring and confirming the presence of the marker residue of the sponsored compound in the target tissue of the target animal. [21 CFR § 500]

Regulatory System

The body of legal requirements for GMP's, inspections, and enforcements that ensure public health protection and legal authority to assure adherence to these requirements. [21 CFR § 26]

Related Drug(s)

Includes other brands, potencies, dosage forms, salts, and esters of the same drug moiety, including articles prepared or manufactured by other manufacturers: and any other drug containing a component so related by chemical structure or known pharmacological properties that, in the opinion of experts qualified by scientific training and experience to evaluate the safety and effectiveness of drugs, it is prudent to assume or ascertain the liability of similar side effects and contraindications. [21 CFR § 310]

Release

The product is released after FDA examination. This message does not constitute assurance the product complies with all provisions of the Food, Drug and Cosmetic Act, or other related Acts, and does not preclude action should the product later be found violative." (A compliance decision has been made.) [IOM Chapter 6]

Relevant Communicable Disease Agent or Disease

(1)(i) For all human cells and tissues, a communicable disease or disease agent listed as follows:
(A) Human immunodeficiency virus, types 1 and 2;
(B) Hepatitis B virus;
(C) Hepatitis C virus;
(D) Human transmissible spongiform encephalopathy, including Creutzfeldt-Jakob disease; and
(E) *Treponema pallidum* .

(ii) For viable, leukocyte-rich cells and tissues, a cell-associated disease agent or disease listed as follows:
(A) Human T-lymphotropic virus, type I; and
(B) Human T-lymphotropic virus, type II.

(iii) For reproductive cells or tissues, a disease agent or disease of the genitourinary tract listed as follows:
(A) *Chlamydia trachomatis* ; and
(B) *Neisseria gonorrhea* .

(2) A disease agent or disease not listed in paragraph (r)(1) of this section:
(i) For which there may be a risk of transmission by an HCT/P, either to the recipient of the HCT/P or to those people who may handle or otherwise come in contact with it, such as medical personnel, because the disease agent or disease:

(A) Is potentially transmissible by an HCT/P and

(B) Either of the following applies:

(*1*) The disease agent or disease has sufficient incidence and/or prevalence to affect the potential donor population, or

(*2*) The disease agent or disease may have been released accidentally or intentionally in a manner that could place potential donors at risk of infection;

(ii) That could be fatal or life-threatening, could result in permanent impairment of a body function or permanent damage to body structure, or could necessitate medical or surgical intervention to preclude permanent impairment of body function or permanent damage to a body structure; and

(iii) For which appropriate screening measures have been developed and/or an appropriate screening test for donor specimens has been licensed, approved, or cleared for such use by FDA and is available. [21 CFR § 1271]

Relevant Medical Records

A collection of documents including a donor medical history interview, a physical assessment of the donor, laboratory test results, medical records, existing coroner and autopsy reports, or information obtained from any source or records which may pertain to donor suitability regarding high risk behaviors, clinical signs and symptoms for HIV and hepatitis, and treatments related to medical conditions suggestive of such risk. [21 CFR § 1270]

Remanufacturer

Any person who processes, conditions, renovates, repackages, restores, or does any other act to a finished device that significantly changes the finished device's performance or safety specifications, or intended use. [21 CFR § 820]

Removal

The physical removal of a device from its point of use to some other location for repair, modification, adjustment, relabeling, destruction, or inspection. [21 CFR § 806]

Removal Report Number or Correction

The number that uniquely identifies each report submitted. [21 CFR § 806]

Reportable Experience

An experience involving any allergic reaction, or other bodily injury, alleged to be the result of the use of a cosmetic product under the conditions of use prescribed in the labeling of the product, under such conditions of use as are customary or reasonably foreseeable for the product or under conditions of misuse, that has been reported to the manufacturer, packer, or distributor of the product by the affected person or any other person having factual knowledge of the incident, other than an alleged experience which has been determined to be unfounded or spurious when evaluated by a filed screening procedure. [21 CFR § 700]

R

Representative

> An employee or agent of a drug manufacturer or distributor who promotes the sale of prescription drugs to licensed practitioners and who may solicit or receive written requests for the delivery of drug samples. A detailer is a representative. [21 CFR § 203]

Representative of the News Media

> Any person actively gathering news for an entity that is organized and operated to publish or broadcast news to the public. News is information about current events or information that would be of interest to the public. Examples of the news media include television or radio stations that broadcast to the public at large and publishers of news periodicals that make their products available to the general public for purchase or subscription. Freelance journalists may be regarded as working for the news media where they demonstrate a reasonable basis for expecting publication through that organization, even though not actually employed by it. [21 CFR § 1401]

Representative Sample

> A sample that consists of a number of units that are drawn based on rational criteria such as random sampling and intended to assure that the sample accurately portrays the material being sampled. [21 CFR § 210]

Representative Sampling of Advertisements

> Typical advertising material (excluding labeling as determined in 202.1(l) (1) and (2)) that gives a

balanced picture of the promotional claims used for the drug, e.g., if more than one medical journal advertisement is used but the promotional content is essentially identical, only one need be submitted. [21 CFR § 207]

Representative Sampling of Advertisements

Typical advertising material that gives the promotional claims made for the device. [21 CFR § 807]

Representative Sampling of any Other Labeling

Typical labeling material (excluding labels and package inserts) that gives a balanced picture of the promotional claims used for the drug, e.g., if more than one brochure is used but the promotional content is essentially identical, only one need be submitted. [21 CFR § 207]

Representative Sampling of any Other Labeling

Typical labeling material (excluding labels and package inserts) that gives the promotional claims made for the device. [21 CFR § 807]

Request

A letter or other written communication seeking records or information under FOIA. [21 CFR § 1401]

R

Residue

Any compound present in edible tissues of the target animal which results from the use of the sponsored compound, including the sponsored compound, its metabolites, and any other substances formed in or on food because of the sponsored compound's use. [21 CFR § 500]

Residue of Carcinogenic Concern

All compounds in the total residue of a demonstrated carcinogen excluding any compounds judged by FDA not to present a carcinogenic risk. [21 CFR § 500]

Respondent

A person named in a notice who presents views concerning an alleged violation either in person, by designated representative, or in writing. [21 CFR § 7]

Responsible Agency Official

The agency decision maker designated in the delegated authority for the underlying actions. [21 CFR § 25]

Responsible Individual

Those in positions of power or authority to detect, prevent, or correct violations of the Federal Food, Drug, and Cosmetic Act. [21 CFR § 7]

Restricted Device

A device for which the Commissioner, by regulation under 801.109 of this chapter or otherwise under section 520(e) of the act, has restricted sale, distribution, or use only upon the written or oral authorization of a practitioner licensed by law to administer or use the device or upon such other conditions as the Commissioner may prescribe. [21 CFR § 807]

Responsible Person

A person who is authorized to perform designated functions for which he or she is trained and qualified. [21 CFR § 1270]

Resubmission

Submission by the applicant of all materials needed to fully address all deficiencies identified in the complete response letter. An application or abbreviated application for which FDA issued a complete response letter, but which was withdrawn before approval and later submitted again, is not a resubmission. [21 CFR § 314]

Resubmission

A submission by the biologics license applicant or supplement applicant of all materials needed to fully address all deficiencies identified in the complete response letter. A biologics license application or supplement for which FDA issued a complete response letter, but which was withdrawn before

R

approval and later submitted again, is not a
resubmission. [21 CFR § 600]

Reverse Distributor

A registrant who receives controlled substances
acquired from another DEA registrant for the purpose
of--

(i) Returning unwanted, unusable, or outdated
controlled substances to the manufacturer or the
manufacturer's agent; or

(ii) Where necessary, processing such substances or
arranging for processing such substances for disposal.
[21 CFR § 1300]

Review

The process of examining documents that are located
during a search to determine if any portion should
lawfully be withheld. It is the processing of
determining disclosability. [21 CFR § 1401]

Review Physician

A physician who, by meeting the requirements set out
in 900.4(c)(5), is qualified to review clinical images on
behalf of the accreditation body. [21 CFR § 900]

Rework

Clean, unadulterated food that has been removed
from processing for reasons other than insanitary
conditions or that has been successfully reconditioned

by reprocessing and that is suitable for use as food. [21 CFR § 110]

Rework

Action taken on a nonconforming product so that it will fulfill the specified DMR requirements before it is released for distribution. [21 CFR § 820]

Right of Reference or Use

The authority to rely upon, and otherwise use, an investigation for the purpose of obtaining approval of an application, including the ability to make available the underlying raw data from the investigation for FDA audit, if necessary. [21 CFR § 314]

Risk

The combination of the probability of occurrence of harm and the severity of that harm [source: Quality Systems Guidance]

Risk Assessment

A systematic process for organizing information to support a risk decision that is made within a risk management process. The process consists of the identification of hazards and the analysis and evaluation of risks associated with exposure to those hazards. [source: Quality Systems Guidance]

Risk Management

The systematic application of quality management policies, procedures, and practices to the tasks of

R

assessing, controlling, communicating, and reviewing risk [source: Quality Systems Guidance]

Risk to Health

(1) A reasonable probability that use of, or exposure to, the product will cause serious adverse health consequences or death; or

(2) That use of, or exposure to, the product may cause temporary or medically reversible adverse health consequences, or an outcome where the probability of serious adverse health consequences is remote. [21 CFR § 806]

Rm

The concentration of the marker residue in the target tissue when the residue of carcinogenic concern is equal to Sm. [21 CFR § 500]

Routine Servicing

Any regularly scheduled maintenance of a device, including the replacement of parts at the end of their normal life expectancy, e.g., calibration, replacement of batteries, and responses to normal wear and tear. Repairs of an unexpected nature, replacement of parts earlier than their normal life expectancy, or identical repairs or replacements of multiple units of a device are not routine servicing. [21 CFR § 806]

Safe Level

A conservative estimate of a drug residue level in edible animal tissue derived from food safety data or other scientific information. Concentrations of residues in tissue below the safe level will not raise human food safety concerns. A safe level is not a safe concentration or a tolerance and does not indicate that an approval exists for the drug in that species or category of animal from which the food is derived. [21 CFR § 530]

Safe-moisture Level

A level of moisture low enough to prevent the growth of undesirable microorganisms in the finished product under the intended conditions of manufacturing, storage, and distribution. The maximum safe moisture level for a food is based on its water activity (aw). An aw will be considered safe for a food if adequate data are available that demonstrate that the food at or below the given aw will not support the growth of undesirable microorganisms. [21 CFR § 110]

Safe and Suitable

The ingredient:

(1) Performs an appropriate function in the food in which it is used.

(2) Is used at a level no higher than necessary to achieve its intended purpose in that food.

(3) Is not a food additive or color additive as defined in section 201 (s) or (t) of the Federal Food, Drug, and Cosmetic Act as used in that food, or is a food additive or color additive as so defined and is used in conformity with regulations established pursuant to section 409 or 721 of the act. [21 CFR § 130]

Safe or Safety

Means that there is a reasonable certainty in the minds of competent scientists that the substance is not harmful under the intended conditions of use. It is impossible in the present state of scientific knowledge to establish with complete certainty the absolute harmlessness of the use of any substance. Safety may be determined by scientific procedures or by general recognition of safety. In determining safety, the following factors shall be considered:

(1) The probable consumption of the substance and of any substance formed in or on food because of its use.

(2) The cumulative effect of the substance in the diet, taking into account any chemically or pharmacologically related substance or substances in such diet.

(3) Safety factors which, in the opinion of experts qualified by scientific training and experience to evaluate the safety of food and food ingredients, are generally recognized as appropriate. [21 CFR § 170]

Safety

The word means the relative freedom from harmful effect to persons affected, directly or indirectly, by a product when prudently administered, taking into consideration the character of the product in relation to the condition of the recipient at the time. [21 CFR § 600]

Same Drug

(i) If it is a drug composed of small molecules, a drug that contains the same active moiety as a previously approved drug and is intended for the same use as the previously approved drug, even if the particular ester or salt (including a salt with hydrogen or coordination bonds) or other noncovalent derivative such as a complex, chelate or clathrate has not been previously approved, except that if the subsequent drug can be shown to be clinically superior to the first drug, it will not be considered to be the same drug.

(ii) If it is a drug composed of large molecules (macromolecules), a drug that contains the same principal molecular structural features (but not necessarily all of the same structural features) and is intended for the same use as a previously approved drug, except that, if the subsequent drug can be shown to be clinically superior, it will not be considered to be the same drug. This criterion will be applied as follows to different kinds of macromolecules:

(A) Two protein drugs would be considered the same if the only differences in structure between them were due to post-translational events or infidelity of translation or transcription or were minor differences in amino acid sequence; other potentially important differences, such as different glycosylation patterns or different tertiary structures, would not cause the drugs to be considered different unless the differences were shown to be clinically superior.

(B) Two polysaccharide drugs would be considered the same if they had identical saccharide repeating units, even if the number of units were to vary and even if there were postpolymerization modifications, unless the subsequent drug could be shown to be clinically superior.

(C) Two polynucleotide drugs consisting of two or more distinct nucleotides would be considered the same if they had an identical sequence of purine and pyrimidine bases (or their derivatives) bound to an identical sugar backbone (ribose, deoxyribose, or modifications of these sugars), unless the subsequent drug were shown to be clinically superior.

(D) Closely related, complex partly definable drugs with similar therapeutic intent, such as two live viral vaccines for the same indication, would be considered the same unless the subsequent drug was shown to be clinically superior. [21 CFR § 316]

Same Drug Product Formulation

The formulation of the drug product submitted for approval and any formulations that have minor differences in composition or method of manufacture from the formulation submitted for approval, but are similar enough to be relevant to the agency's determination of bioequivalence. [21 CFR § 320]

Sample

Consists of 10 subsamples (consumer units), one taken from each of 10 different randomly chosen shipping cases to be representative of a given lot, unless otherwise specified in a specific standard in this part. [21 CFR § 165]

Sample Size

The total number of sample units drawn for examination from a lot. [21 CFR § 145]

Sample Unit

A container, a portion of the contents of a container, or a composite mixture of product from small containers that is sufficient for the examination or testing as a single unit. [21 CFR § 145]

Sample Unit

A packet, card, blister pack, bottle, container, or other single package comprised of one or more dosage units of a prescription drug sample, intended by the manufacturer or distributor to be provided by a licensed practitioner to a patient in an unbroken or unopened condition. [21 CFR § 203]

Sampling and Acceptance Procedure

Means the following:

(1) *Definitions* --(i) *Lot.* A collection of primary containers or units of the same size, type, and style manufactured or packed under similar conditions and handled as a single unit of trade.

(ii) *Lot size.* The number of primary containers or units in the lot.

(iii) *Sample size.* The total number of sample units drawn for examination from a lot.

(iv) *Sample unit.* A container, a portion of the contents of a container, or a composite mixture of product from small containers that is sufficient for the examination or testing as a single unit.

(v) *Defective.* Any sample unit shall be regarded as defective when the sample unit does not meet the criteria set forth in the standards.

(vi) *Acceptance number* (c). The maximum number of defective sample units permitted in the sample in order to consider the lot as meeting the specified requirements.

(vii) *Acceptable quality level* (*AQL*). The maximum percent of defective sample units permitted in a lot that will be accepted approximately 95 percent of the time.

(2) Sampling plans:

Lot size (primary containers)	Size in container	
	n^1	c^2

Lot size (primary containers)	Size in container	
	n^1	c^2
net weight equal to or less than 1 kg (2.2 lb)		
4,800 or less	13	2
4,801 to 24,000	21	3
24,001 to 48,000	29	4
48,001 to 84,000	48	6
84,001 to 144,000	84	9
144,001 to 240,000	126	13
Over 240,000	200	19
net weight greater than 1 kg (2.2 lb) but not more than 4.5 kg (10 lb)		
2,400 or less	13	2
2,401 to 15,000	21	3
15,001 to 24,000	29	4
24,001 to 42,000	48	6
42,001 to 72,000	84	9
72,001 to 120,000	126	13
Over 120,000	200	19
net weight greater than 4.5 kg (10 lb)		
600 or less	13	2
601 to 2,000	21	3
2,001 to 7,200	29	4
7,201 to 15,000	48	6
15,001 to 24,000	84	9

Lot size (primary containers)	Size in container	
	n^1	c^2
24,001 to 42,000	126	13
Over 42,000	200	19

[1] n=number of primary containers in sample.

[2] c=acceptance number.

Sanitize

To adequately treat food-contact surfaces by a process that is effective in destroying vegetative cells of microorganisms of public health significance, and in substantially reducing numbers of other undesirable microorganisms, but without adversely affecting the product or its safety for the consumer. [21 CFR § 110]

Scientific or Medical Journal

A scientific or medical publication:

(1) That is published by an organization that has an editorial board, that uses experts who have demonstrated expertise in the subject of an article under review by the organization and who are independent of the organization, to review and objectively select, reject, or provide comments about proposed articles, and that has a publicly stated policy, to which the organization adheres, of full disclosure of any conflict of interest or biases for all authors or contributors involved with the journal or organization;

---

(2) Whose articles are peer-reviewed and published in accordance with the regular peer-review procedures of the organization;

(3) That is generally recognized to be of national scope and reputation;

(4) That is indexed in the Index Medicus of the National Library of Medicine of the National Institutes of Health; and

(5) That is not in the form of a special supplement that has been funded in whole or in part by one or more manufacturers. [21 CFR § 99]

Scientific Procedures

Include those human, animal, analytical, and other scientific studies, whether published or unpublished, appropriate to establish the safety of a substance. [21 CFR § 170]

Search

To review, manually or by automated means, agency records for the purpose of locating those records responsive to a request. [21 CFR § 1401]

Secretary

The Secretary of Health and Human Services and any other officer or employee of the Department of Health and Human Services to whom the authority involved has been delegated. [21 CFR § 600]

Seizing Agency

The Federal agency which has seized the property or adopted the seizure of another agency, and has the responsibility for administratively forfeiting the property. [21 CFR § 1316]

Seizing District

The district where seizure is actually accomplished. The seizing district is not necessarily the collecting district, as in the case of intransit samples. [IOM Chapter 2]

Seizure

Seizure is a judicial civil action directed against specific offending goods, in which goods are "arrested." Originally designed to remove violative goods from consumer channels, it was intended primarily as a remedial step; however, the sanction often has a punitive and deterrent effect. [IOM Chapter 2]

Selling Agent or Distributor

Any person engaged in the unrestricted distribution, other than by sale at retail, of products subject to license. [21 CFR § 600]

Senior Management

Top management officials in a firm who have the authority and responsibility to mobilize resources [source: Quality Systems Guidance]

Serious, Adverse Health Consequence

Any significant adverse experience, including those
that may be either life-threatening or involve
permanent or long-term injuries, but excluding
injuries that are nonlife-threatening and that are
temporary and reasonably reversible. [21 CFR § 810]

Serious Adverse Experience

Any adverse experience occurring at any dose that
results in any of the following outcomes: Death, a life-
threatening adverse experience, inpatient
hospitalization or prolongation of existing
hospitalization, a persistent or significant
disability/incapacity, or a congenital anomaly/birth
defect. Important medical events that may not result
in death, be life-threatening, or require hospitalization
may be considered a serious adverse experience when,
based upon appropriate medical judgment, they may
jeopardize the patient or subject and may require
medical or surgical intervention to prevent one of the
outcomes listed in this definition. Examples of such
medical events include allergic bronchospasm
requiring intensive treatment in an emergency room
or at home, blood dyscrasias or convulsions that do
not result in inpatient hospitalization, or the
development of drug dependency or drug abuse. [21
CFR § 600]

Serious Complaint

A report of a serious adverse event. [21 CFR § 900]

Serious Risk or Serious Adverse Effect

> An adverse drug experience, or the risk of such an experience, as that term is defined in 310.305, 312.32, 314.80, and 600.80 of this chapter. [21 CFR § 208]

Shall

> Is used to state mandatory requirements. [21 CFR § 110]

Shellfish

> Any fresh, frozen, or incompletely cooked oysters, clams, or mussels, either shucked or in the shell, and any fresh, frozen, or incompletely cooked edible products thereof. [21 CFR § 1250]

Shellfish Control Authority

> A Federal, State, or foreign agency, or sovereign tribal government, legally responsible for the administration of a program that includes activities such as classification of molluscan shellfish growing areas, enforcement of molluscan shellfish harvesting controls, and certification of molluscan shellfish processors. [21 CFR § 1240]

Should

> is used to state recommended or advisory procedures or identify recommended equipment. [21 CFR § 110]

Significant Departure

For the purpose of interpreting 21 U.S.C.
333(g)(1)(B)(i), means a departure from requirements
that is either a single major incident or a series of
incidents that collectively are consequential. [21 CFR
§ 17]

Significant Risk Device

An investigational device that:

(1) Is intended as an implant and presents a potential
for serious risk to the health, safety, or welfare of a
subject;

(2) Is purported or represented to be for a use in
supporting or sustaining human life and presents a
potential for serious risk to the health, safety, or
welfare of a subject;

(3) Is for a use of substantial importance in
diagnosing, curing, mitigating, or treating disease, or
otherwise preventing impairment of human health
and presents a potential for serious risk to the health,
safety, or welfare of a subject; or

(4) Otherwise presents a potential for serious risk to
the health, safety, or welfare of a subject. [21 CFR §
812]

Site Advance Agent

The Secret Service person responsible for security
arrangements at a specific site to be visited by the
protectee. This person is part of the protective detail

---

headed by the Lead Advance Agent. Note: the term Site Advance Agent will include any agent designated by the Site Advance Agent to be the contact with the FDA Lead Investigator. [IOM Chapter 3]

Sm

The concentration of residue in a specific edible tissue corresponding to a maximum lifetime risk of cancer in the test animals of 1 in 1 million. [21 CFR § 500]

So

The concentration of the test compound in the total diet of test animals that corresponds to a maximum lifetime risk of cancer in the test animals of 1 in 1 million. For the purpose of this subpart, FDA will also assume that this Sowill correspond to the concentration of residue of carcinogenic concern in the total human diet that represents no significant increase in the risk of cancer to people. [21 CFR § 500]

Solid Oral Dosage Form

Capsules, tablets, or similar drug products intended for oral use. [21 CFR § 206]

Solid Pack

The product contains practically all fruit with only the very little free flowing liquid that is expressed from the fruit and to which no packing media have been added. [21 CFR § 145]

Special Packaging

As defined in section 2(4) of the Poison Prevention Packaging Act of 1970 means packaging that is designed or constructed to be significantly difficult for children under 5 years of age to open or obtain a toxic or harmful amount of the substance contained therein within a reasonable time and not difficult for normal adults to use properly, but does not mean packaging which all such children cannot open or obtain a toxic or harmful amount within a reasonable time. [21 CFR § 310]

Specification

The quality standard (*i.e.*, tests, analytical procedures, and acceptance criteria) provided in an approved application to confirm the quality of drug substances, drug products, intermediates, raw materials, reagents, components, in-process materials, container closure systems, and other materials used in the production of a drug substance or drug product. For the purpose of this definition, *acceptance criteria* means numerical limits, ranges, or other criteria for the tests described. [21 CFR § 314]

Specification

As used in 601.12 of this chapter, means the quality standard (i.e., tests, analytical procedures, and acceptance criteria) provided in an approved application to confirm the quality of products, intermediates, raw materials, reagents, components, in-process materials, container closure systems, and other materials used in the production of a product. For the purpose of this definition, acceptance criteria means numerical limits, ranges, or other criteria for the tests described. [21 CFR § 600]

Specification

Any requirement with which a product, process, service, or other activity must conform. [21 CFR § 820]

Specimen

Any material derived from a test system for examination or analysis. [21 CFR § 58]

Sponsor

A person who initiates a clinical investigation, but who does not actually conduct the investigation, i.e., the test article is administered or dispensed to or used involving, a subject under the immediate direction of another individual. A person other than an individual (e.g., corporation or agency) that uses one or more of its own employees to conduct a clinical investigation it has initiated is considered to be a sponsor (not a sponsor-investigator), and the employees are considered to be investigators. [21 CFR § 50]

Sponsor

Means:

(1) A person who initiates and supports, by provision of financial or other resources, a nonclinical laboratory study;

(2) A person who submits a nonclinical study to the Food and Drug Administration in support of an application for a research or marketing permit; or

(3) A testing facility, if it both initiates and actually conducts the study. [21 CFR § 58]

Sponsor

The person or agency who assumes responsibility for an investigation of a new drug, including responsibility for compliance with applicable provisions of the act and regulations. The "sponsor" may be an individual, partnership, corporation, or Government agency and may be a manufacturer, scientific institution, or an investigator regularly and lawfully engaged in the investigation of new drugs. [21 CFR § 310]

Sponsor

A person who takes responsibility for and initiates a clinical investigation. The sponsor may be an individual or pharmaceutical company, governmental agency, academic institution, private organization, or other organization. The sponsor does not actually conduct the investigation unless the sponsor is a sponsor-investigator. A person other than an individual that uses one or more of its own employees to conduct an investigation that it has initiated is a sponsor, not a sponsor-investigator, and the employees are investigators. [21 CFR § 312]

Sponsor-investigator

> An individual who both initiates and actually conducts, alone or with others, a clinical investigation, i.e., under whose immediate direction the test article is administered or dispensed to, or used involving, a subject. The term does not include any person other than an individual, e.g., corporation or agency. [21 CFR § 50]

Sponsor-Investigator

> An individual who both initiates and conducts an investigation, and under whose immediate direction the investigational drug is administered or dispensed. The term does not include any person other than an individual. The requirements applicable to a sponsor-investigator under this part include both those applicable to an investigator and a sponsor. [21 CFR § 312]

Sponsored Compound

> Any drug or food additive or color additive proposed for use, or used, in food-producing animals or in their feed. [21 CFR § 500]

Stakeholder

> An individual or organization having an ownership or interest in the delivery, results, and metrics of the quality system framework or business process improvements [source: Quality Systems Guidance]

Standard Breast

A 4.2 centimeter (cm) thick compressed breast consisting of 50 percent glandular and 50 percent adipose tissue. [21 CFR § 900]

Standards

Specifications and procedures applicable to an establishment or to the manufacture or release of products, which are prescribed in this subchapter or established in the biologics license application designed to insure the continued safety, purity, and potency of such products. [21 CFR § 600]

State

A State or the District of Columbia, Puerto Rico, or the Virgin Islands. [21 CFR § 600]

State

A State, American Samoa, the Canal Zone, the Commonwealth of Puerto Rico, the District of Columbia, Guam, Johnston Island, Kingman Reef, Midway Island, the Trust Territory of the Pacific Islands, the Virgin Islands, and Wake Island. [21 CFR § 808]

Statement of Material Fact

A representation that tends to show that the safety or effectiveness of a device is more probable than it would be in the absence of such a representation. A false affirmation or silence or an omission that would lead a reasonable person to draw a particular

---

conclusion as to the safety or effectiveness of a device also may be a false statement of material fact, even if the statement was not intended by the person making it to be misleading or to have any probative effect. [21 CFR § 814]

Statutory Rights or Defenses to the Forfeiture

All legal and equitable rights and remedies available to a claimant of property seized for forfeiture. [21 CFR § 1316]

Stock Recovery

A firm's removal or correction of a product that has not been marketed or that has not left the direct control of the firm, i.e., the product is located on premises owned by, or under the control of, the firm and no portion of the lot has been released for sale or use. [21 CFR § 7]

Stock Recovery

The correction or removal of a device that has not been marketed or that has not left the direct control of the manufacturer, i.e., the device is located on the premises owned, or under the control of, the manufacturer, and no portion of the lot, model, code, or other relevant unit involved in the corrective or removal action has been released for sale or use. [21 CFR § 806]

Straight Color

A color additive listed in parts 73, 74, and 81 of this chapter, and includes lakes and such substances as are permitted by the specifications for such color. [21 CFR § 70]

Strength

(i) The concentration of the drug substance (for example, weight/weight, weight/volume, or unit dose/volume basis), and/or

(ii) The potency, that is, the therapeutic activity of the drug product as indicated by appropriate laboratory tests or by adequately developed and controlled clinical data (expressed, for example, in terms of units by reference to a standard). [21 CFR § 210]

Sterility

The word is interpreted to mean freedom from viable contaminating microorganisms, as determined by the tests prescribed in 610.12 of this chapter. [21 CFR § 600]

Study Completion Date

The date the final report is signed by the study director. [21 CFR § 58]

Study Director

The individual responsible for the overall conduct of a nonclinical laboratory study. [21 CFR § 58]

Study Initiation Date

The date the protocol is signed by the study director. [21 CFR § 58]

S

Subject

a human who participates in an investigation, either as a recipient of the investigational new drug or as a control. A subject may be a healthy human or a patient with a disease. [21 CFR § 312]

Subpoena Duces Tecum

A writ commanding a person to appear in court bringing with him certain designated documents or things pertinent to the issues of a pending controversy. [IOM Chapter 2]

Substance

In the definition of the term "food additive" includes a food or food component consisting of one or more ingredients. [21 CFR § 170]

Substantially Identical to

Refers to the fact that a State or local requirement does not significantly differ in effect from a Federal requirement. [21 CFR § 808]

Substratum

The substance on which the pure color in a lake is extended. [21 CFR § 70]

Sugar

Refined sucrose. [21 CFR § 145]

Summary of Records

A condensed version of the required testing and screening records that contains the identity of the testing laboratory, the listing and interpretation of all required infectious disease tests, and a listing of the documents reviewed as part of the relevant medical records, and the name of the person or establishment determining the suitability of the human tissue for transplantation. [21 CFR § 1270]

Supervising District

The district which exercises supervision over reconditioning lots in connection with seizure actions. [IOM Chapter 2]

Supplement

A request to approve a change in an approved license application. [21 CFR § 600]

Supplemental Application

(1) For drugs, a supplement to support a new use to an approved new drug application;

(2) For biologics, a supplement to an approved license application;

(3) For devices that are the subject of a cleared 510(k) submission and devices that are exempt from the 510(k) process, a new 510(k) submission to support a new use or, for devices that are the subject of an approved premarket approval application, a

supplement to support a new use to an approved premarket approval application. [21 CFR § 99]

Supplemental Data Sheet

Information compiled by a classification panel or submitted in a petition for reclassification, including:

(1) A summary of the reasons for the recommendation (or petition);

(2) A summary of the data upon which the recommendation (or petition) is based;

(3) An identification of the risks to health (if any) presented by the device;

(4) To the extent practicable in the case of a class II or class III device, a recommendation for the assignment of a priority for the application of the requirements of performance standards or premarket approval;

(5) In the case of a class I device, a recommendation whether the device should be exempted from any of the requirements of registration, record-keeping and reporting, or good manufacturing practice requirements of the quality system regulation;

(6) In the case of an implant or a life-supporting or life-sustaining device for which classification in class III is not recommended, a statement of the reasons for not recommending that the device be classified in class III;

(7) Identification of any needed restrictions on the use of the device, e.g., whether the device requires special

labeling, should be banned, or should be used only upon authorization of a practitioner licensed by law to administer or use such device; and

(8) Any known existing standards applicable to the device, device components, or device materials. [21 CFR § 860]

Supplier

Any registered person entitled to fill order forms pursuant to 1305.08 of this chapter. [21 CFR § 1300]

Support Personnel

FDA persons deemed necessary by FDA in order to properly inspect a food service function. [IOM Chapter 3]

Survey

An onsite physics consultation and evaluation of a facility quality assurance program performed by a medical physicist. [21 CFR § 900]

System of Commercial Distribution

Of a cosmetic product means any distribution outside the establishment manufacturing the product, whether for sale, to promote future sales (including free samples of the product), or to gage consumer acceptance through market testing, in excess of $1,000 in cost of goods. [21 CFR § 700]

S

Sworn to

As used in 1316.92(e) and 1316.95(c) refers to the oath as provided by Title 28, U.S.C., section 1746. [21 CFR § 1316]

Tag

A record of harvesting information attached to a
container of shellstock by the harvester or processor.
[21 CFR § 1240]

Target Animals

The production class of animals in which a sponsored
compound is proposed or intended for use. [21 CFR
§ 500]

Target Tissue

The edible tissue selected to monitor for residues in
the target animals, including, where appropriate, milk
or eggs. [21 CFR § 500]

Termination

A discontinuance, by sponsor or by withdrawal of IRB
or FDA approval, of an investigation before
completion. [21 CFR § 812]

Test Animals

The species selected for use in the toxicity tests. [21
CFR § 500]

T

Test Article

Any drug (including a biological product for human use), medical device for human use, human food additive, color additive, electronic product, or any other article subject to regulation under the act or under sections 351 and 354-360F of the Public Health Service Act (42 U.S.C. 262 and 263b-263n). [21 CFR § 50]

Test System

Any animal, plant, microorganism, or subparts thereof to which the test or control article is administered or added for study. *Test system* also includes appropriate groups or components of the system not treated with the test or control articles. [21 CFR § 58]

Testing Facility

A person who actually conducts a nonclinical laboratory study, i.e., actually uses the test article in a test system. *Testing facility* includes any establishment required to register under section 510 of the act that conducts nonclinical laboratory studies and any consulting laboratory described in section 704 of the act that conducts such studies. *Testing facility* encompasses only those operational units that are being or have been used to conduct nonclinical laboratory studies. [21 CFR § 58]

The List

The list of drug products with effective approvals published in the current edition of FDA's publication "Approved Drug Products with Therapeutic

Equivalence Evaluations" and any current supplement to the publication. [21 CFR § 314]

Therapeutic Serum

A product obtained from blood by removing the clot or clot components and the blood cells. [21 CFR § 600]

A product is analogous to a therapeutic serum, if composed of whole blood or plasma or containing some organic constituent or product other than a hormone or an amino acid, derived from whole blood, plasma, or serum.

Theoretical Yield

The quantity that would be produced at any appropriate phase of manufacture, processing, or packing of a particular drug product, based upon the quantity of components to be used, in the absence of any loss or error in actual production. [21 CFR § 210]

Threshold Assessment

FDA's review of data and information about a sponsored compound to determine whether chronic bioassays in test animals are necessary to resolve questions concerning the carcinogenicity of the compound. [21 CFR § 500]

Time Cycle

The film development time. [21 CFR § 900]

Toxin

A product containing a soluble substance poisonous to laboratory animals or to man in doses of 1 milliliter or less (or equivalent in weight) of the product, and having the property, following the injection of non-fatal doses into an animal, of causing to be produced therein another soluble substance which specifically neutralizes the poisonous substance and which is demonstrable in the serum of the animal thus immunized. [21 CFR § 600]

A product is analogous to a toxin or antitoxin, if intended, irrespective of its source of origin, to be applicable to the prevention, treatment, or cure of disease or injuries of man through a specific immune process.

Traceable to a National Standard

An instrument is calibrated at either the National Institute of Standards and Technology (NIST) or at a calibration laboratory that participates in a proficiency program with NIST at least once every 2 years and the results of the proficiency test conducted within 24 months of calibration show agreement within +/-3 percent of the national standard in the mammography energy range. [21 CFR § 900]

Transfer

The placement of human reproductive cells or tissues into a human recipient. [21 CFR § 1271]

Transitional Device

A device subject to section 520(l) of the act, that is, a device that FDA considered to be a new drug or an antibiotic drug before May 28, 1976. [21 CFR § 812]

Trivalent Organic Arsenicals

Means arsphenamine and its derivatives (or any other trivalent organic arsenic compound) applicable to the prevention, treatment, or cure of diseases or injuries of man. [21 CFR § 600]

Type A Medicated Article

Intended solely for use in the manufacture of another Type A medicated article or a Type B or Type C medicated feed. It consists of a new animal drug(s), with or without carrier (e.g., calcium carbonate, rice hull, corn, gluten) with or without inactive ingredients. The manufacture of a Type A medicated article requires an application approved under 514.105 of this chapter or an index listing granted under 516.151 of this chapter. [21 CFR § 558]

Type B Medicated Feed

Intended solely for the manufacture of other medicated feeds (Type B or Type C). It contains a substantial quantity of nutrients including vitamins and/or minerals and/or other nutritional ingredients in an amount not less than 25 percent of the weight. It is manufactured by diluting a Type A medicated article or another Type B medicated feed. The maximum concentration of animal drug(s) in a Type B medicated feed is 200 times the highest continuous use level for Category I drugs and 100 times the highest continuous use level for Category II drugs. The term "highest continuous use level" means the highest dosage at which the drug is approved for continuous use (14 days or more), or, if the drug is not approved for continuous use, it means the highest level used for disease prevention or control. If the drug is approved for multiple species at different use levels, the highest approved level of use would govern under this definition. The manufacture of a Type B medicated feed from a Category II, Type A medicated article requires a medicated feed mill license application approved under 515.20 of this chapter.

Type B or Type C medicated feed manufactured from a drug component (bulk or "drum-run" (dried crude fermentation product)) requires an application approved under 514.105 of this chapter or an index listing granted under 516.151 of this chapter. [21 CFR § 558]

Type C Medicated Feed

Intended as the complete feed for the animal or may be fed "top dressed" (added on top of usual ration) on or offered "free-choice" (e.g., supplement) in conjunction with other animal feed. It contains a substantial quantity of nutrients including vitamins, minerals, and/or other nutritional ingredients. It is manufactured by diluting a Type A medicated article or a Type B medicated feed. A Type C medicated feed may be further diluted to produce another Type C medicated feed. The manufacture of a Type C medicated feed from a Category II, Type A medicated

article requires a medicated feed mill license
application approved under 515.20 of this chapter.

Type B or Type C medicated feed manufactured from
a drug component (bulk or "drum-run" (dried crude
fermentation product)) requires an application
approved under 514.105 of this chapter or an index
listing granted under 516.151 of this chapter. [21
CFR § 558]

U

U

Ultra-pasteurized

> when used to describe a dairy product means that such product shall have been thermally processed at or above 280 deg. F for at least 2 seconds, either before or after packaging, so as to produce a product which has an extended shelf life under refrigerated conditions. [21 CFR § 131]

Unanticipated Adverse Device Effect

> Any serious adverse effect on health or safety or any life-threatening problem or death caused by, or associated with, a device, if that effect, problem, or death was not previously identified in nature, severity, or degree of incidence in the investigational plan or application (including a supplementary plan or application), or any other unanticipated serious problem associated with a device that relates to the rights, safety, or welfare of subjects. [21 CFR § 812]

Unauthorized Distributor

> A distributor who does not have an ongoing relationship with a manufacturer to sell or distribute its products. [21 CFR § 203]

Unexpected Adverse Experience

> Any adverse experience that is not listed in the current labeling for the biological product. This includes events that may be symptomatically and

pathophysiologically related to an event listed in the labeling, but differ from the event because of greater severity or specificity. For example, under this definition, hepatic necrosis would be unexpected (by virtue of greater severity) if the labeling only referred to elevated hepatic enzymes or hepatitis. Similarly, cerebral thromboembolism and cerebral vasculitis would be unexpected (by virtue of greater specificity) if the labeling only listed cerebral vascular accidents. "Unexpected," as used in this definition, refers to an adverse experience that has not been previously observed (i.e., included in the labeling) rather than from the perspective of such experience not being anticipated from the pharmacological properties of the pharmaceutical product. [21 CFR § 600]

Unit

The volume of blood or one of its components in a suitable volume of anticoagulant obtained from a single collection of blood from one donor. [21 CFR § 606]

United States Agent

A person residing or maintaining a place of business in the United States whom a foreign establishment designates as its agent. This definition excludes mailboxes, answering machines or services, or other places where an individual acting as the foreign establishment's agent is not physically present. [21 CFR § 207]

United States Agent

> A person residing or maintaining a place of business in the United States whom a foreign establishment designates as its agent. This definition excludes mailboxes, answering machines or services, or other places where an individual acting as the foreign establishment's agent is not physically present. [21 CFR § 807]

Urgent Medical Need

> That no comparable HCT/P is available and the recipient is likely to suffer death or serious morbidity without the HCT/P. [21 CFR § 1271]

Use of a drug may present a risk to the public health

> FDA has information that indicates that use of a drug may cause an adverse event. [21 CFR § 530]

Use of a drug presents a risk to the public health

> FDA has evidence that demonstrates that the use of a drug has caused or likely will cause an adverse event. [21 CFR § 530]

Utensil

> Includes any kitchenware, tableware, glassware, cutlery, containers, or equipment with which food or drink comes in contact during storage, preparation, or serving. [21 CFR § 1240]

V

Validation

Confirmation by examination and provision of objective evidence that the particular requirements for a specific intended use can be consistently fulfilled. [21 CFR § 820]

(1) Process validation means establishing by objective evidence that a process consistently produces a result or product meeting its predetermined specifications.

(2) Design validation means establishing by objective evidence that device specifications conform with user needs and intended use(s).

Validation

Confirmation, through the provision of objective evidence, that the requirements for a specific intended use or application have been fulfilled. (Reference: The ASQ Auditing Handbook, 3rd edition, ASQ Quality Audit Division, J.P. Russell, Editor [source: Quality Systems Guidance]

Vascularized

Containing the original blood vessels which are intended to carry blood after transplantation. [21 CFR § 1270]

Verification

Confirmation by examination and provision of objective evidence that specified requirements have been fulfilled. [21 CFR § 820]

Verification

Confirmation, through the provision of objective evidence, that specified requirements have been fulfilled. (Reference: The ASQ Auditing Handbook, 3rd edition, ASQ Quality Audit Division, J.P. Russell, Editor) [source: Quality Systems Guidance]

Verified

To confirm; to establish the truth or accuracy. [IOM Chapter 5]

Vessel

Any passenger-carrying, cargo, or towing vessel exclusive of:

(1) Fishing boats including those used for shell-fishing;

(2) Tugs which operate only locally in specific harbors and adjacent waters;

(3) Barges without means of self-propulsion;

(4) Construction-equipment boats and dredges; and

(5) Sand and gravel dredging and handling boats. [21 CFR § 1240]

Veterinary Feed Directive

A written statement issued by a licensed veterinarian in the course of the veterinarian's professional practice that orders the use of a VFD drug in or on an animal feed. This written statement authorizes the client (the owner of the animal or animals or other caretaker) to obtain and use the VFD drug in or on an animal feed to treat the client's animals only in accordance with the directions for use approved or indexed by the Food and Drug Administration (FDA). A veterinarian may issue a VFD only if a valid veterinarian-client-patient relationship exists, as defined in 530.3(i) of this chapter. [21 CFR § 558]

Veterinary Feed Directive (VFD) Drug

A new animal drug approved under section 512(b) of the Federal Food, Drug, and Cosmetic Act (the act) or listed in the index under section 572 of the act for use in or on animal feed. Use of a VFD drug must be under the professional supervision of a licensed veterinarian. [21 CFR § 558]

Virus

Interpreted to be a product containing the minute living cause of an infectious disease and includes but is not limited to filterable viruses, bacteria, rickettsia, fungi, and protozoa. [21 CFR § 600]

Voluntary Corrective Action

The observed voluntary repair, modification, or adjustment of a violative condition, or product. For purposes of this definition, violative means the

product or condition does not comply with the Acts
or associated regulations enforced by the Agency.
[IOM Chapter 2]

W, X, Y, Z

Ward

A child who is placed in the legal custody of the State or other agency, institution, or entity, consistent with applicable Federal, State, or local law. [21 CFR § 50]

Wash Water

Water suitable for domestic uses other than for drinking and culinary purposes, and medical care purposes excluding hydrotherapy. [21 CFR § 1250]

Water

Means, in addition to water, any mixture of water and fruit juice in which the fruit juice(s) is less than 50 percent of such mixture, including any water contributed by the use of liquid nutritive carbohydrate sweeteners. [21 CFR § 145]

Water Activity (aw)

a measure of the free moisture in a food and is the quotient of the water vapor pressure of the substance divided by the vapor pressure of pure water at the same temperature. [21 CFR § 110]

Watering Point

The specific place or water boat from which potable water is loaded on a conveyance. [21 CFR § 1240]

W, X, Y, Z

Wholesale Distribution

Distribution of prescription drugs to persons other than a consumer or patient, but does not include:

(1) Intracompany sales;

(2) The purchase or other acquisition by a hospital or other health care entity that is a member of a group purchasing organization of a drug for its own use from the group purchasing organization or from other hospitals or health care entities that are members of such organizations;

(3) The sale, purchase, or trade of a drug or an offer to sell, purchase, or trade a drug by a charitable organization to a nonprofit affiliate of the organization to the extent otherwise permitted by law;

(4) The sale, purchase, or trade of a drug or an offer to sell, purchase, or trade a drug among hospitals or other health care entities that are under common control;

(5) The sale, purchase, or trade of a drug or an offer to sell, purchase, or trade a drug for emergency medical reasons;

(6) The sale, purchase, or trade of a drug, an offer to sell, purchase, or trade a drug, or the dispensing of a drug under a prescription executed in accordance with section 503(b) of the act;

(7) The distribution of drug samples by manufacturers' and authorized distributors' representatives;

(8) The sale, purchase, or trade of blood or blood components intended for transfusion;

(9) Drug returns, when conducted by a hospital, health care entity, or charitable institution in accordance with 203.23; or

(10) The sale of minimal quantities of drugs by retail pharmacies to licensed practitioners for office use. [21 CFR § 203]

Wholesale Distributor

Any person engaged in wholesale distribution of prescription drugs, including, but not limited to, manufacturers; repackers; own-label distributors; private-label distributors; jobbers; brokers; warehouses, including manufacturers' and distributors' warehouses, chain drug warehouses, and wholesale drug warehouses; independent wholesale drug traders; and retail pharmacies that conduct wholesale distributions. [21 CFR § 203]

Wholesale Distributor

Any person (other than the manufacturer or the initial importer) who distributes a device from the original place of manufacture to the person who makes the final delivery or sale of the device to the ultimate consumer or user. [21 CFR § 807]

W, X, Y, Z

About the author

Mindy Allport-Settle has served as a key executive, board member, and consultant for some of the best companies in the pharmaceutical and FDA-regulated industry. As CEO of PharmaLogika, Inc. since 2008 and over the course of her career, she has provided informed guidance in regulatory compliance, corporate structuring, restructuring and turnarounds, new drug submissions, research & development and product commercialization strategies, operational, project and contract management, and new business development. Her experience and dedication have resulted in international recognition as the developer of the only FDA-recognized and benchmarked quality systems training and development business methodology designed for regulated industries. Her education includes a Bachelor's degree from the University of North Carolina, an MBA in Global Management from the University of Phoenix, and completion of the corporate governance course series in audit committees, compensation committees, and board effectiveness at Harvard Business School.

About PharmaLogika

Since 2002, PharmaLogika, Inc has established itself as one of the world's premier consulting firms for Pharmaceutical, Biotech, and Medical Device companies across the globe. In so doing, it has earned the trust of executives in Life Sciences for its integrity, accuracy, and unwavering commitment to independent thought with regard to its products and services as well as those of its customers. Through www.PharmaLogika.com, its involvement in sponsored events, and personal references it has reached millions in print and online. Its mission, to provide flawlessly designed and executed products and services to startups as well as established industry leaders to facilitate their growth from discovery and clinical trial navigation to the commercialization and marketing of their products.

PharmaLogika consults with pharmaceutical, biotech, and medical device quality units to provide third party audits, training, pre approval inspections (PAIs), compliance remediation, and a portfolio of related quality and regulatory affairs products and services. Those products include but are not limited to Quality Assurance Forms, SOP and clinical templates, and the highly successful Integrated Development Training System.

Regulatory action guidance as well as quality systems guidance are delivered as part of its standard products and services. Through the use of highly skilled resources throughout the process, each offering is designed to enact a comprehensive quality systems approach in addressing Quality Assurance (QA) issues. The results insure a close adherence to current Good Manufacturing Practice (cGMP) standards.

PharmaLogika also has a Research and Development OTC line for human consumption that targets alpha 1-antitrypsin deficiency, Fibromyalgia, Restless Legs Syndrome, and Attention Deficit Disorder. A veterinary OTC is currently available that provides canine and feline oral debriding and cleansing agents as well as a stain remover and topical antiseptic. These products combine to provide a strong pipeline of both current and future deliverables.

PharmaLogika, Inc.
PO Box 461
Willow Springs, NC 27592
www.PharmaLogika.com

PharmaLogika

Other books by this author

Current Good Manufacturing Practices: Pharmaceutical, Biologics, and Medical Device Regulations and Guidance Documents Concise Reference

Investigations Operations Manual: FDA Field Inspection and Investigation Policy and Procedure Concise Reference

Course Development 101: Developing Training Programs for Regulated Industries

Compliance Remediation for Pharmaceutical Manufacturing: A Project Management Guide for Re-establishing FDA Compliance

Good Manufacturing Practice (GMP) Guidelines: The Rules Governing Medicinal Products in the Eurpean Union, EudraLex Volume 4 Concise Reference

Please visit www.PharmaLogika.com for additional titles

Other books by this author